ALIVE IN CHRIST

GRADE 4

The Moral Life

aliveinchrist.osv.com

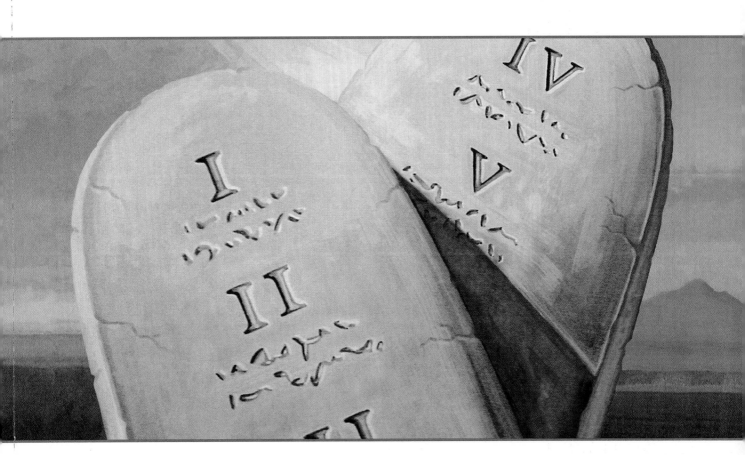

OurSundayVisitor

The Subcommittee on the Catechism, United States Conference of Catholic Bishops, has found this catechetical series, copyright 2014, to be in conformity with the *Catechism of the Catholic Church*.

Nihil Obstat
Rev. Fr. Jeremiah L. Payne, S.Th.L.
Censor Librorum, Diocese of Orlando

Imprimatur
✠ Most Rev. John Noonan
Bishop of Orlando
March 26, 2013

For permission to reprint copyrighted materials, grateful acknowledgment is made to the following sources:

Allelu! Growing and Celebrating with Jesus ® Music CD © Our Sunday Visitor, Inc. Music written and produced by Sweetwater Productions. All rights of the owners of these works are reserved.

English translation of the *Catechism of the Catholic Church for the United States of America* copyright © 1994, United States Catholic Conference, Inc.—Libreria Editrice Vaticana. English translation of the *Catechism of the Catholic Church: Modifications from the Editio Typica* copyright © 1997, United States Catholic Conference, Inc.—Libreria Editrice Vaticana. Used by permission. All rights reserved.

Scripture texts in this work are taken from the *New American Bible, revised edition* © 2010, 1991, 1986, 1970 Confraternity of Christian Doctrine, Washington, D.C., and are used by permission of the copyright owner. All Rights Reserved. No part of the *New American Bible* may be reproduced in any form without permission in writing from the copyright owner.

Excerpts from the *United States Catholic Catechism for Adults*, copyright © 2006, United States Catholic Conference, Inc.—Libreria Editrice Vaticana.

Excerpts from the English translation of *The Roman Missal* © 2010, International Commission on English in the Liturgy Corporation (ICEL): All rights reserved.

The English translation of the Act of Contrition from the *Rite of Penance* © 1974, ICEL: English translation. All rights reserved.

Twenty-Third Publications, A Division of Bayard: "Grail Prayer" from *500 Prayers for Catholic Schools and Parish Youth Groups* by Filomena Tassi and Peter Tassi. Text copyright © Filomena Tassi and Peter Tassi.

United States Conference of Catholic Bishops, Inc., Washington, D.C.: "Hail, Holy Queen" from *Catholic Household Blessings and Prayers*. Translation copyright © 1989 by United States Catholic Conference, Inc.

Additional acknowledgments appear on page 335.

Alive in Christ Parish Grade 4 Student Book
ISBN: 978-1-61278-049-8
Item Number: CU5251

4 5 6 7 8 9 10   015016   21 20 19 18 17
Webcrafters, Inc., Madison, WI, USA; August 2017; Job# 133185

Contents at a Glance

Contents in Detail

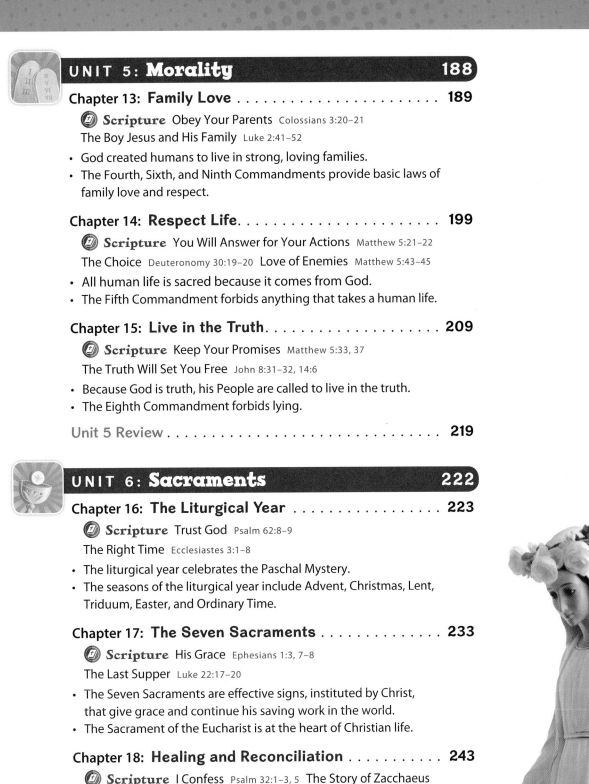

© Our Sunday Visitor

A New Year

 Let Us Pray

Leader: Our Father, out of love you gave us commands to help us honor you and live with others. Help us follow your ways and the teachings of your Son.

"All the paths of the LORD are mercy and truth toward those who honor his covenant and decrees." **Psalm 25:10**

All: Thank you, God, for leading us and forgiving us when we stray from your paths.

Scripture

But because of his great love for us, God, who is rich in mercy, made us alive with Christ even when we were dead in transgressions—it is by grace you have been saved.

Based on Ephesians 2:4–5

? What Do You Wonder?

- Why do we need God's mercy?
- How does God invite us to be in relationship with him?

Fourth Grade

What are we going to learn this year?

You are about to begin the next mile of your faith journey, but you do not travel alone. Your family, friends, and the whole parish community travel with you. And so does God's Word.

 This symbol lets you know that the story or reading that follows is from the Bible. In every lesson you will spend time with God's Word in Scripture. Through these stories you will learn more about God's plan for all people, whom he created in his image and likeness. You will grow closer to Jesus as you learn more about his life and the teachings of his Church.

You will begin and end each lesson with a prayer. Each time you are together, you have the chance to thank God, ask his help, pray for the needs of others, and praise God for being God. God the Holy Spirit helps you pray.

You will sing songs to praise God and celebrate our faith. During the year, you'll explore the feasts and seasons of the Church year, and you will meet many Saints, heroes of the Church.

Every chapter has exercises to help you better understand what's being taught. You may be underlining, circling, writing, matching, or more.

Living as Jesus' Disciples

During this year, you'll be learning a lot about God's **covenant** with his People, and the laws he gave them to live by the covenant. Important Catholic Faith Words are **highlighted** in yellow to focus your attention and defined again on the sides of the pages.

You'll see how Jesus teaches us to love God and others by following the Ten Commandments and living the Beatitudes. Scripture stories will remind you that no matter what we do, God will always forgive us if we are truly sorry and ask his forgiveness.

All you do in class will help you follow Jesus' example and be part of the Church.

Three times a chapter you'll see green words like the ones below. You'll take a break to think about your faith and special people in your life; make connections to what you do at home, with friends, at Church; and see how living your faith can make a difference.

Catholic Faith Words

covenant a sacred promise or agreement between God and humans

 Circle one thing you want to learn more about this year.

Share Your Faith

Reflect Name some teachings of Jesus that you've heard often.

_____

_____

_____

Share Talk with a partner about why these teachings are important and who taught them to you.

Blessed are the peacemakers

God's Word

Another name for the Bible is **Sacred Scripture**. It is the inspired Word of God written by humans. We read and pray with Scripture with our families, during parish gatherings, and in religion classes. We hear readings from Scripture during Mass and the other Sacraments.

The Catholic Bible has seventy-three books—forty-six in the Old Testament and twenty-seven in the New Testament.

The Old Testament

The first part of the Bible is about God's relationship with the Hebrew people before Jesus was born. It includes laws, history, messages of the prophets, and stories of God's faithfulness and actions in the lives of his People.

The Old Testament	
The Pentateuch	Genesis, Exodus, Leviticus, Numbers, Deuteronomy
The Historical Books	Joshua, Judges, Ruth, 1 Samuel, 2 Samuel, 1 Kings, 2 Kings, 1 Chronicles, 2 Chronicles, Ezra, Nehemiah, Tobit, Judith, Esther, 1 Maccabees, 2 Maccabees
The Wisdom Books	Job, Psalms, Proverbs, Ecclesiastes, Song of Songs (Ecclesiasticus), Wisdom, Sirach
The Prophetic Books	Isaiah, Jeremiah, Lamentations, Baruch, Ezekiel, Daniel, Hosea, Joel, Amos, Obadiah, Jonah, Micah, Nahum, Habakkuk, Zephaniah, Haggai, Zechariah, Malachi

Catholic Faith Words

Sacred Scripture another name for the Bible; Sacred Scripture is the inspired Word of God written by humans

Before the invention of the printing press, the Bible had to be copied by hand. Many times when copying the text, monks would also illuminate, or illustrate, Scripture passages.

The New Testament

The second part of the Bible tells of God's love for people after the coming of Jesus. It is about the life and teaching of Jesus, his followers, and the early Church.

The New Testament	
The Gospels	Matthew, Mark, Luke, John
The Acts of the Apostles	
The New Testament Letters	Romans, 1 Corinthians, 2 Corinthians, Galatians, Ephesians, Philippians, Colossians, 1 Thessalonians,
	2 Thessalonians, 1 Timothy, 2 Timothy, Titus, Philemon, Hebrews, James, 1 Peter, 2 Peter, 1 John, 2 John, 3 John, Jude
Revelation	

Connect Your Faith

Locate Bible Passages To practice finding a particular Bible passage, use the example of Luke 10:25–28. Luke is the name of a book in the Bible. The chapter number always comes directly after the name of the book, so 10 is the chapter number. The numbers 25–28 refer to the verses. With a partner, find this passage in your Bible and discuss what this passage means to you. Write some of your thoughts here.

_____

_____

_____

Our Catholic Life

Each chapter in your book has an Our Catholic Life section. It builds on what's in the chapter and focuses in a special way on what it means to be Catholic. Words, images, and activities help us better understand how to grow closer to Jesus and the Church.

 Match the ways to grow as disciples on the left with the descriptions on the right.

Growing as Disciples of Jesus

Know more about our faith	Understand and live the Beatitudes and the Great Commandment
Understand and take part in the Sacraments	Participate in the mission and community life of your parish
Live as Jesus calls us to	Understand and pray in adoration, praise, thanksgiving, petition, and intercession
Talk and listen to God in prayer	Show the Gospel by the choices we make and way we treat others
Be an active member of the Church	Celebrate the Eucharist and participate in Reconciliation
Help others know Jesus through our words and actions	Learn about God's plan for us all through Sacred Scripture and Sacred Tradition

People of Faith

You will also be introduced to People of Faith, holy women and men who loved God very much and did his work on Earth. They are officially recognized by the Church as Venerables, Blesseds, or Saints.

Live Your Faith

Describe what's happening in the picture. How are these people being active members of the Church?

Name some ways you can take part in your parish activities and worship.

Pray Together

Every chapter has a prayer page. Over the course of the year, you'll talk and listen to God using different prayer types. You may listen to God's Word, read from the Bible, pray for the needs of others, call on the Saints to pray for us, and praise God the Father, Son, and Holy Spirit in words and songs.

Gather and begin with the Sign of the Cross.

Leader: Blessed be God.

All: Blessed be God forever.

Leader: Let us pray.

Bow your heads as the leader prays.

All: Amen.

Leader: A reading from the holy Gospel according to Luke.

Read Luke 10:25–28.

The Gospel of the Lord.

All: Praise to you, Lord Jesus Christ.

 Sing "Alive in Christ"

We are Alive in Christ
We are Alive in Christ
He came to set us free
We are Alive in Christ
We are Alive in Christ
He gave his life for me
We are Alive in Christ
We are Alive in Christ

FAMILY+FAITH
LIVING AND LEARNING TOGETHER

YOUR CHILD LEARNED >>>

This page encourages you to share your faith and identify the many ways you already live the faith in daily family life.
In this section, you will find a summary of what your child has learned in the chapter.

Scripture

 This introduces you to the opening Scripture, and provides direction for more reading.

Catholics Believe

- Bulleted information highlights the main points of doctrine of the Chapter.

People of Faith

Here you meet the holy person featured in People of Faith.

CHILDREN AT THIS AGE >>>

This section gives you a sense of how your child will likely be able to understand the topics taught. It suggests ways you can help your child better understand and live their faith.

How They Understand Children this age typically want to be independent, and doing things together with their peers is important to them. However, they are just beginning to "come out of themselves." Some days they will appear older than their years and other days they will seem younger. Remember to be patient with your child as he or she experiments with new ways of talking or behaving.

At this age children will have begun to internalize and express a moral code that is shaped in your family as well as in school and by the Church. They may seem very concerned about fairness and rights. Rules and regulations are the measure of right and wrong for them. At times they may appear legalistic and judgmental of themselves and others.

You can nurture your child's sense of Catholic morality. Give him or her opportunities to consider better or best choices, not just right or wrong choices. Help him or her see how their words and actions can affect others.

CONSIDER THIS >>>

These questions invite you to reflect on your own experience and consider how the Church speaks to you on your faith journey.

LET'S TALK >>>

Here you will find some practical questions that prompt discussion about the lesson's content, faith sharing, and making connections with your family life.

- What are you and your child looking forward to learning about your faith this year?

LET'S PRAY >>>

 Encourages family prayer connected to the example of our People of Faith.

Holy men and women, you model faith, hope, and love. Pray for us as we journey through this year. Amen.

 For a multimedia glossary of Catholic Faith Words, Sunday readings, seasonal and Saint resources, and chapter activities go to **aliveinchrist.osv.com**.

Sorrowful Mother

 Let Us Pray

Leader: Lord God,

In times of doubt, sadness and difficulty.

We trust in you, as our Mother Mary did.

We know you are with us.

"But I trust in you, LORD;

I say, 'You are my God.'" **Psalm 31:15**

All: Amen.

Scripture

The child's father and mother were amazed at what was being said about him. Then Simeon blessed them and said to his mother Mary, "This child is destined for the falling and the rising of many in Israel, and to be a sign that will be opposed so that the inner thoughts of many will be revealed—and a sword will pierce your own soul too." **Based on Luke 2:33–35**

? What Do You Wonder?

- How do you think Mary felt after listening to Simeon's words?

- What do you think Mary thought was going to happen after Simeon's prophecy?

Michelangelo's sculpture *Pietà*, on display in St. Peter's Basilica in Vatican City, depicts Mary holding Jesus after his body had been taken down from the Cross.

Ordinary Time

- The life and ministry of Jesus are the focus of Ordinary Time. Mary and the Saints are also remembered throughout the year.

- In Ordinary Time, the priest wears green, a sign of growth and life.

- The priest wears white on Mary's feast days.

Ordinary Time

The Church honors Mary in every season. The feast days of Mary often remember happy events in her life, such as the day we celebrate her birth or her Assumption into Heaven. But on September 15 during Ordinary Time, the Church honors Mary as Our Lady of Sorrows. This feast is a time to recall some of the sorrows in Mary's life.

Mary, Our Model of Faith

There were seven especially sad times in Mary's life. They are called the seven sorrows of Mary.

Three of the sorrows happened during Jesus' childhood. The first was Simeon's prophecy that Jesus' life would make Mary sad. Next was the difficult trip into Egypt to escape Herod's plan to kill Jesus. Later, Mary worried when Jesus was missing and teaching in the Temple.

The last four sorrows came at the end of Jesus' life. Mary must have been sad to see Jesus carrying his Cross and being crucified. As any mother would, she must have felt sorrow when he was taken down from the Cross and buried in the tomb. But in difficult and sad times, Mary always believed in her Son. She acted with courage and cared for others. Mary can be a model for you, too, in the sad times of your life.

➤ **What can we do when we have difficult times?**

Number the Seven Sorrows of Mary above.

Compassion

Mary watched as her Son suffered and died at the hands of those who did not understand him. Sorrow is still felt today whenever someone sees a loved one hurting. But from your sorrow can grow greater caring and compassion for the suffering of others. Compassion for others is more powerful than pain. We hear this message in the Gospels.

Activity

Link Virtues and Actions Match each virtue with an action that will develop it. Talk with a friend about how each action could make the virtue stronger.

Developing Virtues

Virtues	Actions
repentance	standing up for someone who is being bullied
purity	avoiding movies that are not appropriate for you
courage	earning money and then giving it to the poor
patience	saying you are sorry for hurting someone
self-denial	helping a younger person learn something

People of Faith

Chapter	Person	Feast Day
1	Saint Kateri Tekakwitha	July 14
2	Saint Bridget of Sweden	July 23
3	Saint Raymond of Peñafort	January 7
4	Saint Germaine Cousin	June 15
5	Saint Dominic	August 8
6	Saint Charles Lwanga	June 3
7	Saint Yi Sung-hun	September 20
8	Saint Katharine Drexel	March 3
9	Saint Mary Ann of Quito	May 26
10	Blessed Frédéric Ozanam	September 9
11	Saint Bernadette Soubirous	April 16
12	Saint Mary Magdalen Postel	July 16
13	Blessed Louis Martin and Blessed Marie-Azélie Martin	July 12
14	Saint Gianna Beretta Molla	April 28
15	Saint Joan of Arc	May 30
16	Saint Juan Diego	December 9
17	Saint Margaret Mary Alacoque	October 16
18	Venerable Matt Talbot	
19	Queen Saint Margaret of Scotland	November 16
20	Blessed Junípero Serra	July 1
21	Saint Martin de Porres	November 3

Let Us Pray

Prayer for Mercy

Gather and pray the Sign of the Cross together.

Leader: Blessed be God.

All: Blessed be God forever.

Sing together.

Leader: Christ Jesus, you have given us Mary as a model of courage and patience. As we remember Mary's sorrows, we express sorrow for our failure to love. Lord, have mercy.

All: Lord, have mercy.

Guided Reflection

Sit in silence before the cross as the leader leads you in a reflection on Our Lady of Sorrows.

Leader: Let us pray . . .

All: Amen.

Go Forth!

Leader: Let us go forth in Mary's spirit of faith, hope, and love for her Son.

All: Thanks be to God.

 Sing "Holy Mary"

TALKING ABOUT ORDINARY TIME >>>

Feasts of Mary and the Saints occur throughout the Church Year. Ordinary Time is the longest of all the Church seasons. It occurs over thirty-three or thirty-four Sundays. It is called Ordinary Time because all the Sundays are numbered in order. Ordinary Time is divided into two parts. The first is from the end of the Christmas season until Ash Wednesday. The second is from the end of the Easter season until the first Sunday of Advent, which begins the next cycle, or a new liturgical year. Following the Feast of the Holy Cross, the Church celebrates the Feast of Our Lady of Sorrows on September 15. This feast invites us to contemplate the suffering that Mary endured as the Mother of God.

Scripture

 Luke 2:33–35 describes the presentation of Jesus in the Temple and Simeon's prophecy to Mary. How has your faith helped you deal with any suffering?

HELPING YOUR CHILD UNDERSTAND >>>

Mary

- Usually at this age, children begin to take on role models. They may begin to see Mary as a role model for their own spiritual life.

- Most children at this age develop a strong sense of fairness. It is difficult for them to grasp that bad things do happen to good people. This can lead to many discussions about how one handles suffering and injustice as a Christian.

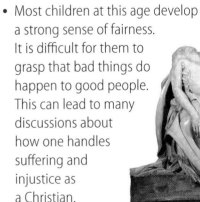

FEASTS OF THE SEASON >>>

Saint Mother Theodore Guérin
October 3

Saint Mother Theodore Guérin was a woman of many talents. Born in France, she accepted an assignment to travel to the Indiana wilderness. She taught, administered medicines, and founded several orphanages and schools. Her group prospered despite anti-Catholic feelings and difficulties on the frontier. She was canonized in 2006.

FAMILY PRAYER >>>

 Pray this prayer as you gather for mealtime throughout September.

Mary Mother of Sorrows,

We pray for all those we know who are suffering—our family members and friends, and all those throughout the world, especially for those who have no one to help them. We ask you to intercede for them before God that he will send them what they need.

Amen.

 For a multimedia glossary of Catholic Faith Words, Sunday readings, seasonal and Saint resources, and chapter activities go to **aliveinchrist.osv.com**.

Prepare for Jesus

 Let Us Pray

Leader: Lord God, as we prepare for the feast of Christmas. We thank you for the gift of your Son, Emmanuel, God with us.

"The LORD has done great things for us;
    Oh, how happy we were!" **Psalm 126:3**

All: Amen.

Scripture

"In the sixth month, the angel Gabriel was sent from God to a town of Galilee called Nazareth, to a virgin betrothed to a man named Joseph, of the house of David, and the virgin's name was Mary. And coming to her, he said, 'Hail, favored one! The Lord is with you.' Then the angel said to her, 'Do not be afraid, Mary, for you have found favor with God. Behold, you will conceive in your womb and bear a son, and you shall name him Jesus. He will be great and will be called Son of the Most High . . .'" **Luke 1:26–32a**

? What Do You Wonder?

• What do you have to be or do to be favored?

• What great things has God done for you, your family, or people you know?

Change Our Hearts

Advent is the first season of the Church year. During the four weeks of Advent, the whole Church prepares to celebrate Jesus' Second Coming into the world at the end of time.

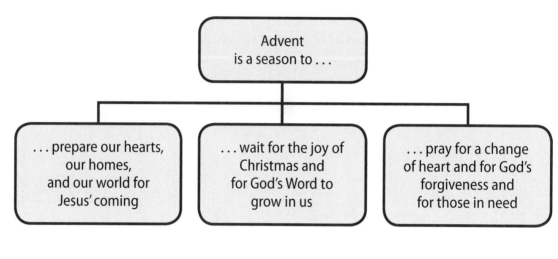

Advent is a season to . . .

. . . prepare our hearts, our homes, and our world for Jesus' coming

. . . wait for the joy of Christmas and for God's Word to grow in us

. . . pray for a change of heart and for God's forgiveness and for those in need

Purple is the Advent color. The priest wears purple vestments. The church is decorated with purple decorations.

During this season, Catholics prepare for Christmas by reflecting on the gift of the Incarnation, when God sent his only Son to become one of us and to be the Savior of all people.

➤ What is one way you will prepare for Jesus' coming during Advent this year?

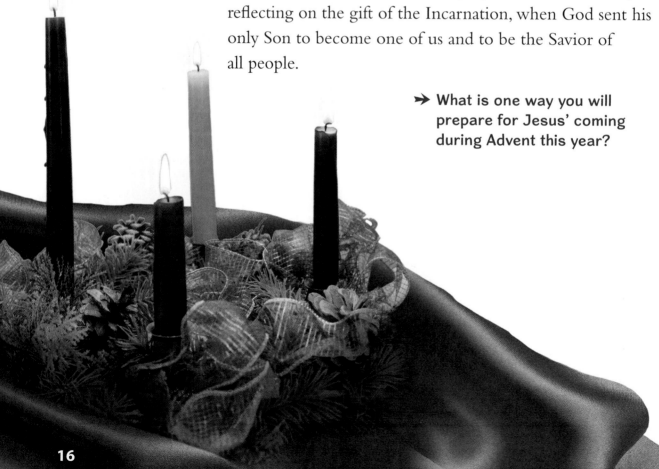

The Path of Love

Taking time for daily prayer before the Advent wreath with your family gives you time to reflect on Jesus' love. Small acts of sacrifice and penance can help you turn your heart toward Jesus and show greater love for others.

John told the people who were waiting for the Messiah that they would have to change. He said, "Prepare the way of the Lord, make straight his paths" (**Mark 1:3**).

➤ **What changes can you make to straighten your path and bring you closer to Jesus?**

Activity

Show Your Love In the space below, create a list of loving actions you can do for members of your family. You might include things like reading a book to a younger sibling, washing the dog, cleaning up your room without complaining, or taking someone else's turn doing the dishes. Create a coupon book to give to each member of your family this Christmas.

Celebrate Forgiveness

This prayer is a penitential prayer. In a penitential prayer, we ask for God's loving mercy and forgiveness.

 Let Us Pray

Gather and pray the Sign of the Cross together.

Leader: Our help is in the name of the Lord.

All: Who made Heaven and Earth.

Leader: Let us pray.

Bow your heads as the leader prays.

All: Amen.
I confess to almighty God
and to you, my brothers and sisters,
that I have greatly sinned,
in my thoughts and in my words,
in what I have done and in what I have failed to do,

Gently strike your chest with a closed fist.

through my fault, through my fault,
through my most grievous fault;
therefore I ask blessed Mary ever-Virgin,
all the Angels and Saints,
and you, my brothers and sisters,
to pray for me to the Lord our God.

Amen.

 Sing "Through My Fault"

Listen to God's Word

Leader: A reading from the holy Gospel according to Mark.

Read Mark 1:1–8.

The Gospel of the Lord.

All: Praise to you, Lord Jesus Christ.

Prayer Before the Wreath

Sit before the wreath in silence and reflect on ways you will try to change your heart.

Leader: Lord, change our hearts to prepare for your coming. Be with us as we pray.

Stand, raise your hands, and pray the Lord's Prayer.

Leader: Let us offer one another a greeting of peace as a sign of our desire to change our hearts.

All exchange a sign of peace.

Go Forth!

Leader: Let us go forth to prepare the way of the Lord.

All: Thanks be to God.

FAMILY+FAITH
LIVING AND LEARNING TOGETHER

TALKING ABOUT ADVENT >>>

The four weeks of Advent give us a chance to reflect on ways we need to change our hearts to grow closer to God. He sent his only Son to become one of us. Jesus the Messiah saved us from sin and showed us the way to live as children of his light.

Scripture

Read **Luke 1:26–38**. We hear about the angel's invitation to Mary to be the Mother of God, and we hear Mary's unconditional "yes." How has God shown favor in your life?

HELPING YOUR CHILD UNDERSTAND >>>
Advent

- Typically at this age, children enjoy group activities and are inclined to do service for others. Look for a service opportunity that your family can do together during Advent.

- Most children at this age are in the process of developing a conscience and are becoming more aware of choices they make that are not part of God's plan for our lives. Watch for opportunities to praise them for good choices.

CATHOLIC FAMILY CUSTOMS >>>

It is important to mark the season of Advent as a family. Here are some things you can do together with your children during the weeks before Christmas to keep the focus on preparing for the coming of Christ.

- Take time out for a discussion on how you prepare when a special guest is coming to your house for Christmas. Talk about what family members can do during the season of Advent to spiritually prepare for the coming of Jesus. What thoughts or actions need to be "cleaned up"?

- Write the name of each family member on a small piece of paper. Fold these papers and place them in a bowl. At mealtime, ask each family member to choose a name. For the next week, secretly do something extra for the person whose name you chose, such as putting away toys, taking on a chore, or treating the person kindly.

FAMILY PRAYER >>>

Praying the Lord's Prayer slowly and thinking about each phrase is a good way to start the process of changing one's heart. Before or after dinner, light a candle on your Advent wreath, and pray together the Lord's Prayer. Then exchange a Sign of Peace.

For a multimedia glossary of Catholic Faith Words, Sunday readings, seasonal and Saint resources, and chapter activities go to **aliveinchrist.osv.com**.

God's Greatest Gift

 Let Us Pray

Leader: Faithful God, you loved us so much you sent us your only Son. Strengthen us to return your love by living as his faithful followers.

"I will sing of your mercy forever, LORD proclaim your faithfulness through all ages."
Psalm 89:2

All: Amen.

 Scripture

But when the goodness and loving-kindness of Jesus our Savior came to Earth, he saved us. Humans did not do anything to deserve being saved. God sent Jesus to save us just because he wanted to. He saved us because he was merciful and forgiving. We were saved by his grace so we might inherit the hope of eternal life.   **Based on Titus 3:4–7**

? What Do You Wonder?

- What makes it possible that a person forgives over and over again?
- What does it mean to inherit good things?

The Season of Christmas

The Church's season of Christmas begins with the Christmas Eve Vigil on December 24. Christmas is a joyful and festive season. The priest wears white or gold vestments. During the Christmas season, Jesus' birth and childhood are proclaimed and celebrated.

The Feast of Epiphany comes in the middle of the Christmas season. The season ends in January with the Feast of the Baptism of the Lord, after Epiphany.

Precious Gifts

The word Epiphany means "showing forth." On Epiphany the Church remembers the visit of the three Magi, often called wise men, to the Infant Jesus.

The Magi came from distant lands, followed a bright star to find the Infant Jesus, honored him, and gave glory to God. Epiphany celebrates the belief that Jesus came to Earth to save everyone.

To honor the Savior and show him reverence, the Magi brought him gifts of gold, frankincense, and myrrh.

➜ **What gifts of reverence and worship can you offer Jesus?**

© Our Sunday Visitor

The gift of gold, a precious metal, showed that the Magi thought of Jesus as worthy of the highest honor.

Frankincense, an incense with a pleasing smell, represented the holiness of Jesus.

Myrrh is a symbol of preserving and saving. This gift was a sign that Jesus would die for the salvation of all people.

Let Us Pray

Celebrate Jesus

Gather and pray the Sign of the Cross together.

Leader: Blessed be the name of the Lord.

All: Now and forever.

Sing together the refrain.

Leader: Let us pray.

Bow your heads as the leader prays.

All: Amen.

Listen to God's Word

Reader: A reading from the holy Gospel according to Matthew.

Read Matthew 2:9–11.

The Gospel of the Lord.

All: Praise to you, Lord Jesus Christ.

Go Forth!

Leader: Let us go forth to bring the Christmas gifts of peace, love, and joy to all we meet.

 All: Sing "We Three Kings"
O star of wonder, star of light,
star with royal beauty bright;
westward leading, still proceeding,
guide us to thy perfect light.

FAMILY+FAITH
LIVING AND LEARNING TOGETHER

TALKING ABOUT CHRISTMAS >>>

As a family, you can celebrate the season of Christmas in your home in many ways. The Christmas season is a festive one. It lasts from the Christmas Eve Vigil until the feast of the Baptism of the Lord in January. In today's culture, the meaning of Christmas may get lost. The Feast of Epiphany in January helps shift the focus from material gifts to the gift that is Jesus. Epiphany means "showing forth." The visit of the Magi on Epiphany is a symbol and a prophecy that God sent Jesus for the salvation of all peoples.

Scripture

Read **Titus 3:1–8**. Paul describes to Titus how a Christian should live as we await Jesus' second coming. How do you try to live the Christian life that Paul describes?

HELPING YOUR CHILD UNDERSTAND >>>
Epiphany

- Most children love the drama of the Feast of Epiphany. The following of the star, the visit to Herod, the presentation of gifts, and the secret return of the Magi enthrall them.

- Children this age often enjoy learning how other cultures celebrate Epiphany. In families with Spanish heritage, children put hay or grass and water under a child's bed. This is meant to be food for the Magi's camels. During the night, the Magi exchange the food for presents.

- Give your child the example of the municipality of Juana Diaz, in Puerto Rico, which holds a festival to honor the Magi. Hundreds of people dress as shepherds to welcome the Magi, who are dressed in fancy costumes.

CATHOLIC FAMILY CUSTOMS >>>

One way to celebrate the Feast of Epiphany is by marking the home's doorway with the initials of the Magi. While the names of the Magi are not found in Scripture, our tradition has handed on the names: Caspar, Melchior, and Balthazar.

Obtain a piece of chalk and gather your family around the front door of your home. Then pray: "Lord, bless this doorway and all who enter here. Help us to be generous and welcoming to those who cross this threshold." Use the chalk to mark the doorway with the initials of the Magi (C, M, B). This tradition reminds family members to bring Christ to all whom they encounter.

FAMILY PRAYER >>>

Don't put away that manger scene until the end of the Christmas season. Each Sunday of the Christmas season, before a family meal, gather as a family around the scene. Light a candle or a lamp and sing a favorite family Christmas hymn as your prayer.

For a multimedia glossary of Catholic Faith Words, Sunday readings, seasonal and Saint resources, and chapter activities go to **aliveinchrist.osv.com**.

A Time To Pray

 Let Us Pray

Leader: Lord God, send your Holy Spirit to open our hearts to see what we need to change. We pray the Holy Spirit will show us where we can be less selfish and more like your Son. Through Christ, our Lord.

"I shall walk before the LORD in the land of the living." **Psalm 116:9**

All: Amen.

 Scripture

"What then shall we say to this? If God is for us, who can be against us? He who did not spare his own Son but handed him over for us all . . .

It is Christ [Jesus] who died, rather, was raised, who also is at the right hand of God, who indeed intercedes for us." **Romans 8:31–32, 34**

? What Do You Wonder?

- In what ways is God on your side?
- Why doesn't God always give you what you ask for?

An Unselfish Spirit

Trees and vines can grow wild when no one takes care of them. They produce fruit too small or too sour to enjoy. That is why it is important to prune trees and vines. Pruning means cutting off dead and unhealthy branches so that the best fruit can grow. Trees and vines also require plenty of soil, water, and sunlight.

Spiritual Discipline

During the Season of Lent, the Church reminds us that good pruning is needed to produce good fruit. You can produce good fruit by cutting away bad habits and selfishness. Then the good fruit of love, sharing, and forgiveness can grow in you.

Prayer, fasting, and almsgiving are the three principal practices of Lent. These are the practices of disciples of Jesus. Prayer is the foundation for all spiritual discipline. It is like the soil a tree needs to grow. It gives you spiritual nourishment and deepens your relationship with God.

Lent

- Lent is a forty-day season set aside for the People of God to reflect on our relationship with God and others.

- Purple, the liturgical color for Lent, reminds us we are called to change. It is a sign of penance.

- During Lent, the Church fasts, prays, and gives alms.

➔ **What good can you produce if you cut away bad habits?**

Growing Spiritually

Your body is growing every day. Growing in spirit is equally important. Just as you feed your body, so must your soul be fed. The spiritual discipline of prayer strengthens you so that you can avoid sin and prepare for the joy of Easter.

Activity

On Good Soil Around the tree, list two or three ways you could try to deepen your life of prayer during Lent. Try a different way during each of the six weeks of Lent.

Celebrate Lent

In this prayer form, a celebration of the Word, you listen and reflect on God's Word.

 ## Let Us Pray

Gather and pray the Sign of the Cross together.

Leader: Oh Lord, open my lips.

All: That my mouth shall proclaim your praise.

Leader: Let us pray.

Raise your hands as the leader prays.

All: Amen.

Listen to God's Word

Leader: A reading from the holy Gospel according to Matthew.

Read Matthew 6:5–8.

The Gospel of the Lord.

All: Praise to you, Lord Jesus Christ.

Dialogue

Why does Jesus say that it is better to pray in secret? How can prayer help you to yield "good fruit"?

Kneel in Silence

Ask God to strengthen you to turn toward his love and to be faithful to the Gospel.

All: Sing "Ashes"

We rise again from ashes,
from the good we've failed to do.
We rise again from ashes,
to create ourselves anew.
If all our world is ashes,
then must our lives be true,
an offering of ashes, an offering to you.

Prayer of the Faithful

Leader: God does not desire our death, but rather that we should turn from our sins and have life. Let us pray that we may sin no more, and so bear good fruit.

All: Lord, hear our prayer.

Go Forth!

Leader: Lord, may our Lenten prayer strengthen us so that we may bear good fruit and be Good News.

All: Thanks be to God.

FAMILY+FAITH
LIVING AND LEARNING TOGETHER

TALKING ABOUT LENT >>>

Lent is a forty-day journey that begins on Ash Wednesday. The receiving of ashes on one's forehead marks the promise to repent or change to grow closer to God and the Church. Lent is a time of inner change for us. Most adults have had some life experiences that have prompted a change of bad habits to habits of selflessness. Lent is a time to change old ways in preparation for Easter. Prayer, fasting, and almsgiving, the three Lenten practices, help families grow in Christ.

Scripture

 Read **Romans 8:31** and reflect on past events in your family that have shown evidence that God is with you. How can your family show gratitude for God's being present for you?

HELPING YOUR CHILD UNDERSTAND >>>

Lent

- Most children at this age understand that Lent is a season for changes of both heart and behavior, and they are capable of applying these concepts to themselves.

- Usually children at this age are curious and interested in facts. They would enjoy looking up more information about Lent.

- Ordinarily, children of this age love ritual and will be able to fully engage in the Stations of the Cross, the practice of remembering Jesus' Death that begins with Pilate's condemnation and ends with placing Jesus' dead body in the tomb.

CATHOLIC FAMILY CUSTOMS >>>

Lent is a time to reflect on how we need to change. As a parent, you can guide your child to develop spiritual strength by exercising spiritual discipline.

- Spend some time in quiet prayer to discern areas where your child may need spiritual guidance.

- Talk with your child about specific actions that he or she might do to build up spiritual strength.

- Periodically talk with your child about his or her progress.

FAMILY PRAYER >>>

God of love, as we journey through this holy season of Lent, be with us, open our hearts. Help us to look deeply at our lives, through prayer, fasting, and almsgiving. Help us to recognize the needs of others and respond to those needs.

In the name of your Son, Jesus, Amen.

For a multimedia glossary of Catholic Faith Words, Sunday readings, seasonal and Saint resources, and chapter activities go to **aliveinchrist.osv.com**.

Triduum

Let Us Pray

Leader: Lord, God, sometimes we do things we
should not do.
We are sorry. Send your Holy Spirit
to guide us to right and loving actions.
Through Christ, our Lord.

"The Lord God is my help,
therefore I am not disgraced."   Isaiah 50:7a

All: Amen.

Scripture

"He humbled himself,
becoming obedient to death,
even death on a cross.
Because of this, God greatly exalted him
and bestowed on him the name
that is above every name."   Philippians 2:8–9

? What Do You Wonder?

- Why did Jesus choose to be obedient?

- What helps people do the right thing?

The Cross

On Palm (Passion) Sunday, with the procession of palms and the reading of the Passion of Jesus, the Church begins the holiest week of the year. We call to mind all the events that led to Jesus' dying and rising to new life.

The last three days of Holy Week are called the Triduum. Triduum starts with the Holy Thursday Mass, moves into Good Friday, continues through the Easter Vigil, and ends with evening prayer on Easter Sunday.

Suffering Servant

On Good Friday the Church remembers the suffering Jesus endured for the sake of every person.

Jesus' journey carrying his Cross from the place he was condemned to the place where he was crucified is called the Way of the Cross. It was a painful journey. The Romans used the crucifixion as an instrument of punishment and death. Yet through Jesus the cross became a sign of new life.

A Good Friday procession reenacts Jesus carrying the Cross to Golgotha, the place of his Crucifixion.

Because of Jesus' Death on the Cross and his Resurrection to new life, you receive forgiveness and share in God's life.

Today, the cross is a symbol of Jesus' love for all. The cross can inspire you to love in both word and action.

➜ **Where do you see crosses?**

New Life

The passage from the Book of Isaiah was written long before Jesus was born. Isaiah told the people that someday one of God's servants would suffer for the sins of many. Jesus suffered and died to free all people from sin and to bring them back to God's friendship. That is why the Church calls Jesus the Suffering Servant.

Activity

In Word and Action Think about an act of kindness or sacrifice that you will make during Holy Week. Then write some more ways you can imitate the love of Jesus in word and action.

_____

_____

_____

_____

_____

_____

_____

_____

Celebrate Triduum

This prayer form reverences the cross in a celebration of the Word. In the celebration you reflect on God's Word. In reverencing the cross, you use movement to pray.

Let Us Pray

Gather and pray the Sign of the Cross together.

Leader: O Lord, open my lips.

All: That my mouth may proclaim your praise.

Leader: Let us pray.

Bow your heads as the leader prays.

All: Amen.

Listen to God's Word

Leader: A reading from the Book of the prophet Isaiah.

Read Isaiah 53:10b–12.

The word of the Lord.

All: Thanks be to God.

Sing together.

 Sing "Were You There?"

Dialogue

The Book of Isaiah was written long before the birth of Jesus. Why do you think the Church reads this passage on Good Friday?

Prayer of the Faithful

Kneel for a moment after each prayer, then stand as the leader prays.

Honor the Cross

Leader: Behold the wood of the Cross, on which hung the salvation of the world.

All: Come, let us worship.

Stand and say this acclamation three times, bowing deeply first to the left, then to the right, then to the center, always facing the cross.

All: Holy is God! Holy and Strong!

Step forward in silence, one by one, and reverence the cross by bowing, kissing the cross, or offering some other sign of reverence.

Go Forth!

Leader: Confessing that Jesus is Lord to the glory of God, go forth in the peace of Christ.

All: Thanks be to God.

Depart in silence.

FAMILY+FAITH
LIVING AND LEARNING TOGETHER

TALKING ABOUT TRIDUUM >>>

Holy Week is the holiest week of the Church year. It begins on Palm Sunday and continues until Evening Prayer on Easter Sunday. The Triduum, or "three days," marks the most sacred time of Holy Week. It begins at sundown on Holy Thursday and ends at sundown on Easter Sunday. During these three days, the whole Church fasts and prays with anticipation and hope. The Holy Thursday Mass has a unique connection with parish sacramental life. At this Mass, the holy oils that will be used for the next year are presented. These oils are blessed by the bishop at the Chrism Mass held in each diocese. The oils are used during the Sacraments of Baptism, Confirmation, Holy Orders, and the Anointing of the Sick.

Scripture

Read **Philippians 2:6–11**. It describes Jesus' attitudes of humility and obedience to his Father. When your family makes decisions, do you consider what God might want you to do?

HELPING YOUR CHILD UNDERSTAND >>>

Triduum

- Most children this age have developed a sense of sin and are aware of the need for salvation.

- Usually children this age are capable of meditation using the Sorrowful Mysteries of the Rosary or the Stations of the Cross.

CATHOLIC FAMILY CUSTOMS >>>

This lesson teaches about the importance of the Cross as a means of salvation. It makes the point that each person deals with difficult things, or "carries a cross," at some point.

- Reinforce this idea when your child has a difficult task to face, such as giving up a treat or tolerating a medical procedure.

- Honor the crosses and crucifixes in your home by dusting and cleaning them before Easter.

FAMILY PRAYER >>>

 During Triduum, you might place a crucifix or cross on the dinner table. Before your meatless meal on Good Friday, have each family member kiss or reverently touch the cross. This is similar to the actions done to honor the Cross during the Good Friday services. Pray together:

We adore you, O Christ, and we bless you, because by your Cross, you have redeemed the world.

Amen.

For a multimedia glossary of Catholic Faith Words, Sunday readings, seasonal and Saint resources, and chapter activities go to **aliveinchrist.osv.com**.

He Lives

 Let Us Pray

Leader: Lord, God, bless all your people with the joy of Easter and the continued presence of your Son forever. Through Christ our Lord.

"Give thanks to the LORD, for he is good,
his mercy endures forever." **Psalm 118:1**

All: Amen.

 Scripture

"The community of believers was of one heart and mind, and no one claimed that any of his possessions was his own, but they had everything in common. With great power the apostles bore witness to the resurrection of the Lord Jesus, and great favor was accorded them all. There was no needy person among them, for those who owned property or houses would sell them, bring the proceeds of the sale, and put them at the feet of the apostles, and they were distributed to each according to need." **Acts 4:32–35**

? What Do You Wonder?

• Why do you think the first believers lived this way?

• How easy or difficult would it be for you to live like they did?

At Easter, we often see Resurrection crosses inside and outside churches. White cloths and flowers to help proclaim Jesus' being raised to new life.

Light of the World

On Easter the Church celebrates Jesus' Resurrection. When Jesus was raised from the dead on the third day, he conquered sin and death. The Church celebrates Easter for fifty days, from Easter Sunday to Pentecost.

The Easter season is one of joy and gladness. Alleluias are sung once again. Flowers and plants fill the churches, as signs of the new life Christ brings. Choirs sing Glory to God! and the altar is draped in white cloth. All are signs of the light that Jesus brings into the world.

In the northern hemisphere, Easter comes as the darkness of winter gives way to spring. Leaves appear on trees, and flowers blossom. Spring is a season of new life.

Let Your Light Shine

Jesus' Resurrection is a sign of the new life that bursts forth in the bright light of the sun. Jesus triumphed over the selfishness that leads people away from God. He turned the darkness of sin into the light of love. That is why Jesus is called the Light of the World.

Did you ever notice that outside on a dark night, away from the lights of the city, the stars seem brighter? In a similar way, the light of Christ brightens the darkness of the world. In the midst of sadness and violence, Christ's light shines even more brightly. In the midst of loneliness or rejection, the light of Christ's love is there to warm the heart that is hurting.

➜ **What are some ways Jesus is light for you?**

➜ **How can you help others to know the light of Christ's love?**

The Light of the World Decorate the candle with symbols of Jesus as the Light of the World.

In the seven rays of light radiating from the candle flame, write things you and your family can do each week during the Easter season to bring Christ's light into your neighborhood and community. Share your ideas with your family.

Celebrate Easter

This prayer is a celebration of the Word and an act of praise and thanksgiving. A celebration of the Word is a moment of prayer with the Church using the Scriptures.

 Let Us Pray

Gather and pray the Sign of the Cross together.

Leader: Light and peace in Jesus Christ our Lord. Alleluia.

All: Thanks be to God, Alleluia.

Reader: Christ is our light in the darkness!

All: Alleluia, Alleluia, Alleluia.

Reader: Christ is the Way, the Truth, and the Life!

All: Alleluia, Alleluia, Alleluia.

Leader: Let us pray.

Bow your heads as the leader prays.

All: Amen, Alleluia.

Listen to God's Word

Reader: A reading from the holy Gospel according to Matthew.

Read Matthew 28:1–10.

The Gospel of the Lord.

All: Praise to you, Lord Jesus Christ.

Dialogue

What was your first thought as you heard this Gospel? What did Jesus tell the women?

Blessing with Holy Water

Step forward and bow before the candle. Then dip your hand in the blessed water and make the Sign of the Cross.

Leader: Let us pray.

Bow your heads as the leader prays.

All: Amen.

Go Forth!

Leader: Let us go forth and share the Good News that Christ our light has risen! Alleluia!

All: Thanks be to God. Alleluia!

 Sing "He Is Risen, Alleluia!"
He is Risen, Alleluia!
He is here with us today!
He is Risen, Alleluia!
He brings new life on this day.
Jesus, you bring new life on this day.
© 2011, John Burland. All rights reserved.

TALKING ABOUT EASTER >>>

The celebration of the Easter season includes the fifty days following the Triduum. The Easter liturgies reflect the joy of salvation. The Alleluia is sung often. The Gospels proclaim the Easter event and celebrate what God did for us through his Son, Jesus. When the priest and deacon bless the assembly with the sprinkling of holy water, all renew their baptismal commitments. The Church celebrates together as an Easter people.

Scripture

Read **Acts 4:32–35**. It describes life in the early Christian community. In what ways does your family live in harmony and provide for the needs of one another and the wider community?

HELPING YOUR CHILD UNDERSTAND >>>
Easter

- Usually fourth-graders will respond well to helping those in need.

- At this age, most children are interested in and want to participate in rituals and ritual activity.

- As a rule, children this age are alert to the sensate. They will be aware of and motivated by expansive Easter symbols and music.

CATHOLIC FAMILY CUSTOMS >>>

Depending on when Easter occurs, some part of the season will occur during the month of May. The Feast of Saint Joseph the worker is celebrated on May 1. This is a good day to honor workers who give service to your family (waste removal, fire and police, plumbers, or electricians) with a word of thanks.

FAMILY PRAYER >>>

The Alleluia is a prayer of praise and thanksgiving. Celebrate in the Resurrection at your evening meal. Encourage your child to lead you. Turn off all lights, then light a candle to symbolize the light of Christ.

Leader: Jesus, we praise you for your Easter victory over sin and death.

All: Alleluia!

Leader: Increase our joy during these fifty days of Easter, and transform us by the light of your Resurrection.

All: Alleluia!

For a multimedia glossary of Catholic Faith Words, Sunday readings, seasonal and saint resources, and chapter activities go to **aliveinchrist.osv.com**.

Ascension

 Let Us Pray

Leader: Dear Lord,
Help us to understand that your will is for us to enjoy eternal happiness with you in Heaven. Give us the help of the Holy Spirit to live as faithful followers here, so that one day we will enjoy that happiness. In your name we pray.

"The LORD has set his throne in heaven; his dominion extends over all."   **Psalm 103:19**

All: Amen.

 Scripture

"'I am the resurrection and the life; whoever believes in me, even if he dies, will live, and everyone who lives and believes in me will never die. Do you believe this?' She said to him, 'Yes, Lord. I have come to believe that you are the Messiah, the Son of God, the one who is coming into the world.'"   **John 11:25–27**

 What Do You Wonder?

- What would it be like to live forever?
- How do you imagine Heaven?

Death and Dying

Jesus died and rose and then ascended into Heaven to be with his Father forever. All of us will die some day, too. But we have the chance to be with Jesus and his Father in Heaven. We are always sad when someone close to us dies because we miss that person. Jesus' Resurrection and his Ascension give us faith and hope that when a person dies, his or her life continues, but it is different.

Death is a passing from this life to new life. Our body dies but our soul lives on. However, our bodies will also rise at the end of time On the Feast of the Ascension, the Church celebrates Jesus' return to his Father in Heaven. Ascension Thursday is celebrated forty days after Easter.

Check off the things that you already do. Circle something you will do in the future. Then add one idea to the list.

The Offer

God calls everyone at all times and offers us the gift of salvation. We accept God's gift of salvation through our faith in Jesus Christ. Real faith will show itself in the things we do.

☐ We take time to listen and talk to God.

☐ We are kind and respectful to others.

☐ We take care of all God's gifts.

☐ We reach out to the poor, to those who are sick, and to those who are outcasts.

_____

_____

Let Us Pray

Remember the Ascension

Gather to sing and pray the Sign of the Cross together.

Leader: We proclaim your Death, O Lord,
and profess your Resurrection
until you come again.
Let us pray.

Bow your heads as the leader prays.

All: Amen.

Listen to God's Word

Leader: A reading from the holy Gospel according to John.

Read John 14:1–3

Silent Reflection

Presentation of Names

Leader: One way to give witness to the Resurrection is to commend those who have died to God. Write the names of people who have died whom you wish to remember in prayer. Then place your list in the bowl in the front of the room.

After the last child has come forward, the intercessions begin. Respond to each intercession with these words.

All: I place my trust and hope in God.

Go Forth!

Leader: Let us offer a prayer of praise to God—Father, Son, and Holy Spirit.

 Sing "Rise Up with Him"

FAMILY+FAITH
LIVING AND LEARNING TOGETHER

TALKING ABOUT ASCENSION >>>

Catholics celebrate the Feast of Ascension Thursday forty days after Easter. In some dioceses and parishes, the feast is moved from Thursday to the seventh Sunday of Easter. The Feast of the Ascension celebrates the Risen Jesus returning to his Father in Heaven. In the United States, Ascension Thursday is a Holy Day of Obligation.

Scripture

Read **John 11:25–27**. It says that those who believe in Jesus will live, and that everyone who lives and believes in Jesus will never die. Who are your loved ones you hope to see again after death?

HELPING YOUR CHILD UNDERSTAND >>>

Ascension

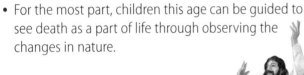

- Often children this age picture only the wondrous elements of the story of the Ascension. They need assistance making it appropriate to their own lives.

- Sometimes children this age find it difficult to talk about death and dying.

- For the most part, children this age can be guided to see death as a part of life through observing the changes in nature.

FEASTS OF THE SEASON >>>
Saint Mathias

On May 14, the Church celebrates the Feast of Saint Matthias. He was the Apostle chosen to replace Judas. He was chosen because he was with the disciples throughout Jesus' life, and he was a witness to the Resurrection.

FAMILY PRAYER >>>

 Pray this traditional prayer to the Holy Spirit as a dinner or bedtime prayer every day between Ascension Thursday and Pentecost Sunday. Each time, make note of the names of family members or friends who have died.

Eternal rest grant to them, O Lord
and let perpetual light shine upon them.
May they rest in peace.

Amen.

For a multimedia glossary of Catholic Faith Words, Sunday readings, seasonal and Saint resources, and chapter activities go to **aliveinchrist.osv.com**.

Pentecost

Let Us Pray

Leader: Come Holy Spirit
send us your power and your gifts,
that we may be instruments
of the coming of God's Kingdom.
Through Christ, our Lord.

"Bless the LORD, my soul!
LORD, my God, you are great indeed!"
Psalm 104:1

All: Amen.

Scripture

"No one can say, 'Jesus is Lord,' except by the holy Spirit. There are different kinds of spiritual gifts but the same Spirit; there are different forms of service but the same Lord; there are different workings but the same God who produces all of them in everyone. To each individual the manifestation of the Spirit is given for some benefit." **1 Corinthians 12:3b–7, 12–13**

? What Do You Wonder?

- What gifts has the Spirit given you?
- How do people use their gifts for the common good?

Pentecost Today

Today the Church rejoices in the Resurrection of the Lord for fifty days after Easter. Then on Pentecost, the Church celebrates the gift of the Holy Spirit to the Church. The Holy Spirit gave the first disciples the wisdom and courage they needed to preach the Gospel.

Underline the Holy Spirit's action in and for the Church from Pentecost through to today.

- The Feast of Pentecost celebrates the coming of the Holy Spirit on Mary and the Apostles.

- Pentecost occurs fifty days after Easter and marks the end of the Easter season.

- On Pentecost the priest wears red vestments. Red reminds us of the fire of the Holy Spirit.

The coming of the Holy Spirit marked the beginning of the Apostles' active ministry of spreading the Gospel after Jesus' Ascension. From this time onward, the Church has been empowered by the Holy Spirit to spread the Good News by word and action. He builds up the Church, empowers her for service, and is the source of her holiness.

➜ **How is the Holy Spirit active in the world today?**

© Our Sunday Visitor

Let Us Pray

Celebrate Pentecost

Gather and pray the Sign of the Cross together.

Leader: Light and peace in Jesus Christ our Lord, Alleluia.

All: Thanks be to God, Alleluia.

Leader: Let us pray.

Bow your heads as the leader prays.

All: Amen.

Listen to God's Word

Reader: A reading from the Acts of the Apostles.

Read Acts 2:1–11.

The word of the Lord.

All: Thanks be to God.

Prayer of the Faithful

Leader: Let us pray for the Church and the world, that all will be open to the power of the Holy Spirit.

Respond to each prayer with these words.

All: Send us your Spirit, O Lord.

Go Forth!

Leader: Let us go forth in love, Alleluia.

All: Thanks be to God, Alleluia!

 Sing "Come, Holy Ghost"

FAMILY+FAITH
LIVING AND LEARNING TOGETHER

TALKING ABOUT PENTECOST >>>

At Pentecost we remember the coming of the Holy Spirit on the Apostles and Mary. The liturgical color for this celebration is red, which symbolizes the fire of Pentecost and the power of the Holy Spirit. In Scripture readings, music, and gestures, the Church celebrates God's empowering actions through the Gifts of the Holy Spirit. Pentecost Sunday is an uplifting celebration of God's ongoing work in the world.

Scripture

 Read **1 Corinthians 12:3b–13**. It describes the varieties of gifts members of the Church are given to use for the good of the community. What gifts does your family have that can be used in service to others?

HELPING YOUR CHILD UNDERSTAND >>>
Pentecost

- Most children this age are beginning to develop a sense of their own gifts and want to use them to help others.

- Usually children this age find guided meditation helpful to enter into a Scripture passage.

- Children this age will be interested in creating art and poetry images of the Holy Spirit.

FEASTS OF THE SEASON >>>
Saint Bernardine of Siena

May 20 is the Feast of Saint Bernardine of Siena. Bernardine had two gifts he used for others. In his younger life, he had a gift for healing, which he used in a hospital with patients who were dying during a plague. Later, he received a gift for preaching, and he traveled extensively preaching about, sin, virtue, and God's mercy.

FAMILY PRAYER >>>

 Say this prayer before your family Pentecost meal.

Come, Holy Spirit, fill the hearts of your faithful.
And kindle in them the fire of your love.
Send forth your Spirit and they shall be created.
And you will renew the face of the earth.

Lord, by the light of the Holy Spirit you have taught the hearts of your faithful. In the same Spirit, help us to relish what is right and always rejoice in your consolation. We ask this through Christ our Lord, Amen.

For a multimedia glossary of Catholic Faith Words, Sunday readings, seasonal and Saint resources, and chapter activities go to **aliveinchrist.osv.com**.

Units at a Glance

Revelation

Our Catholic Tradition

- God communicates a loving plan for all of creation. We learn of this in Sacred Scripture and Sacred Tradition. (CCC, 50, 81)

- God stays true and faithful to his promises. Through his covenants, God keeps telling and showing people that he will be faithful, even though we sin. (CCC, 211)

- God helps us understand how to be faithful to him. Through the Ten Commandments, God revealed how he wants all of his children to live. (CCC, 2060)

How does God show he is faithful to his covenant through the lives of Abraham, Joseph, and Moses?

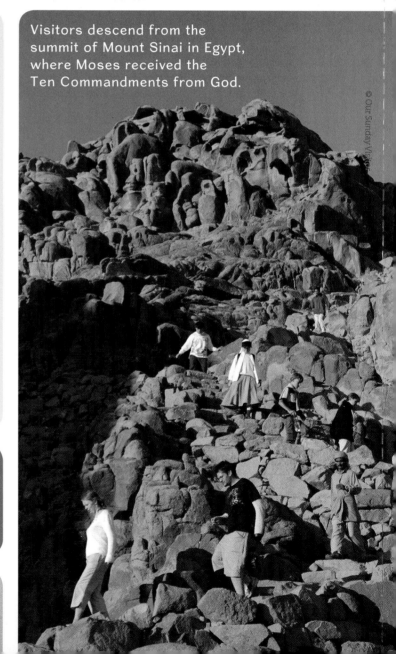

Visitors descend from the summit of Mount Sinai in Egypt, where Moses received the Ten Commandments from God.

© Our Sunday Visitor

God's Providence

 Let Us Pray

Leader: Gracious God, we thank you for caring for and guiding us.

"I will instruct you and show you the way
   you should walk,
   give you counsel with my eye upon you."
Psalm 32:8

All: God our Father, your great love for us never ends. We trust that following your plan for us will bring us happiness and peace. Amen.

 Scripture

"For [God] spoke and it came to be,
   commanded, and it stood in place.

But the plan of the LORD stands forever,
   the designs of his heart through all generations.

Blessed is the nation whose God is the LORD,
   the people chosen as his inheritance."
Psalm 33:9, 11–12

? What Do You Wonder?

- How many things did God create that we don't even know about?

- How do you know God's plan?

God's Creation

What did God say about all that he had made?

The world is something like a kaleidoscope. Its complex patterns and movements give clues to God's amazing plan for creation. This Scripture account teaches us about God and his creation.

ⓣ Scripture

The Story of Creation

In the beginning, when God created the heavens and the earth, the earth was a formless wasteland. It was completely dark. A mighty wind swept over the waters.

Then God said, "Let there be light," and there was light. He separated the light from the darkness. God called the light "day" and the darkness "night." God saw that it was good. This was the first day.

Then God said, "Let there be a dome in the middle of the waters." God made the dome. It separated the water above from the water below. God called the dome "the sky." God saw that it was good. This was the second day.

Then God said, "Let the water under the sky be gathered into a single basin." The water was gathered into a single basin and dry land appeared. God called the dry land "earth." He called the water "the sea." God saw that it was good.

Then God said, "Let there be plants, and trees of every kind." The earth brought forth every kind of plant and every kind of fruit tree. God saw that it was good. This was the third day.

Then God said, "Let there be lights in the dome of the sky, to separate day from night." God made two great lights. He made the sun for the day and the moon for the night. Then God made the stars. God saw that it was good. This was the fourth day.

Then God said, "Let the seas be filled with living creatures and the sky with flying birds." God created all kinds of swimming creatures and all kinds of birds. God saw that it was good. This was the fifth day.

Then God said, "Let the earth be filled with all kinds of living creatures." God made wild animals, cattle, and all kinds of creeping things. God saw that it was good. Then God said, "Let there be people, made in my own image and likeness." God created people, a man and a woman. He blessed them and told them to take care of the earth, the seas, and all the plants and living creatures. God looked at everything he made and saw that it was very good! This was the sixth day.

After God had finished creating the world, he rested. He blessed the seventh day and made it holy.

Based on Genesis 1:1–31, 2:1–3

1. Circle the word *good* every time it appears in the Scripture passage.

2. Tell what you learned about God from this Scripture passage.

Share Your Faith

Reflect On the globe, fill in some of the ways the world shows God's love and care for his creation.

Share Talk about some of these ways with a partner.

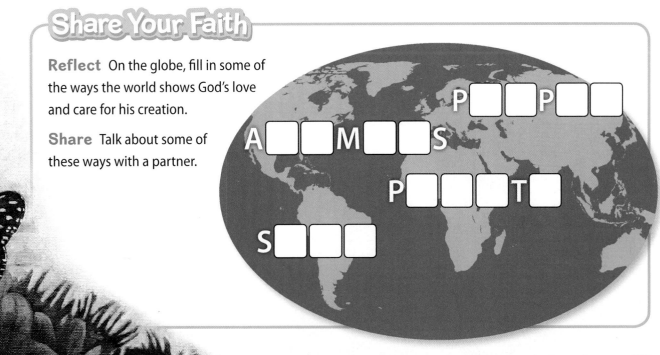

P □ □ P □ □

A □ □ M □ □ S

P □ □ □ T □

S □ □ □

A Plan of Loving Goodness

How does God reveal his plan to us?

Catholic Faith Words

providence God's loving care for all things; God's will and plan for creation

From the beginning, God has had a loving plan for all creation. As God's plan unfolds, he keeps everyone and everything in his loving care. This is called **providence**. God has a plan for you and for everyone.

Once, long before Jesus was born, there was a young man who lived in the tiny kingdom of Judah, where the nation of Israel is today. His name was Jeremiah, which means "the Lord raises up." Jeremiah was called by God to speak the truth to his people in a time of great danger. They had lost their way and were being invaded by powerful nations. This is how Jeremiah remembered God calling him.

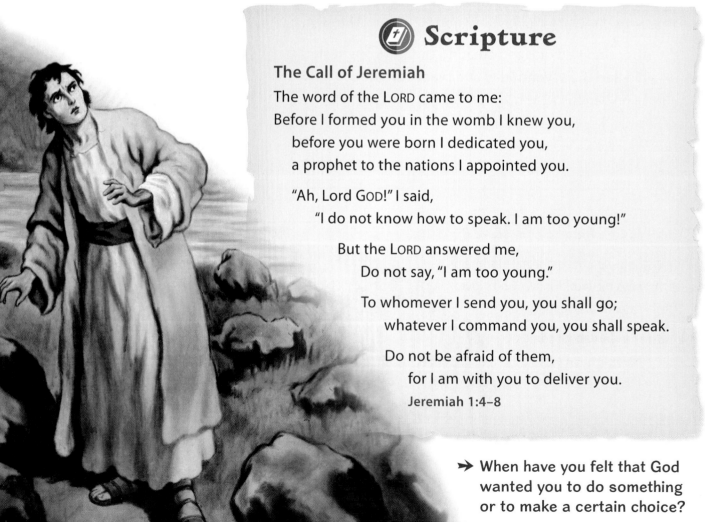

Scripture

The Call of Jeremiah
The word of the LORD came to me:
Before I formed you in the womb I knew you,
    before you were born I dedicated you,
    a prophet to the nations I appointed you.

"Ah, Lord GOD!" I said,
    "I do not know how to speak. I am too young!"

But the LORD answered me,
    Do not say, "I am too young."

To whomever I send you, you shall go;
    whatever I command you, you shall speak.

Do not be afraid of them,
    for I am with you to deliver you.
Jeremiah 1:4–8

➜ When have you felt that God wanted you to do something or to make a certain choice?

➜ How did you know?

Jeremiah answered God's call, or command, and followed his plan. The story of Jeremiah is in the Old Testament of the Bible. The Bible, also called **Sacred Scripture**, is God's Word written in human words. There are many more stories in the Old Testament that can show you how others have followed God's plan.

Then, in the New Testament, you can see God's Son, Jesus, answering his Father's call perfectly. Through Jesus, you can learn how you are to respond to God's plan for you. The Holy Spirit, whom Jesus sent to the Church, will help you.

God's Revelation

God has made himself known gradually throughout history by words and deeds and in the experience of people. The way God shares the truth about himself and his plan is called **Divine Revelation**. Revelation is found in Sacred Scripture and in the **Sacred Tradition** of the Church.

© Our Sunday Visitor

Catholic Faith Words

Sacred Scripture another name for the Bible; Sacred Scripture is the inspired Word of God written by humans

Divine Revelation the way God makes himself, and his plan for humans, known to us

Sacred Tradition God's Word to the Church, safeguarded by the Apostles and their successors, the bishops, and handed down verbally—in her creeds, Sacraments, and other teachings—to future generations

Connect Your Faith

Define Providence Explain *providence* in your own words.

Our Catholic Life

Where do you pray?

Prayer is talking and listening to God. It is raising your mind and heart to God. Prayer helps you learn about God's plan for you. Quiet time and a special place make it easier to think and pray. A prayer space is a place you can go to feel close to God.

 Add your ideas in the spaces provided.

Make Your Own Prayer Space

1. Find a Space	Think of a quiet place where you will not be disturbed. The space needs to be a place that you have permission to use and can get to by yourself. It can be in your home, your yard, or any place where you will feel safe. Name where your space would be. _____ _____
2. Prepare the Space	After you choose a prayer space, decide how you want to prepare it. If you are indoors, you might want to close the curtains or blinds, allowing only soft light. Perhaps you would like to add a religious picture, a cross, or an object from nature to help you quiet your mind and focus.
3. Prepare Yourself	Be sure to prepare yourself for prayer. Focus your eyes and listen to your breathing. Remember that God breathed his life into you when you were created. Think about a story of Jesus from the Bible, or imagine that he is sitting there with you. Tell which story might help you prepare yourself best. _____
4. Pray	Pray from your heart. Listen for God. Give thanks to him for his constant presence in your life. If you start to think of something else, remind yourself that this is a time for prayer, and go back to thinking about God.

People of Faith

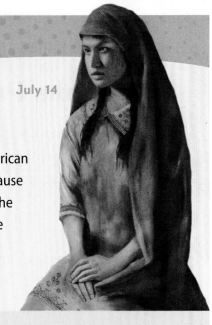

July 14

Saint Kateri Tekakwitha, 1656–1680

Saint Kateri Tekakwitha's father was a Mohawk warrior. Her mother was an Algonquian woman who was Christian. Kateri is the first Native American to be canonized. She learned about Jesus from Jesuit missionaries. Because she lived so close to nature and found God in the natural world, she is the patron of ecology, nature, and the environment. Kateri often spent time praying in the woods, where she would talk to God. She would hear him in her heart and through the wonders of creation. One of her titles is the "Lily of the Mohawks."

Discuss: What in nature reminds you of God?

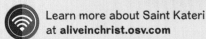 Learn more about Saint Kateri at **aliveinchrist.osv.com**

Live Your Faith

Design a prayer space for your room. What would be important to have in this space?

Identify three things on your sketch.

♥ Let Us Pray

Psalm Prayer of Praise

This prayer, taken from the Book of Psalms in the Bible, is a prayer of praise. We give praise to our loving and compassionate God, who is more than we can ever imagine.

Gather and begin with the Sign of the Cross.

Leader: Compassionate God, we praise you for your wondrous works, your kindness and love, your marvelous plan for your creation.

Reader 1: The Lord is gracious and compassionate, filled with great kindness and rich in love.

Reader 2: The Lord is good to all and compassionate toward all his works.

All: The Lord is compassionate toward all his works.

Reader 3: Let all your works give you thanks, O Lord, and let your holy People bless you.

Reader 4: The eyes of all look to you and you give them all they need.

All: The Lord is compassionate toward all his works.

Reader 5: The Lord is just in all his ways and loving toward all that he has created.

All: The Lord is compassionate toward all his works. **Based on Psalm 145**

Leader: Let us pray.

 All: Sing "I Sing the Mighty Power of God"

FAMILY+FAITH
LIVING AND LEARNING TOGETHER

YOUR CHILD LEARNED >>>

This chapter explains that God reveals himself through Sacred Scripture and the Sacred Tradition of the Church.

Scripture

 Read **Psalm 25:1–2a, 4–5** to find out about God's plan for us.

Catholics Believe

- God loves and cares for all creation and has a plan for the world.
- Everything God wants you to know about him is contained in Scripture and in the Tradition of the Church.

To learn more, go to the *Catechism of the Catholic Church #80–83, 302–308* at **usccb.org.**

People of Faith

This week, your child learned about Saint Kateri Tekakwitha, a patron of ecology and the first Native American to be canonized.

CHILDREN AT THIS AGE >>>

How They Understand God's Plan The logical nature of children's thinking at this age leads them to a sensible conclusion about God's creation: If God made everything, then he made everything for a reason. It's helpful to talk with your child about the purpose behind created things and especially the idea that he or she is made for a unique purpose as well.

CONSIDER THIS >>>

Do you ever wonder about God's plan for you?

You are God's greatest creation because he has created you in his image. He created you with a plan and purpose for your life. As Catholics, we know that "God guides his creation toward its completion or perfection through what we call his *Divine Providence*. This means that God has absolute sovereignty over all that he has made and guides his creation according to the divine plan of his will" (*USCCA, p. 56*).

LET'S TALK >>>

- Ask your child to tell you the Bible account of creation in his or her own words.
- Share a way that God has made himself known to you recently.

LET'S PRAY >>>

 O God, help us to learn to know and love you through your creation as Saint Kateri did. Amen.

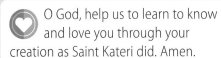 For a multimedia glossary of Catholic Faith Words, Sunday readings, seasonal and Saint resources, and chapter activities go to **aliveinchrist.osv.com.**

Chapter 1 Review

A **Work with Words** Fill in the circle next to the answer that best completes each statement.

1. God's plan for _____ is revealed gradually.
   - ○ the Bible
   - ○ creation
   - ○ animals

2. People experience God _____ .
   - ○ throughout their lives
   - ○ only after death
   - ○ never

3. God's plan for everything that exists _____ .
   - ○ continues today
   - ○ is finished
   - ○ has not started

4. God's loving care and plan for all creation is called _____ .
   - ○ Scripture
   - ○ Tradition
   - ○ providence

5. Jesus always _____ God the Father's plan for him.
   - ○ ignored
   - ○ followed
   - ○ changed

B **Check Understanding** Complete the following statements.

6. God's Divine Revelation is found in Sacred Scripture and _____ _____ .

7. _____ _____ is the inspired Word of God written in human words.

8. _____ _____ is the way God makes himself, and his plan for humans, known to us.

9. Prayer is _____ and listening to God.

10. _____ involves raising your heart and mind to God.

© Our Sunday Visitor

 Go to **aliveinchrist.osv.com** for an interactive review.

God Is Faithful

 Let Us Pray

Leader: Lord of all faithfulness, gather us as your people and keep us close to your heart.

"I will sing of your mercy forever, LORD
   proclaim your faithfulness through all ages.
For I said, 'My mercy is established forever;
   my faithfulness will stand as long as the
      heavens.'" **Psalm 89:2–3**

All: Faithful God, thank you for making us your own.
Thank you for believing in us. Thank you for
giving us faith. Amen.

 Scripture

"This is the covenant I will establish with
   them after those days, says the Lord:

'I will put my laws in their hearts,
and I will write them upon their minds. . . .
Their sins and their evildoing I will remember no more.'

Let us hold unwaveringly to our confession that gives us
hope, for he who made the promise is trustworthy."
Hebrews 10:16–17, 23

 What Do You Wonder?

- How did God show his faithfulness to the first humans?

- Who or what helps you strengthen your faith in God?

In the biblical Creation accounts, we learn about our first parents, known as Adam and Eve.

The First Sin

How did Adam and Eve's choice affect all of us?

For Adam and Eve, there was a time when every day was a good day. But one day, Satan, a fallen angel who was God's enemy, came to Eve in the form of a snake and tempted her. We learn from the Book of Genesis what Adam and Eve did. Genesis is the first book of the Bible. Together, the first five books of the Bible are called the Pentateuch. The five books are: Genesis, Exodus, Leviticus, Numbers, and Deuteronomy.

Catholic Faith Words

Original Sin the sin of our first parents, Adam and Eve, which led to the sinful condition of the human race from its beginning

salvation the loving action of God's forgiveness of sins and the restoration of friendship with him brought by Jesus

 **Scripture**

In the Garden

In the Garden of Eden was one special tree that God told Adam and Eve not to touch. But Satan convinced Eve that if she and Adam ate the fruit of that tree, they could be more like God. Adam and Eve did as Satan said; but after they sinned, they felt ashamed. They learned how it felt to do something wrong.

Everything got harder for Adam and Eve. God sent them away from the garden. They had to work to find food and shelter. From then on, jealousy, sadness, and fighting were in the world. **Based on Genesis 3**

Consequences

Humans were created to share God's life and to be happy with God forever. By disobeying God, Adam and Eve broke their friendship with God. This sin of our first parents is called **Original Sin** because ever since that choice was made, sin has been present throughout the world. Original Sin affects every human. The inclination to sin, suffering, and death all came into the world as a result of Original Sin.

Even though God sent Adam and Eve away from the garden, he did not abandon them. He remained faithful and promised **salvation**. He wanted all humans to be free and faithful to him, so they could be happy forever.

The Book of Genesis then tells another important story, the story of Noah. The point of Noah's story is that even when people continued to sin and to disobey God, God was faithful.

Underline what happened because of Original Sin.

Share Your Faith

Reflect Find some stories in the news that are examples of the effects of Original Sin in the world today.

Share In a small group, talk about ways that people can act as God wants them to in these situations.

A Sacred Promise

What did God ask of and promise to Abram?

After a long time, God called a man named Abram to help humans remain faithful.

 **Scripture**

Abram's Call and Journey

The LORD called Abram, promising to bless him and make of him a great nation. Abram took his wife, Sarai, his brother's son Lot, and their possessions on the long journey to the new land as God directed.

Abram and his family were never alone on their difficult journey. They knew that God was always with them. Every time Abram reached a stop on the journey, he built an altar of thanksgiving to the LORD. **Based on Genesis 12:1–8**

God's Promise

Many years later, after Abram had settled in the land of Canaan, the LORD spoke again to him, saying, "Don't be afraid! I will protect and reward you."

Abram replied, "LORD, you have given me everything I could ask for, except children."

The LORD told Abram, "Look at the sky and count the stars. That is how many descendants you will have."

God spoke to Abram again. God made a covenant with Abram and his descendants for all time. God told Abram, "To your descendants I give this land . . . I am making you the father of a multitude of nations." The land of Canaan would belong to Abram and his descendants forever, and these people would be God's people.

Based on Genesis 15:1–5, 18; 17:5–9, 15; 21:1–3

God's Covenant with Abraham

God revealed his plan to Abram in a new way by making a **covenant**, or sacred promise or agreement, with him. As a sign of the covenant, God changed the names of Abram and Sarai to Abraham and Sarah. Soon after that, even though Sarah was old, she had a son, whom the couple named Isaac.

Abraham and Sarah never turned away from God. Like Abraham and Sarah, you are **faithful** to God every time you obey his laws and make loving choices.

Abraham is considered an ancestor in faith of Christianity, Judaism, and Islam. These religions see their origins in Abraham's free response to God's revelation that he was the one God Abraham should believe in and follow.

In prayer before the Blessed Sacrament, we are in the presence of Christ, who remained faithful to God the Father and fulfilled the covenant.

Catholic Faith Words

covenant a sacred promise or agreement between God and humans

faithful to be constant and loyal in your commitments to God and others, just as he is faithful to you

Connect Your Faith

Show Faith Write your first name in colorful letters below. Around your name, write words that tell how you show that you are faithful to God.

Our Catholic Life

How do you remain faithful?

Often we ask God for help and guidance. Sometimes his help does not come as quickly as we would like. Or it may not be the help we expect. It may be difficult to be faithful. But, we continue to pray and trust that God will give us the help we need to get through whatever we face.

Abraham and Sarah prayed and waited for many years before they had their first child. They were shocked to learn they would have a child so late in life. But, their son, Isaac, arrived according to the timing of God's plan.

At times, God's answer is not easy to see. Many times when you ask for his help, God gives you the ability to help yourself. Jessica learns this in the following situation.

 Write about a time when you asked God for help and later realized that he had given you what you needed to help yourself.

Jessica's story

Jessica wanted the video game she saw at the store. She prayed, asking God for the game. She continued to pray for several weeks, but still she did not get the game. One day her neighbor offered Jessica $5 to water his plants while he was out of town. Another neighbor asked Jessica to walk her dog. At the end of the week, Jessica had $10. She realized that she could save her money for the game. With her parents' permission, Jessica started asking neighbors whether they had odd jobs for her to do. After two months, Jessica had enough money to buy the video game.

Your story

_____
_____
_____
_____
_____
_____
_____
_____
_____

People of Faith

Saint Bridget of Sweden, ~1303–1373

July 23

Saint Bridget was born to one of the wealthiest landowners in all of Sweden. In fact, her family was related to the king. Her parents made sure that she was taught religion. By the time she was seven, she was known to have religious dreams, or visions, of Jesus and the Holy Family. For an entire year, she prayed fifteen Our Fathers and fifteen Hail Marys every day, along with other prayers Jesus taught her.

Discuss: Tell about a time when you waited for God to answer a prayer.

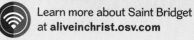
Learn more about Saint Bridget at **aliveinchrist.osv.com**

Live Your Faith

Circle the actions below that describe how you can follow God's example, being loyal and trustworthy to friends, family, and most especially God.

lying

being friendly

helping in class

telling the truth

sharing possessions

stealing

Let Us Pray

Covenant Prayer

This covenant prayer recalls and promises some of the ways we are faithful to our loving God.

Gather and begin with the Sign of the Cross.

Leader: God Ever Faithful, we gather, aware of your constant faithfulness to us.

All: Thank you for your gift of faithfulness, O God. Help us to trust in you. We are your covenant People.

Name ways you have made loving choices and been faithful. Then respond:

God Ever Faithful, we are your covenant People.

Leader: Let us pray.

 All: Sing "God Keeps His Promises"
God keeps his promises.
God keeps his promises
God keeps his promises to us
God keeps his promises
God keeps his promises
Every word he says you can trust!
© 2010, Chet A. Chambers. Published by Our Sunday Visitor, Inc.

FAMILY+FAITH
LIVING AND LEARNING TOGETHER

YOUR CHILD LEARNED >>>

This chapter explains Original Sin, its consequences, and how God loves us despite our choices to act against his plan for our happiness and salvation.

Scripture

Read **Hebrews 10:16–17, 23** to find out about God's promises of love.

Catholics Believe

- God's covenant with Abraham reveals that God is always faithful to his People.

- Sin is present in the world because of human choice.

To learn more, go to the *Catechism of the Catholic Church #59–61, 385–389* at **usccb.org.**

People of Faith

This week, your child learned about Saint Bridget of Sweden. She is known for her faithfulness in prayer.

CHILDREN AT THIS AGE >>>

How They Understand God's Faithfulness As he or she grows in social skills and awareness, your child has deeper friendships than before. Your child understands that trust and loyalty are essential to being in relationship with someone else. This provides a natural context in which to learn about God's covenants and his faithfulness in keeping his promises— even when we as human beings do not always live up to our commitments to God.

CONSIDER THIS >>>

How can making good choices make you happy?

God created us to live in happiness with him forever. When we sin, we turn away from God and our relationship with him. As Catholics, we realize that "though venial sin does not completely destroy the love we need for eternal happiness, it weakens that love and impedes our progress in the practice of virtue and the moral good. Thus, over time, it can have serious consequences" (*USCCA*, p. 313).

LET'S TALK >>>

- Ask your child to tell you about God's covenant with his People and why it was needed.

- Talk with each other about what it means to be trustworthy and loyal to God and one another.

LET'S PRAY >>>

Dear God, help us to pray faithfully to you like Saint Bridget did. Amen.

For a multimedia glossary of Catholic Faith Words, Sunday readings, seasonal and Saint resources, and chapter activities go to **aliveinchrist.osv.com**.

Chapter 2 Review

A **Work with Words** Complete each sentence with the correct word from the Word Bank.

Word Bank
· · · · · · · · · · ·
faithful

sin

covenant

names

friendship

1. By disobeying God, Adam and Eve broke their

   _____ with him.

2. One consequence of the disobedience of Adam and Eve is

   the inclination to _____ .

3. God always remains _____ to his People.

4. God made a _____ with Abraham and

   his descendants.

5. As a sign of the covenant, God changed the _____

   of Abram and Sarai.

B **Check Understanding** Fill in the circle of the choice that best completes each sentence.

6. God created humans to be _____ with him forever.

   ○ **happy**   ○ **confused**   ○ **out of relationship**

7. _____ is the child of Abraham and Sarah.

   ○ **Adam**   ○ **Isaac**   ○ **Eve**

8. The choice of our first parents, Adam and Eve, to disobey God is called _____ .

   ○ **Original Sin**   ○ **Original Temptation**   ○ **Original Suffering**

9. _____ is the loving action of God's forgiveness of sins and the restoration
   of friendship with God through Jesus.

   ○ **Happiness**   ○ **Honesty**   ○ **Salvation**

10. Abraham is an _____ in faith.

    ○ **author**   ○ **ancestor**   ○ **official**

© Our Sunday Visitor

Go to **aliveinchrist.osv.com** for an interactive review.

God's Commandments

 ## Let Us Pray

Leader: Loving Father, you made us to know you and your desire for us.

"I delight to do your will, my God;
your law is in my inner being!" **Psalm 40:9**

All: O God, help us to learn how to listen for your voice so that we will know how to follow you. Amen.

🔖 Scripture

"When [Moses] looked, although the bush was on fire, it was not being consumed. . . . When the LORD saw that he had turned aside to look, God called out to him from the bush: Moses! Moses! He answered, 'Here I am.' God said: Do not come near! Remove your sandals from your feet, for the place where you stand is holy ground." **Exodus 3:2b, 4–5**

❓ What Do You Wonder?

- How does God speak to people today?
- How do the Ten Commandments help you to know God and what he wants for you?

From Slavery to Freedom

How does God give his people freedom?

God created human beings to be free. He asks us to use the gift of free will to answer his call to live as his People. Because of sin, we know that there are times when others try to take away our freedom. Here are two Bible stories about how God led his People from slavery to freedom.

God gave Joseph the ability to interpret dreams. After he explained the Pharaoh's dreams, Pharaoh called Joseph "a man so endowed with the spirit of God" (Genesis 41:38).

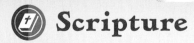

Scripture

Joseph and His Brothers

Jacob, one of Abraham's descendants, had twelve sons. Jacob's older sons hated their younger brother Joseph because he was their father's favorite.

One day Joseph's brothers threw him into a dry well. Then, they sold him as a slave in Egypt. They told their father that wild animals had killed Joseph. Now, more of their father's goods would belong to them.

Over the years, Joseph's power to tell the meaning of dreams won him a place of honor with Pharaoh, the leader of Egypt. During a famine, Joseph's brothers came to the court to beg for grain. The brothers did not recognize Joseph, but Joseph knew them.

To test them, Joseph had servants fill the brothers' sacks with grain and put a silver cup into the sack of his brother Benjamin. Later, he had his servants follow them and discover the silver cup in the sack. Joseph then told the brothers that Benjamin was to be his slave.

Benjamin's brother Judah pleaded for him, saying that their father would be brokenhearted if Benjamin did not return. At this news, Joseph wept and told the men that he was their brother. He forgave them.

Based on Genesis 37:1–4, 42:6–8, 44:1–12, 45:4–5

➜ **When have you forgiven someone as Joseph did?**

God Calls Moses

When Joseph's brothers sold him as a slave, they caused problems for themselves as well. It was only when Joseph forgave his brothers that his family knew real freedom and happiness again.

 Scripture

The Exodus from Egypt

Many years later, God's People, the Israelites, were slaves in Egypt. Their male children were being killed, so one Israelite mother hid her baby boy in a basket near the Nile River. When Pharaoh's daughter found the baby, she kept him and named him Moses. She raised him at court as her son.

When Moses grew older, God called him to be a leader of his people. God asked Moses to tell Pharaoh to stop hurting the Israelites, but Pharaoh did not listen.

Finally, Moses was able to lead the Israelites out of Egypt. At the Red Sea, Moses raised his staff and the waters parted for the Israelites to pass through.

Based on Exodus 2:1–10, 14:10–31, 15:19–21

➜ **Who was Moses and what did he do?**

Share Your Faith

Reflect How did forgiveness help Joseph's family experience happiness again?

Share Tell how you felt after you were forgiven for something you'd done or said.

Laws to Guide Us

How do the Ten Commandments help us to be faithful?

The Israelites were free from slavery, but they still needed God's help. After they crossed the Red Sea, they wandered in the desert for years. They forgot that God had saved them from slavery in Egypt. Moses struggled to keep order among God's People and to find food and water for them. He complained to God about his hard job, and God helped him.

In the desert, God called Moses up to Mount Sinai. After God showed his power with thunder and lightning, he gave Moses the **Ten Commandments** as laws to show the people how they were to live.

Moses and the Israelites built a special container, called the **ark of the covenant**, to house the tablets of the Ten Commandments. They carried the ark with them wherever they went as a reminder that God was with them.

Living God's Covenant

Just as the Ten Commandments helped the Israelites live their covenant relationship with God, the Commandments are also a guide for you. They tell you the minimum that is required to love God and others. The first three Commandments show you how to be faithful to God. The last seven show you how to treat other people with love. The chart on the next page names the Ten Commandments and explains what each one means for you.

 Underline why God gave his People the Ten Commandments.

© Our Sunday Visitor

Catholic Faith Words

Ten Commandments the summary of laws that God gave Moses on Mount Sinai. They tell what is necessary in order to love God and others.

ark of the covenant a wooden chest that housed the tablets of the Ten Commandments. The Israelites carried it wherever they went as a reminder that God was with them.

The Ten Commandments

The Commandment	What the Commandment Means
1. I am the Lord your God. You shall not have strange gods before me.	• Place your faith in God alone. • Worship, praise, and thank the Creator. • Believe in, trust, and love God.
2. You shall not take the name of the Lord your God in vain.	• Speak God's name with reverence. • Don't curse. • Never call on God to witness to a lie.
3. Remember to keep holy the Lord's Day.	• Gather to worship at the Eucharist. • Rest and avoid unnecessary work on Sunday.
4. Honor your father and your mother.	• Respect and obey your parents, guardians, and others who have proper authority.
5. You shall not kill.	• Respect and protect the lives of others and your own life.
6. You shall not commit adultery.	• Be faithful and loyal to friends and family. • Be pure and act appropriately to respect God's gift of sexuality.
7. You shall not steal.	• Respect the things that belong to others. • Share what you have with those in need.
8. You shall not bear false witness against your neighbor.	• Be honest and truthful. • Do not brag about yourself. • Do not say untruthful or negative things about others.
9. You shall not covet your neighbor's wife.	• Practice modesty in thoughts, words, and dress.
10. You shall not covet your neighbor's goods.	• Rejoice in others' good fortune. • Do not be jealous of others' possessions. • Do not be greedy.

Connect Your Faith

Commandments and You Talk with a partner about a decision you made this week, and tell which Commandment you followed when you made that decision.

Our Catholic Life

How can you live as the Ten Commandments require?

God gave Moses the Ten Commandments to share with his People. These Commandments help us live in a way that is pleasing to God.

Page 77 lists explanations of each Commandment. Here are some other ways to live out the Commandments.

Write the correct Commandment number next to each example. Then fill in the last section with one way to live out the Fourth Commandment.

The Ten Commandments

☐	Remember that religious holidays, such as Christmas and Easter, are about Jesus, not about gifts and candy.
☐	When someone lends you something, treat it with great care. Always return it in good condition.
☐	On Sunday, go to Mass and spend time in quiet reflection about your week.
☐	Listen when your parents ask you to do something. Don't make them ask you repeatedly.
☐	Use the names of God and Jesus with reverence and respect.
☐	Treat people and animals with care.
☐	Behave with decency.
☐	Follow Jesus' example of respecting himself and his friends.
☐	Be thankful for what you have, and share with others.
☐	Speak honestly about others.
☐	_____

People of Faith

January 7

Saint Raymond of Peñafort, c. 1175–1275

Many of our Church laws are based on the Ten Commandments. Laws that are written for the Church are called "canon laws." Saint Raymond of Peñafort was a priest who studied canon law. There were many canon laws, but they were not organized into one place. The Pope asked Raymond to put all the canon laws in one book. He had to make sure no law was repeated. It was a big job! When all the laws were in one book, Saint Raymond became the head of the Dominican Order. He lived about 800 years ago.

Discuss: How do you follow the Ten Commandments?

Learn more about Saint Raymond
at **aliveinchrist.osv.com**

Live Your Faith

Write the number of the Commandment that is not being followed in each of the two pictures below.

Talk with a partner about what you would do in each situation. Then draw a picture of yourself keeping one Commandment.

Let Us Pray

Psalm Prayer of Praise

Gather and begin with the Sign of the Cross.

Leader: The Lord gives us the Commandments as a way of living. Let us praise God for the gift of salvation.

Reader 1: Then was our mouth filled with laughter, on our lips there were songs.

All: God has done great things for us.

Reader 2: What marvels the Lord worked for us! Indeed, we were glad.

All: God has done great things for us.

Reader 3: Those who are sowing in tears will sing when they reap.

All: God has done great things for us.

Reader 4: They go out, they go out, full of tears; they come back, they come back, full of song.

All: God has done great things for us.

Leader: Let us pray.

Bow your head as the leader prays.

All: Amen. **Based on Psalm 126**

 Sing "My Ten Commandments"

FAMILY+FAITH
LIVING AND LEARNING TOGETHER

YOUR CHILD LEARNED >>>

This chapter explains that the Ten Commandments teach us how to respond to God, who first loved us, and how to love others.

Scripture

 Read **Exodus 3:2b, 4–5** to find out how God communicated to Moses through the burning bush.

Catholics Believe

• God gave you the Ten Commandments to help you be faithful to him and his covenant.

• The Commandments tell you ways to love God and others.

To learn more, go to the *Catechism of the Catholic Church #2055, 2060–2061* at **usccb.org.**

People of Faith

This week, your child learned about Saint Raymond of Peñafort. Saint Raymond was known for compiling all the Church's canon laws into one book.

CHILDREN AT THIS AGE >>>

How They Understand the Ten Commandments Your child is probably a practical, concrete thinker, but children this age are also beginning to understand that morality involves more than what people see on the outside. Commandments of the heart such as "You shall not covet" are beginning to make sense as your child internalizes an understanding of living a Christian life. In this process, conscience formation and character building are moving toward the next stage of development.

CONSIDER THIS >>>

What does setting limits for your child teach him or her about love?

Out of love, we set limits for our children to keep them safe and healthy as well as teach them how to treat others with respect. As Catholics, we understand that "before God gave the Commandments at Sinai, he entered into a covenant of love with the community of Israel (cf. Exodus 19:3–6). Once the covenant was established, God gave the people the Ten Commandments in order to teach them the way to live the covenant of love" (*USCCA, p. 325*).

LET'S TALK >>>

• Ask your child to tell you about Joseph and his brothers.

• Talk together about what positive things we can do when we are feeling jealous.

LET'S PRAY >>>

 Dear God, help us to always keep your Commandments. Amen.

 For a multimedia glossary of Catholic Faith Words, Sunday readings, seasonal and Saint resources, and chapter activities go to **aliveinchrist.osv.com**.

Chapter 3 Review

A **Work with Words** Match each description in Column 1 with the correct term in Column 2.

Column 1   Column 2

1. forgave his brothers   Moses

2. place of law–giving   Pharaoh

3. Israelites' place of slavery   Mount Sinai

4. leader of Egypt   Joseph

5. led Israelites to freedom   Egypt

B **Check Understanding** Circle True if a statement is true, and circle False if a statement is false. Correct any false statements.

6. God gave Moses the Ten Commandments on Mount Sinai.

   True   **False**

   _____

7. The Third Commandment requires you to avoid gossip.

   True   **False**

   _____

8. The Ten Commandments were only for Moses to keep for himself.

   True   **False**

   _____

9. Moses led his followers out of Egypt.

   True   **False**

   _____

10. Joseph was the leader of Egypt.

   True   **False**

   _____

Go to **aliveinchrist.osv.com** for an interactive review.

Unit Review

A **Work with Words** Use the clues to solve the puzzle. Write the answer to each clue in the boxes. When you have finished, read down the column with the circles to find the hidden word you can use to answer number 10.

1. Original _____ is what we call Adam and Eve's choice to disobey God.

2. "You shall not have strange gods before me" is part of the _____.

3. _____ Tekakwitha is the first Native American to be canonized.

4. The Fifth Commandment forbids us to do this.

5. God's loving care for all things; his will and plan for creation

6. Divine _____ is the way God makes himself and his plan for humans known.

7. Steadfast and loyal in your commitment to God

8. What Joseph did after his brothers pleaded for Benjamin to be spared

9. A sacred promise or agreement between God and humans

10. Sacred _____ is another name for the Bible, or the inspired Word of God written in human words.

B **Check Understanding** Complete each sentence with the correct word from the Word Bank.

Word Bank

plan

Pharaoh's

journey

Moses

jealous

11. God asked Abram and Sarai to go on a long

_____ and live in a new land called Canaan.

12. God has a _____ for all of his People.

13. Joseph's brothers sold him into slavery because they

were _____ .

14. God gave the Ten Commandments to _____

to share with his People.

15. As a baby, Moses was left in a basket by the Nile River, where he

was found by _____ daughter.

C **Make Connections** Write a response to each question.

16. Why is it important for you to find a quiet place to pray?

_____

_____

_____

_____

17. What is the lesson of the story of Abraham and Sarah's waiting many
years to have a child?

_____

_____

_____

_____

Use the terms in the Word Bank in a paragraph to explain how you keep the Third Commandment.

18–20. _____

_____

_____

_____

_____

_____

_____

_____

_____

_____

_____

_____

_____

Word Bank

Sunday

worship

rest

Lord's Day

Trinity

Our Catholic Tradition

- You are made in God's image and likeness and are to live and love in community. (CCC, 1604)

- Showing love to others is a way we reflect the love of the Holy Trinity. The failure to do so is sin. (CCC, 735)

- The Divine Persons of the Holy Trinity help you to do good and avoid evil. You do this by using your free will and following your conscience. (CCC, 1704)

How does a conscience, informed by Sacred Scripture and Sacred Tradition, interpreted by the Church, help us to love as God loves?

In God's Image

 Let Us Pray

Leader: Creator Father, we give you thanks for making us as we are and who we are.

"You formed my inmost being;
>   you knit me in my mother's womb.
I praise you, because I am wonderfully made;
>   wonderful are your works!" **Psalm 139:13–14**

All: O God, you are more than our maker. You are our loving Father. Help us grow to be like you more and more each day. Amen.

 Scripture

Live in a manner worthy of the Lord, so as to be fully pleasing, in every good work bearing fruit and growing in the knowledge of God, . . . giving thanks to the Father, who has made you fit to share in the inheritance of the holy ones in light. He delivered us from the power of darkness and transferred us to the kingdom of his beloved Son, in whom we have redemption, the forgiveness of sins.

>   He is the image of the invisible God,
>   the firstborn of all creation. **Colossians 1:10, 12–15**

? What Do You Wonder?

- How might sin hurt the way people relate to others?

- How does sin hurt the way people reflect God's image?

Reflect God's Love

What does it mean to be created in God's image?

God has given you life. He has created you and all people to reflect his own image of love. God's image is meant to shine in each of us. As Catholics, we believe that all people have **human dignity** because they are created in God's image.

© Our Sunday Visitor

Catholic Faith Words

human dignity the worth each person has because he or she is made in the image of God

soul the spiritual part of a human that lives forever

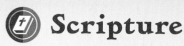

Scripture

God created mankind in his image;
in the image of God he created them;
male and female he created them.   Genesis 1:27

God made you with a human body, and you have a **soul** that will live forever. God gave you the ability to think, to love, and to make choices. You can choose to do good every day and let God's image of love shine through.

In the mirror, draw one way you are an image of love.

Saint Marianne Cope

The story of Saint Marianne Cope shows how one person reflected God's love. She treated others, especially the poor and sick, with dignity and respect.

When she was a child, Barbara Cope knew that she wanted to become a religious sister. Because her family was poor, she worked in a factory to help support them. When her brothers and sisters were finally grown, she entered the religious community of the Sisters of Saint Francis.

In the convent, she was known as Sister Marianne. She taught and helped her Sisters establish hospitals which were special at that time because they treated people of any nationality, religion, or color. In the hospitals, she worked for patients' rights and promoted cleanliness.

The King and Queen of Hawaii invited the Sisters to work in hospitals there. Mother Marianne, as she was then called, took a group of Sisters to answer the call. Within a few years, they transformed a dirty hospital for lepers (people with a contagious skin disease) into a beautiful facility and made other improvements to help lepers and their families.

Over the years, Mother Marianne also helped found hospitals in New York.

➜ **How did Mother Marianne's work honor the dignity of people?**

© Our Sunday Visitor

Share Your Faith

Reflect In your own words, describe what the term *human dignity* means.

Share Explain your description to a partner.

Created to Be with God

What is a failure to love?

God created you to be united to him and to all people. Every time you act in a loving way, you deepen your connection to God and to the members of the Church, the Body of Christ. When you choose to treat someone badly, you hurt this person and the whole community of faith. You choose not to show love and respect.

Sin is always a failure to love. A sinful thought, word, or act also hurts your friendship with God and other people. Sin affects you, too, and keeps you from becoming the person God wants you to be. There are two kinds of personal sin—**mortal sin** and **venial sin**.

Personal Sin	
Venial Sins	**Mortal Sins**
• sins that weaken your friendship with God and others, but do not destroy it	• sins that cause a person's relationship with God to be broken
• things that you do, such as disobeying, cheating, and lying. These are sins of commission.	• serious sins, such as murder
• bad habits that you develop, such as being lazy or dishonest	• In order for a sin to be mortal, (1) the act must be seriously wrong, (2) you must know that it is seriously wrong, and (3) you must freely choose to do it anyway.
• A failure to act sometimes is a sin of omission; for example, to remain silent when someone tells a joke that makes fun of another person or group is a sin.	

Love and Respect

All people are equal. Every person has human dignity and is worthy of respect because he or she is made in God's image. Because he is the Son of God, Jesus is the perfect image of God. You are called to become more like Jesus and to reflect the love and care that he shows all people.

Connect Your Faith

Identify Sins For each statement below, write an M in the blank if it describes a mortal sin. Write a V in the blank if it describes a venial sin.

- ☐ a serious sin

- ☐ lying or cheating

- ☐ destroys a person's relationship with God and others

- ☐ murder

- ☐ hurts a person's relationship with God and others

- ☐ being lazy or disobeying

Catholic Faith Words

sin a deliberate thought, word, deed, or omission contrary to the law of God. Sins hurt our relationship with God and other people.

mortal sin serious sin that causes a person's relationship with God to be broken

venial sin a sin that weakens a person's relationship with God but does not destroy it

Our Catholic Life

Where do you see God's glory?

God shows you something of what he is like through his image in people and through the world he created. If you pay attention you will learn many things about him.

1. Inside the flower, write one way nature is a sign of God's glory.

2. Inside the soccer ball, write about a time when you have seen a reflection of God in another person.

Nature Gives Glory to God

The loveliness of a flower or the brilliance of a sunset tells you something about God's power and goodness. Reflecting on his glory may bring about feelings of gratitude or peace. Take time to look closely at and appreciate nature.

People Show the Glory of God

Think about people who have shown you love: your parents or guardians, a good friend, an understanding teacher, or a devoted grandparent. A baby may make you think of God's power and wonder. An older person may remind you of God's wisdom.

People of Faith

Saint Germaine Cousin, 1579–1601

June 15

Saint Germaine Cousin reminds us that each of us is made in God's image and worthy of respect. She had a crippled hand and a deformed neck. After her mother died, her father remarried. Her stepmother made her sleep in a cupboard under the stairs. Germaine never complained. Instead, she prayed for her stepmother. Finally, her stepmother realized that Germaine was very holy and wanted her to live in the house. But Germaine stayed in her cupboard and was a model of prayer and holiness.

Discuss: What can you do to help someone who has a disability?

Learn more about Saint Germaine at **aliveinchrist.osv.com**

Live Your Faith

Create a poster that explains how you can treat others with dignity and see the glory of God in everyone.

DIGNITY

Let Us Pray

Prayer for Dignity and Respect

Gather and begin with the Sign of the Cross.

Reader 1: God of life,

All: We pray for the dignity of life.

Reader 2: God of creation,

All: We pray for the dignity of life.

Reader 3: God, the source of all life,

All: We pray for the dignity of life.

Reader 4: God, the protector of humanity,

All: We pray for the dignity of life.

Leader: God, we give you praise and thanks for all creation.   **Based on Psalm 139**

All: Amen.

 Sing "O God, You Search Me"

O God, you search me and you know me.
All my thoughts lie open to your gaze.
When I walk or lie down you are before me:
Ever the maker and keeper of my days.

FAMILY+FAITH
LIVING AND LEARNING TOGETHER

YOUR CHILD LEARNED >>>

This chapter explains that God created all people in his image and therefore each of us has human dignity and deserves respect.

Scripture

 Read **Colossians 1:10, 12–15** to find out how God created us to live.

Catholics Believe

• Every person is worthy of respect because he or she is created in God's image.

• Each person has a soul that will live forever.

To learn more, go to the *Catechism of the Catholic Church #355–357, 362–366* at **usccb.org.**

People of Faith

This week, your child learned about Saint Germaine Cousin, who was born with some severe disabilities.

CHILDREN AT THIS AGE >>>

How They Understand Being Created in God's Image
Your child is probably now past those early childhood years in which he or she thought anything was possible. Some children this age are becoming painfully aware of their limitations and need to remember that they are valuable human beings by virtue of their creation in God's image. Knowing this, they can also begin to explore the idea that they were created for a purpose, and that God has a design for their lives.

CONSIDER THIS >>>

Is it easier to show respect to a stranger or to someone in your own family?

It may be more difficult to show respect to people with whom we live because we see their flaws up close. All people deserve our respect because they are made in the image of God. As Catholics, we know that "to be made in the image of God includes specific qualities. Each of us is capable of self-knowledge and of entering into communion with other persons through self-giving. These qualities—and the shared heritage of our first parents—also form a basis for a bond of unity among all human beings" (*USCCA, p. 67*).

LET'S TALK >>>

• Ask your child to explain why all people have dignity.

• Share a personal story about a time when you were not treated with dignity and how you felt.

LET'S PRAY >>>

 O God, may we always be respectful of all people, knowing we are all your children. Amen.

For a multimedia glossary of Catholic Faith Words, Sunday readings, seasonal and Saint resources, and chapter activities go to **aliveinchrist.osv.com.**

Chapter 4 Review

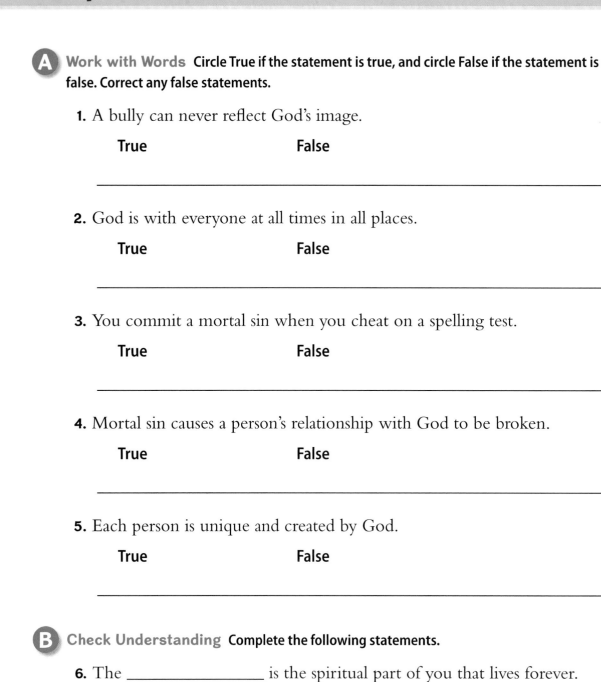

A Work with Words Circle True if the statement is true, and circle False if the statement is false. Correct any false statements.

1. A bully can never reflect God's image.

   True   **False**

   _____

2. God is with everyone at all times in all places.

   True   **False**

   _____

3. You commit a mortal sin when you cheat on a spelling test.

   True   **False**

   _____

4. Mortal sin causes a person's relationship with God to be broken.

   True   **False**

   _____

5. Each person is unique and created by God.

   True   **False**

   _____

B Check Understanding Complete the following statements.

6. The _____ is the spiritual part of you that lives forever.

7. Human _____ is the worth each person has because he or she is made in God's image.

8. A _____ sin hurts your friendship with God.

9. _____ and _____ show the glory of God.

10. You are _____ to show God's love and care to others, as Jesus did.

Go to **aliveinchrist.osv.com** for an interactive review.

Living in Community

 Let Us Pray

Leader: God of unity and communion, God who is one and three-in-one, unite us in love.

"How good and how pleasant it is,
    when brothers dwell together as one!"

Psalm 133:1

All: God of unity and communion, God who is one and three-in-one, unite us in love. Amen.

 Scripture

In this way the love of God was revealed to us: God sent his only Son into the world so that we might have life through him. . . . Beloved, if God so loved us, we also must love one another. No one has ever seen God. Yet, if we love one another, God remains in us, and his love is brought to perfection in us. This is how we know that we remain in him and he in us, that he has given us of his Spirit. . . . God is love, and whoever remains in love remains in God and God in him.

1 John 4:9, 11–13, 16b

? What Do You Wonder?

- What are some things you do to keep a friendship going strong?

- Where can you look for help in living a moral life, or a life of love?

Created to Love

What does love of neighbor have to do with love of God?

© Our Sunday Visitor

Catholic Faith Words

Holy Trinity the mystery of one God in three Divine Persons: Father, Son, and Holy Spirit

Underline the mission of God the Son and God the Holy Spirit.

You learned in the last chapter that God made all people in his image. You are more clearly an image of God when you reflect the love of the **Holy Trinity** to others. The Holy Trinity is the mystery of one God in three Divine Persons: God the Father, God the Son, and God the Holy Spirit. God reveals himself as three unique Divine Persons, but the Father, Son, and Holy Spirit are one God.

Jesus is both divine and human, God and man. Jesus tells us that the mission of God the Son and God the Holy Spirit is to bring people into the love of the Holy Trinity—the perfect love that exists in the Father, Son, and Holy Spirit. God's plan is for people to live together in love.

From the time of the first humans, people have formed groups. When a group of people live together in love, it is a community. In a community like this, the people have common beliefs, hopes, and goals.

Jesus teaches his disciples.

Right and Responsibility

Each person has individual rights that are balanced with a responsibility to respect and protect the rights of others. No one has unlimited freedom or an unlimited right to the Earth's goods. When everyone's rights are in balance, the Kingdom of God is close at hand.

You can see a good example of this in the story of the early Christians. In this passage, we learn how they lived in the years just after Jesus' Resurrection and Ascension— praying, teaching, and caring for others.

 ## Scripture

The Communal Life

They devoted themselves to the teaching of the apostles and to the communal life, to the breaking of the bread and to the prayers. Awe came upon everyone, and many wonders and signs were done through the apostles. All who believed were together and had all things in common; they would sell their property and possessions and divide them among all according to each one's need. Acts 2:42–45

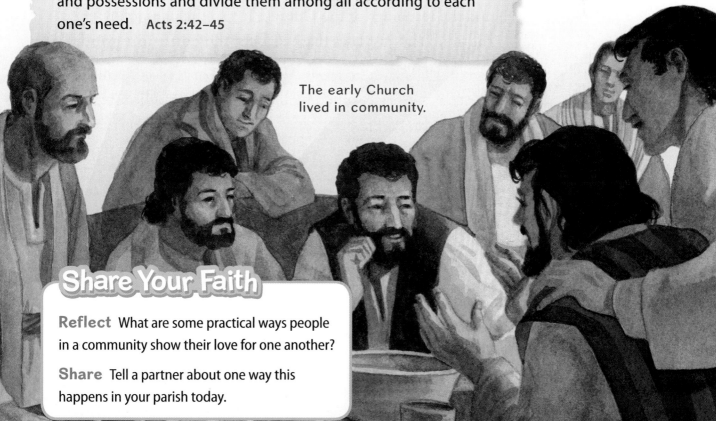

The early Church lived in community.

Share Your Faith

Reflect What are some practical ways people in a community show their love for one another?

Share Tell a partner about one way this happens in your parish today.

Living as Catholics

What does it mean to live a moral life?

Love One Another

The early Christians formed a community based on a common faith in Jesus Christ and his message. Their faith and love are an example for you today. Faith is your "yes" to all that God has revealed. God created all men and women equal in dignity and in his image. So respect for the rights and needs of others is part of faith.

Just as you cannot live in isolation from others, so you cannot believe alone. You believe as part of a larger community of faith. As a Catholic, you are called to live a good moral life.

Moral Living

The moral life is a way of living in right relationship with God, yourself, and others. Catholic **morality** includes following the Ten Commandments, the teachings of Jesus, and the teachings of the Church. It also includes following the good and just laws that work for the **common good**.

Catholic families and your parish community are places where you can learn to live the Catholic moral life.

➡ **How are you called to live as part of a larger community of faith?**

An altar server places the Procession Cross during the Introductory Rites of the Mass.

Catholic Faith Words

morality living in right relationship with God, yourself, and others. It is putting your beliefs into action.

common good the good of everyone, with particular concern for those who might be most vulnerable to harm

The Common Good

People who live in true communities work for the common good by

- respecting the human dignity of each person and acknowledging each person's right to freedom and self-expression, as long as others are not hurt.

- making sure that every person has a way to get the things that are necessary for life, such as food, shelter, clothing, and access to doctors.

- providing peace, security, and order in the community.

Connect Your Faith

For the Common Good Beside each picture, explain how these people in your neighborhood or parish work for the common good.

respecting the human dignity of each person

_____

_____

_____

making sure that people can get the things that are necessary for life

_____

_____

_____

providing peace, security, and order

_____

_____

_____

Our Catholic Life

How should you live as part of a community?

Your actions affect the lives of others. As part of the community of God's family, you have a responsibility to those around you. When you act responsibly, you help create a more loving community.

Here are some guidelines for becoming a good member of the community.

1. Choose words from the Word List to complete the sentences.
2. Circle what you are already doing to live as a good community member.
3. Write one way you can be a better community member.

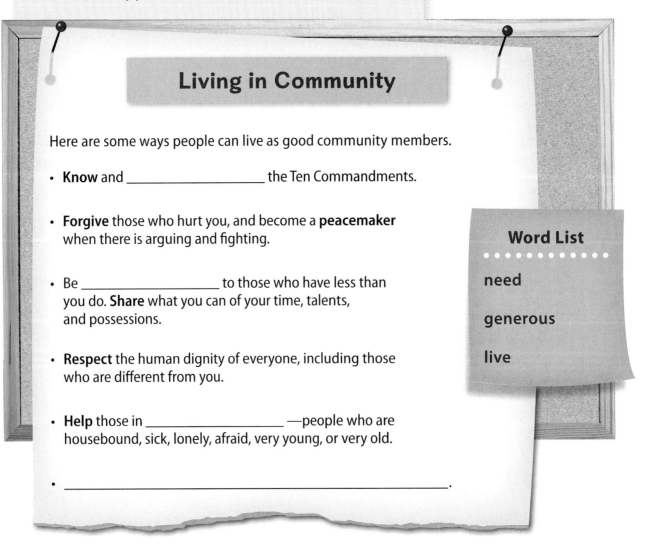

Living in Community

Here are some ways people can live as good community members.

- **Know** and _____ the Ten Commandments.

- **Forgive** those who hurt you, and become a **peacemaker** when there is arguing and fighting.

- Be _____ to those who have less than you do. **Share** what you can of your time, talents, and possessions.

- **Respect** the human dignity of everyone, including those who are different from you.

- **Help** those in _____ —people who are housebound, sick, lonely, afraid, very young, or very old.

- _____.

Word List

need

generous

live

People of Faith

Saint Dominic, 1170 –1221

Saint Dominic knew that it was important for people who work for God to be together. He founded a religious order called the Order of Preachers. Sometimes they are called *Dominicans*, after him. His motto was: "to praise, to bless, to preach." He wanted his followers to always praise God, bless everyone they met, and preach the Gospel. He also wanted them to live together in community. They shared all they had, like the earliest followers of Jesus did. Even today, Dominicans dedicate their lives to telling people the Good News, and they still live in community.

Discuss: How does your family work together for the good of each person?

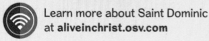

Learn more about Saint Dominic at **aliveinchrist.osv.com**

Live Your Faith

Look at what the people in the pictures are doing to help one another.

Decide on one thing you can do next week to help create a more loving community.

List the steps you will take to make this happen.

To do list

- ☐
- ☐
- ☐
- ☐
- ☐

Let Us Pray

Lectio Divina

This ancient prayer of the Church is a slow praying of the Scriptures in which we listen for what the Holy Spirit wants us to hear.

Gather and begin with the Sign of the Cross.

Leader: Come Holy Spirit. Open our ears;

All: open our minds; open our hearts.

Leader: Read John 14:27

First Reflection

Leader: Read John 14:27

Second Reflection

Leader: United as one community, committed to grow as one in God, we pray:

Side 1: Glory be to the Father

Side 2: and to the Son

Side 1: and to the Holy Spirit,

Side 2: as it was in the beginning

Side 1: is now, and ever shall be

Side 2: world without end.

All: Amen.

▶ Sing "Raise Your Voice for Justice"

FAMILY+FAITH
LIVING AND LEARNING TOGETHER

YOUR CHILD LEARNED >>>

This chapter explains that the Holy Trinity—God the Father, God the Son, and God the Holy Spirit—shows us how to live in right relationship with God, ourselves, and one another.

Scripture

 Read **1 John 4:9, 11–13, 16b** to find out why God sent his Son, Jesus, to live among us.

Catholics Believe

- God created people for one another, and all must work for the common good. Such love of neighbor reflects the love of the Holy Trinity.

- No one can believe alone, just as no one can live alone.

To learn more, go to the *Catechism of the Catholic Church #1905–1912* at **usccb.org.**

People of Faith

This week, your child learned about Saint Dominic, the founder of the Dominican Order. His life motto was "to praise, to bless, to preach."

CHILDREN AT THIS AGE >>>

How They Understand Being Created for One Another Most children this age are very social. But the social skills of your child have probably moved beyond the early childhood years of simply wanting to play with other children to forming real bonds of friendship. This is a time of "best friends," when children form close relationships with one or a few children they prefer to spend their time with. It is the beginning of the deeper relationships they will hopefully enjoy for the rest of their lives.

CONSIDER THIS >>>

When a Catholic says, "God is love," what do we mean?

As Catholics, we believe God's nature is a relationship of perfect love— a communion of love between Father, Son, and Holy Spirit. God, "ever-faithful and forgiving, is ultimately experienced by human beings through his Son, Jesus Christ, and the Holy Spirit. His love is stronger than a mother's love for her child or a bridegroom for his beloved. [. . .] Jesus has revealed that God's very being is love" (*USCCA, p. 51*).

LET'S TALK >>>

- Ask your child to explain the connection between love of neighbor and love of God.

- Talk about how people in your community work for the common good.

LET'S PRAY >>>

 Dear God, help us always live in peace and work for the good of each person in our family. Amen.

 For a multimedia glossary of Catholic Faith Words, Sunday readings, seasonal and Saint resources, and chapter activities go to **aliveinchrist.osv.com.**

Chapter 5 Review

A Work with Words Solve the crossword puzzle.

Down

1. A group of people with similar beliefs, working together toward a common goal

2. Living in right relationship with God, self, and others

4. Members of a community _____ on one another.

Across

3. The result of respecting and working for everyone's rights in a community

5. When we show this to others, we follow God's way and live a moral life.

B Check Understanding Circle the word that best completes each statement.

6. Your **(beliefs/actions)** affect the lives of others.

7. Your individual rights are **(balanced/unconnected)** with your responsibility to respect and protect the rights of others.

8. God created **(some/all)** men and women equal in human dignity and in his image.

9. A Catholic community where you can worship and learn is called a **(parish/city)**.

10. As a Catholic, you are called to live a **(good/partly)** moral life.

© Our Sunday Visitor

Go to **aliveinchrist.osv.com** for an interactive review.

Making Good Choices

♥ Let Us Pray

Leader: O God, give us a faith strong
enough to see what is right and just.

"Teach me wisdom and knowledge,
for in your commandments
I trust." **Psalm 119:66**

All: O God, give us the wisdom and knowledge to
make choices that are true to that faith. Amen.

Scripture

A shoot shall sprout from the stump of Jesse,
and from his roots a bud shall blossom.
The spirit of the LORD shall rest upon him:
a spirit of wisdom and of understanding,
A spirit of counsel and of strength,
a spirit of knowledge and of fear of the LORD,
and his delight shall be the fear of the LORD.
Not by appearance shall he judge,
nor by hearsay shall he decide,
But he shall judge the poor with justice,
and decide fairly for the land's afflicted.
Isaiah 11:1–4a

? What Do You Wonder?

- Who or what helps you choose what is right and just?

- What are some ways you can form your conscience in
order to choose what is right and just?

Choices and Consequences

What is the proper use of free will?

You have the freedom to make choices, but all choices have consequences. In this story, Julia learns a lesson from a choice she makes.

Julia Decides

"Come on, Julia!" said Monica. "I really want to see the new movie at the Crosstown Cinema. I thought you wanted to see it, too."

"I do want to see it," Julia replied. "Maybe we can see it next week.

My coach just called an extra soccer practice for this afternoon. I have to go."

"Well, you can go to soccer practice if you want to," said Monica. "I am going to the movie."

After Monica left, Julia got ready for practice. "I can see that movie later with my sister Lila," she thought as she tied her shoes. "Right now I have to work on my goal tending. The team is counting on me."

When Julia finally saw the movie, she enjoyed it. However, not as much as she enjoyed winning the award for most improved player at the end of the season!

Freedom and Responsibility

Julia's story shows that all choices have consequences. You are responsible for your choices, too.

When God created you in his image, he gave you **free will**. With your free will, you make choices. Sometimes your choices are between right and wrong. Sometimes, as in Julia's case, they are between better and best. Whenever you make a good choice, you use God's gift of free will properly and you grow closer to God.

God Helps You

God gives you many gifts to help you make good choices. God's most important gift is **grace**, which is God's free and loving gift to you of his own life and help. You received grace in a special way in the Sacrament of Baptism. You grow in God's grace through the Sacraments, prayer, and good moral choices.

In addition to his grace, God gives you the Ten Commandments and the Church to help you. God is always helping you develop a more loving relationship with him.

© Our Sunday Visitor

Catholic Faith Words

free will the God-given freedom and ability to make choices. God created us with free will so we can have the freedom to choose good.

grace God's free and loving gift to humans of his own life and help

Underline three ways God helps you make good choices.

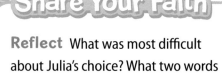

Share Your Faith

Reflect What was most difficult about Julia's choice? What two words would you use to describe how she felt after she made her choice?

_____

_____

Share Design a ribbon for Julia's Most Improved Player award.

God's Gift of Conscience

What is a well-formed conscience?

Good choices help you grow as a moral person. They build good habits and strengthen your relationship with God and others. One day Jesus told this story about showing love, even toward people whom we do not know.

 **Scripture**

The Parable of the Good Samaritan

Jesus told the story of a Jewish traveler going from Jerusalem to Jericho who was attacked by robbers that beat, robbed, and left him on the side of the road.

A priest saw the injured traveler and moved to the other side of the road. Later, a Jewish leader came to the same place, and when he saw the traveler, he too moved to the other side of the road. Finally, a Samaritan came to the place where the traveler lay dying. Unlike the others, the Samaritan stopped. He treated and bandaged the traveler's wounds. He carried him on his own animal to an inn, where he cared for him. The next day, when the Samaritan was leaving, he gave the innkeeper money and told him, "Take care of this man. If you spend more than what I have given you, I will repay you when I return." **Based on Luke 10:30–35**

→ What was difficult about the choice the Samaritan made?

→ When is it difficult for you to make good choices?

Catholic Faith Words

conscience the God-given ability that helps us judge whether actions are right or wrong. It is important for us to know God's laws so our conscience can help us make good decisions.

Know the Difference

Good choices strengthen your relationship with God and others. Sin weakens or destroys that relationship. Sin is always a failure to love God and others. When you use your free will to sin, you always become less free.

You probably know when you have done something wrong, even if no one has seen you. You know that you have acted against God's plan. Your **conscience** is a gift from God that helps you to know the difference between right and wrong. Conscience is your free will and your reason working together. They direct you to choose what is good and avoid what is wrong. It is your job to strengthen, or form, your own conscience. You cannot do this alone.

1. Place a check mark next to one thing you want to know more about.

2. Draw a star next to one way you will form your conscience this week.

Forming Your Conscience

The Holy Spirit	strengthens you to make good choices	☐
Prayer and study	help you think things through	☐
Scripture and Church teaching	guide your decisions	☐
Parents, teachers, and wise people	give you good advice	☐

Connect Your Faith

The Right Choice
For each scenario, what advice would you give to help a friend use God's gift of conscience to make the right choice? Take turns sharing with a partner.

Our Catholic Life

How do you make decisions?

Making good moral decisions takes practice. Remember the words *stop*, *think*, *pray*, and *choose*. They are steps to help you make decisions. These words will remind you what to do when you are faced with a moral choice.

These four steps may not help you make the easiest choice or the most popular choice, but they will help you make the best choice. This choice will strengthen your relationship with God and others.

Making Good Decisions

STOP	THINK
Take your time Do not make a snap decision or act on your first idea. • Important choices can affect you, others, and your relationship with God. • Give yourself time, and you are more likely to make a good decision.	**Consider your choices** Think about what might happen if you make each choice. • Say a prayer to the Holy Spirit for guidance. • Listen to your conscience. • Consider what the Bible and the Church teach you. • Consult with your family and teachers.

PRAY	CHOOSE
Ask for help in choosing Reflect on what God is calling you to do. • Pray again for help and guidance from the Holy Spirit. • Ask for wisdom and courage to make the best choice.	**Make up your mind** Decide what you will do. • Be confident that if you think and pray about your decision, you will make the right choice. • Act on your choice.

People of Faith

Saint Charles Lwanga, d. 1886

June 3

Saint Charles Lwanga was a young servant in the king's court in Uganda. The king hated Christians. He commanded his servants to join in immoral activities. Charles refused, choosing to follow his conscience and obey God, not the king. Charles and twenty-one other Christians were tortured before they were executed in an effort to get them to do what the king wanted. As Charles was dying, he prayed aloud and said that he knew he was going to Heaven. Charles and his companions are known as the African Martyrs.

Discuss: Tell about a time when you followed your conscience.

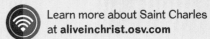 Learn more about Saint Charles at **aliveinchrist.osv.com**

Live Your Faith

Think about a time when your conscience helped you to make a good moral decision. Then draw the steps you took to make that decision.

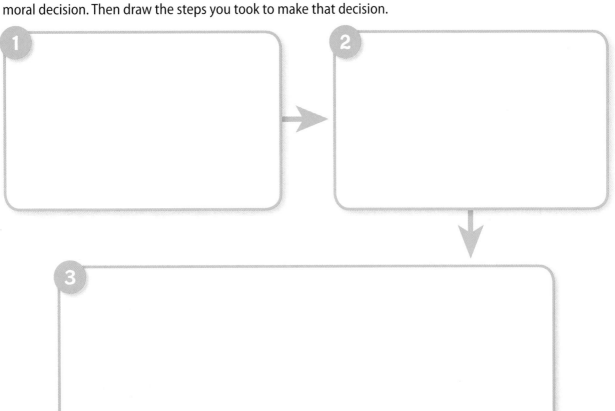

1

2

3

♥ Let Us Pray

Prayer of Reflection

Gather and begin with the Sign of the Cross.

Leader: In prayer, you listen for God's voice to guide you. Close your eyes and think about a time when you were afraid and didn't know what to do. Listen to this story about a man named Elijah, who heard God's voice in a very surprising way when he was afraid.

Reader: Read 1 Kings 19:9–14

Leader: Sit quietly and notice whether you can hear God whispering to you inside your heart. What is God saying to you? What do you want to say to God?

Leader: God of the whispering sound, help us be still and listen for your voice to guide us.

All: Amen.

FAMILY+FAITH
LIVING AND LEARNING TOGETHER

YOUR CHILD LEARNED >>>

This chapter explains that it is necessary to develop a well-formed conscience in order to choose good over evil.

Scripture

 Read **Isaiah 11:1–4a** to find out about the Savior God promised to send.

Catholics Believe

- God's grace helps us use our reason and free will to make good choices.
- Conscience is our God-given ability that helps us judge right from wrong.

To learn more, go to the *Catechism of the Catholic Church #1776–1782* at **usccb.org.**

People of Faith

This week, your child learned about Saint Charles Lwanga, an African martyr who was known for following his conscience.

CHILDREN AT THIS AGE >>>

How They Understand Free Will and Conscience Fourth grade children understand well that adults do not always see what they say and do. They also know that there are limits to the ability of authority figures in their life to enforce their will. Being a moral person, then, becomes a series of choices. They need to understand that these choices are given to us so that we can have the freedom to choose the good. This is also the beginning of the understanding of conscience. As children become more aware of their inner thoughts, they can form and listen to their conscience to help them make good choices.

CONSIDER THIS >>>

Have you ever considered the difference between a well-formed conscience and your opinion?

It can be all too easy to seemingly speak with authority even when we may not be well informed. There is a distinction between opinion and our conscience. As Catholics, we know that "a good conscience makes judgments that conform to reason and the good that is willed by the Wisdom of God. A good conscience requires lifelong formation. Each baptized follower of Christ is obliged to form his or her conscience according to objective moral standards" (*USCCA, p. 314*).

LET'S TALK >>>

- Ask your child to explain how all choices have consequences.
- Talk about a time when someone in the family had to make an important decision. How did the family help him or her?

LET'S PRAY >>>

 Saint Charles, pray for us that we may follow our consciences, even when it hard to do so. Amen.

 For a multimedia glossary of Catholic Faith Words, Sunday readings, seasonal and Saint resources, and chapter activities go to **aliveinchrist.osv.com.**

Chapter 6 Review

A Work with Words Complete each sentence with the correct term from the Word Bank.

1. _____ is the God-given freedom and ability to make choices.

2. Your _____ is the God-given ability that helps us judge actions as right or wrong.

3. Good choices help you grow as a _____ person.

4. Sin weakens or destroys your relationship with _____ and with others.

5. God's gift of his own life and help is _____ .

B Make Connections Write responses on the lines below.

6. What is the lesson of the Parable of the Good Samaritan?

_____

7. How do prayer and study help you?

_____

_____

8. What can help you make good decisions?

_____

_____

9. What happens when you choose to sin?

_____

10. To whom can you go when you need advice?

_____

_____

Go to **aliveinchrist.osv.com** for an interactive review.

A Work with Words Write the correct word after each definition. Then find the word in the word search. Some words may be written backwards.

F	C	D	E	V	Q	T	Y	Y	L
O	L	N	C	P	I	U	H	T	T
C	M	J	A	K	E	P	S	I	R
I	L	M	R	I	X	U	X	N	L
W	D	I	G	N	I	T	Y	U	C
J	D	Y	P	P	V	S	K	M	B
C	R	E	A	T	E	I	N	M	Y
E	C	N	E	I	C	S	N	O	C
X	V	Z	O	O	R	E	S	C	C

1. God's free and loving gift to us of his own life and help _____

2. To make something from nothing _____

3. The God-given ability that helps you judge right from wrong _____

4. A group of people with common beliefs and goals _____

5. The worth each person has from being made in God's image _____

B **Check Understanding** Match each description in Column 1 with the correct term in Column 2. Terms may be used more than once.

Column 1	Column 2
6. cheating on homework	sin of omission
7. staying silent while someone is being teased	venial sin
8. lying to a friend	sin
9. a deliberate thought, word, deed, or omission contrary to the law of God	
10. murder	mortal sin

Match each description in Column 1 with the correct term in Column 2.

Column 1	Column 2
11. the spiritual part of a human that lives forever	conscience
12. ability from God to judge right from wrong	free will
13. a Catholic community with shared spiritual beliefs and worship	morality
14. living in right relationship with God, yourself, and others	parish
15. the freedom God has given you to make choices	soul

© Our Sunday Visitor

C Make Connections Write responses on the lines below.

16. What is the difference between mortal sin and venial sin?

_____

_____

_____

17. How does God help you make good choices?

_____

_____

_____

18. How can you work for the common good?

_____

_____

_____

19. How would you describe morality?

_____

_____

_____

20. How can you develop your conscience?

_____

_____

_____

Jesus Christ

Our Catholic Tradition

- Jesus wants people to be happy and to carry his message of the goodness of God's Kingdom into the world. He shared that message in his teachings, most especially the Beatitudes. (CCC, 851, 1724)

- Jesus calls us to trust in the Father and to be a blessing to others by living the Great Commandment of love. (CCC, 2055)

- Jesus teaches us to praise God with worship, by honoring his name, and by keeping Sunday holy. (CCC, 2083)

How does Jesus' teaching in the Beatitudes help us to live the Ten Commandments?

Hagia Maria Sion Abbey stands just outside the Old City of Jerusalem, on Mt. Zion.

The Beatitudes

 Let Us Pray

Leader: Thank you, O Lord, for you have
blessed us in so many ways.

"Blessed is the nation whose God is the LORD,
the people chosen as his inheritance."
Psalm 33:12

All: You have chosen us, O Lord, and made us to be
happy with you forever. We are truly blessed by
your gifts. Amen.

 Scripture

While [Jesus] was speaking, a woman from the crowd called
out and said to him, "Blessed is the womb that carried you and
the breasts at which you nursed." He replied, "Rather, blessed are
those who hear the word of God and observe it." Luke 11:27–28

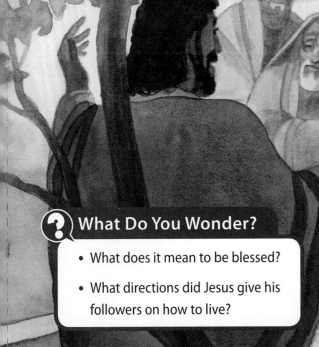

? What Do You Wonder?

- What does it mean to be blessed?
- What directions did Jesus give his
  followers on how to live?

Jesus Brings God's Blessing

What did Jesus teach his disciples about blessings?

In the Gospel according to Matthew, we find a summary of what Jesus taught about how to live by God's Word. We learn who is blessed and how to be a blessing for others, and about the kindness and concern know as **mercy**.

Catholic Faith Words

mercy kindness and concern for those who are suffering. God has mercy on us even though we are sinners.

Beatitudes teachings of Jesus that show the way to true happiness and tell the way to live in God's Kingdom now and always

eternal life life forever with God for all who die in his friendship

Scripture

One day Jesus stood in the midst of his Apostles and a great crowd of followers. He taught them with these words:

"Blessed are the poor in spirit,
    for theirs is the kingdom of heaven.

Blessed are they who mourn,
    for they will be comforted.

Blessed are the meek,
    for they will inherit the land.

Blessed are they who hunger and thirst
        for righteousness,
    for they will be satisfied.

Blessed are the merciful,
    for they will be shown mercy.

Blessed are the clean of heart,
    for they will see God.

Blessed are the peacemakers,
    for they will be called children of God.

Blessed are they who are persecuted for
        the sake of righteousness,
    for theirs is the kingdom of heaven."

Matthew 5:3–10

This statue of Christ the Redeemer overlooks Rio de Janeiro, Brazil. A chapel beneath the statue was consecrated in 2006.

The Beatitudes

The Church calls this teaching of Jesus the **Beatitudes**. The word *beatitude* means "blessing" or "happiness." God put the desire for happiness inside each of us. Sometimes we think certain people or things will make us happy. But true happiness comes when we follow the Beatitudes.

The Beatitudes are about how we act, feel, and think. They are about the lasting happiness God wants for you. God wants us to work with him as he builds his Kingdom. He wants us all to have **eternal life**.

 Match the Beatitude on the left with its meaning on the right.

The Beatitudes

Blessed are the poor in spirit . . .	Forgive others and ask forgiveness.
Blessed are the meek . . .	In difficult times, trust in God and stand up for what is right.
Blessed are the merciful . . .	Share people's sorrows and joys.
Blessed are the peacemakers . . .	Help all people treat others justly, and help change unjust conditions.
Blessed are they who mourn . . .	Depend on God, not on material things.
Blessed are those who hunger and thirst for righteousness . . .	Be faithful to God and to his ways.
Blessed are the clean of heart . . .	Be gentle and humble.
Blessed are those who are persecuted for the sake of righteousness . . .	Work to bring people together. Look for ways to solve problems peacefully.

Share Your Faith

Reflect Imagine you had been there when Jesus gave us the Beatitudes. Think of one question you would ask him about them.

Share Discuss with a partner how Jesus would answer.

Be a Blessing

What does it mean to be a blessing to others?

Because God first blessed us, everyone has a chance to be a blessing to others. This story tells how one humble man was a blessing to many people.

Pope Saint John XXIII

Angelo Roncalli grew up in an Italian farming family. He became a priest in 1904 and he helped a bishop run a diocese. He also taught in a seminary and gave inspirational homilies.

When Italy became involved in World War I, Angelo was drafted. He became a sergeant and chaplain in the medical corps. He prayed with wounded soldiers, gave them Holy Communion, and heard their confessions. When needed, he performed the Sacrament of the Anointing of the Sick.

After the war, he went back to work at the seminary. Soon, Father Angelo was put in charge of an office in the Vatican that helps those who work in the missions.

While in Bulgaria, he visited and worked with Catholic and other Christian groups. When an earthquake struck, he worked to provide relief to the victims. No matter where Father Angelo was, he served those around him by loving them in God's name.

A stamp printed in Italy in 1981 commemorates the 100th anniversary of Pope Saint John XXIII's birth.

Sisters from the Missionaries of Charity amid the rubble of their church after the 2010 earthquake in Port-au-Prince, Haiti.

Sharing Blessings

In the 1930s, Father Angelo worked for the Church in Greece. Then, World War II broke out. He helped prisoners of war communicate with their families. He also helped Jewish families escape by giving them papers that ensured their safe travel.

Angelo was respected in these countries because of his sincere ways and deep holiness. He tried to settle problems by using the teachings about love from the Bible.

In 1958, Father Angelo was elected Pope. He took the name John XXIII. In this position, he was a good servant to his people. He visited people in hospitals and in prisons. He welcomed and met with people from other countries and of other religions. He urged everyone to live in **peace** and settle their problems with kindness and justice. In 1961, Pope Saint John XXIII called a special meeting of all the bishops of the Church. They discussed how the Church could help bring the message of Jesus to the world.

➤ How did Pope Saint John XXIII show that God blesses all people?

➤ What lesson can you learn from Pope Saint John XXIII?

Catholic Faith Words

peace a state of calm when things are in their proper order and people settle problems with kindness and justice

Connect Your Faith

Be a Blessing Write words beginning with the letters of the word PEACE to describe how you can be a blessing to others.

P _____

E _____

A _____

C _____

E _____

Our Catholic Life

How can you share blessings through prayer?

Intercession, or petition, is a kind of prayer in which you ask God for something for another person or for the community. It is a generous, thoughtful kind of prayer, and it is one of the types of prayers that Jesus prayed.

Just before the preparation of the gifts at Mass, the whole assembly offers prayers of intercession to God in the Prayer of the Faithful. These prayers are often said for members of the Church, religious and government leaders, and people in the news. Here are some examples of when you might want to say a prayer of intercession.

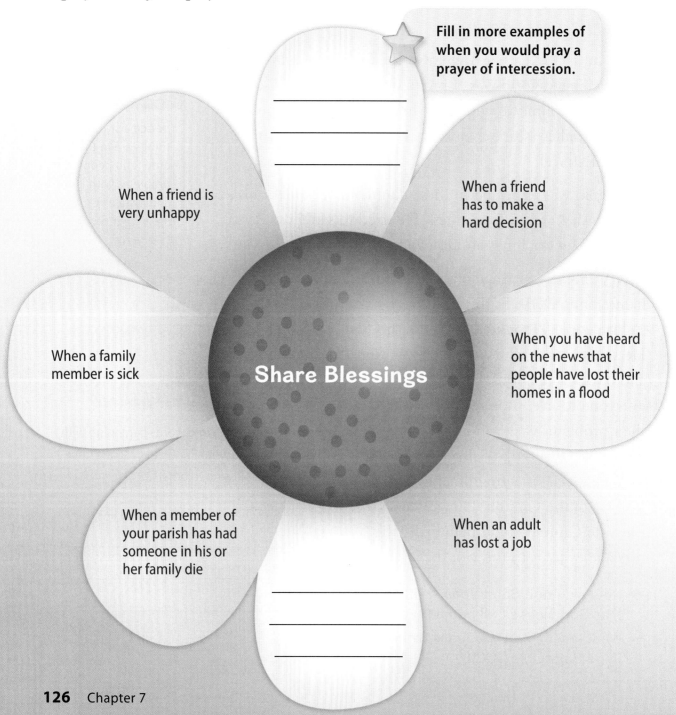

Fill in more examples of when you would pray a prayer of intercession.

_____
_____
_____

When a friend is very unhappy

When a friend has to make a hard decision

When a family member is sick

Share Blessings

When you have heard on the news that people have lost their homes in a flood

When a member of your parish has had someone in his or her family die

When an adult has lost a job

_____
_____

People of Faith

Saint Yi Sung-hun, 1756–1801

Saint Yi Sung-hun lived in Korea. His family was part of the ruling class. When he was traveling with his father to China, he was baptized. He was one of the first people in Korea to become Catholic. The government did not want people to be Christian. When Yi Sung-hun refused to worship a false god, he was arrested. Many other Korean Christians were arrested too. One hundred and three people were killed for being Christian. When Yi Sung-hun died, he told people not to be sad because he would see them again in Heaven. He placed God first, and was a man of the Beatitudes.

Discuss: How does God bless you? How can you share those blessings with others?

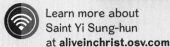 Learn more about Saint Yi Sung-hun at **aliveinchrist.osv.com**

Live Your Faith

Name one Beatitude that you live by regularly and another that is more difficult for you.

_____

_____

_____

Write a short prayer asking God to help you live these Beatitudes.

_____

_____

_____

_____

_____

Let Us Pray

Prayer of Blessing

Gather and begin with the Sign of the Cross.

Leader: Brothers and sisters, praise God, who is rich in mercy.

All: Blessed be God forever.

Reader 1: Read Philippians 4:4–7.

All: Blessed be God forever.

Reader 2: Loving God, you created all the people of the world, and you know each of us by name.

All: Blessed be God forever.

Reader 3: We thank you for our lives. Bless us with your love and friendship.

All: Blessed be God forever.

Reader 4: May we grow in wisdom, knowledge, and grace.

All: Blessed be God forever.

Leader: May we be blessed in the name of the Father, the Son, and the Holy Spirit.
Based on Matthew 5, 7; John 14

All: Amen.

▶ Sing "Lead Me, Lord"

FAMILY+FAITH
LIVING AND LEARNING TOGETHER

YOUR CHILD LEARNED >>>

This chapter explains that Jesus gave us the Beatitudes to show the way to true happiness and to tell how us to live in God's Kingdom now and always.

Scripture

 Read **Luke 11:27–28** to find out who Jesus says is blessed and why.

Catholics Believe

- The Beatitudes are eight teachings that describe the Reign of God that Jesus announced when he lived on Earth.

- The Beatitudes show you how to live and act as a follower of Jesus.

To learn more, go to the *Catechism of the Catholic Church #1716–1724* at **usccb.org**.

People of Faith

This week, your child learned about Saint Yi Sung-hun, a Korean martyr who placed God first and is remembered for sacrificing his life for his belief in Jesus.

CHILDREN AT THIS AGE >>>

How They Understand the Beatitudes Your child is probably beginning to understand that morality, in the Catholic life, is not just about what is not allowed. It is about being something, and specifically *following someone*, Jesus Christ. Jesus offers us a pattern in the Beatitudes, which involve both outward actions and inner dispositions of the heart. Children your child's age are growing in their ability to perceive what is inside their hearts, so this is a good time to use the Beatitudes to talk about who God would call us to be.

CONSIDER THIS >>>

Have you ever felt a blessing in the midst of suffering?

Even in times of suffering, we can count the blessings of those who care for us, listen to us, and share God's love with us. As Catholics, we know that "the Church carries forward Christ's healing ministry in a variety of approaches. Catholic families in countless ways care for family members who are ill. There are numerous inspiring stories of an aging spouse who personally ministers to an ailing spouse in cases of Alzheimer's and other illnesses. Caregivers find that faith and prayer mean a great deal to them in these situations" (*USCCA, p. 252*).

LET'S TALK >>>

- Ask your child to tell you about the Beatitudes.

- Share how God has blessed your family and how your family members are a blessing to one another.

LET'S PRAY >>>

 Saint Yi Sung-hun, pray for us that we may put God first in our lives, and always be a blessing for others. Amen.

 For a multimedia glossary of Catholic Faith Words, Sunday readings, seasonal and Saint resources, and chapter activities go to **aliveinchrist.osv.com**.

Chapter 7 Review

A **Work with Words** Complete the following paragraph with the correct words from the Word Bank.

1–5. Jesus gave us the _____ to show us
the way to _____ happiness.
Through the _____ Beatitudes,
Jesus tell us about being blessed by God and living
for God's _____ now and always.
He said that people who are _____
are blessed because they will inherit the land.

Word Bank

true

eight

Kingdom

Beatitudes

meek

B **Check Understanding** Fill in the circle next to the answer that best completes each statement.

6. People who are poor in spirit are those who depend on _____ .

  ◯ material things   ◯ God   ◯ themselves

7. God wants all people to share _____ with him.

  ◯ eternal life   ◯ Beatitudes   ◯ material things

8. Working to bring people together is a way to be _____ .

  ◯ meek   ◯ poor in spirit   ◯ a peacemaker

9. Kindness and concern for those who are suffering is _____ .

  ◯ mercy   ◯ blessedness   ◯ meekness

10. Prayers of _____ ask God for something for another person or for a community.

  ◯ righteousness   ◯ intercession   ◯ friendship

Go to **aliveinchrist.osv.com**
for an interactive review.

CHAPTER 8

Love God and Neighbor

 Let Us Pray

Leader: Merciful God, help us to know and do your will.

"Lᴏʀᴅ, teach me the way of your statutes;
I shall keep them with care." **Psalm 119:33**

All: You ask us, Lord, to love you with our whole heart and love our neighbor as we love ourselves. Give us the grace to do what you ask. Amen.

 Scripture

"So be imitators of God, as beloved children, and live in love, as Christ loved us." Jesus gave himself as a sacrifice of love to his Father for us. So, you holy ones must live as Jesus commanded. Do not ever be greedy, or swear, or be disrespectful. **Based on Ephesians 5:1–5**

? What Do You Wonder?

- What helps you imitate Christ, to have faith, hope, and love?

- How can you be generous and help people in need?

The Great Commandment

How is the Great Commandment like the Ten Commandments?

Catholic Faith Words

Great Commandment the twofold command to love God above all and your neighbor as yourself. It sums up all God's laws.

We all know that rules are important. We understand that obeying rules, even when we don't like them, helps keep order. But Jesus taught that keeping the Ten Commandments includes more than checking off items on a list. Each Commandment shows you a way to love God and love others with your whole heart and soul.

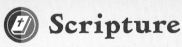

Scripture

The Greatest Commandment

"You shall love the Lord, your God, with all your heart, with all your soul, and with all your mind. This is the greatest and the first commandment. The second is like it: You shall love your neighbor as yourself. The whole law and the prophets depend on these two commandments." Matthew 22:37–40

Therefore, the **Great Commandment** to love God above all and your neighbor as yourself sums up the Ten Commandments, the whole law, and what the prophets taught.

Following Jesus

There are many ways that you can follow Jesus by sharing your love with others. Once, Jesus asked a young man to show his love for others in a very generous way.

Scripture

The Rich Young Man

One day when Jesus was teaching, a young man asked, "What must I do to live forever with God?"

Jesus answered, "Keep the commandments."

"Which commandments?" the young man asked. Jesus listed some of the Ten Commandments for him.

"I keep all those commandments!" the young man said happily. "What else do I need to do?"

"If you wish to be perfect," Jesus said, "go, sell what you have and give to [the] poor, and you will have treasure in heaven. Then come, follow me."

The young man's smile faded, for he was very rich. He could not imagine giving everything away, so he went away sad.   **Based on Matthew 19:16–22**

Jesus knew that the man's love for his possessions could keep him from loving God completely. When Jesus tested him to see how important his possessions were, the man could not part with them.

➡ **Why could the rich young man not give away his possessions?**

Share Your Faith

Reflect Think about what Jesus tells us about the Great Commandment.

Share With a partner, design a billboard that supports this teaching.

Love God

How can you live the Great Commandment?

The first step in living the Great Commandment is to understand that God wants you to love him. The **Theological Virtues** help you to live in a loving relationship with God. Virtues are good spiritual habits that strengthen you and help you to do what is right and good. They develop over time with our practice and openness to God's grace.

The Theological Virtues of **faith**, **hope** and **charity** are gifts from God. When we use these gifts, we are drawn into a deeper relationship with God. We also come to a deeper understanding that loving God leads to sharing God's love with others.

Love Others

God the Father sent his Son to show all people how to live in love. Jesus showed that the power of love can make a difference. Jesus cared most for those who were poor, helpless, and suffering. He calls his followers to do the same.

Catholic Faith Words

Theological Virtues the virtues of faith, hope, and charity, which are gifts from God that guide our relationship with him

faith the theological virtue that makes it possible for us to believe in God and all that he helps us understand about himself. Faith leads us to obey God.

hope the theological virtue that helps us trust in the true happiness God wants us to have and in Jesus' promises of eternal life, and to rely on the help of the Holy Spirit

charity the theological virtue of love. It directs us to love God above all things and our neighbor as ourselves, for the love of God.

Theological Virtues

Faith	God created you with the ability to know and trust him. You make the choice to seek God and believe in him.
Hope	This virtue helps you trust in God and the happiness he wants you to have.
Charity	The greatest of all Theological Virtues. This gift makes it possible for you to love God above everything else, and others as yourself.

Acts of Charity

The strength of the Holy Spirit, whom Jesus sent, gives you the power to reach out to others in love, as Jesus did. The Holy Spirit breathed charity into you at your Baptism.

Jesus' Great Commandment tells you to love others as you love yourself. Christians see the needs of others and help meet those needs. The Church has named seven acts of kindness you can do to meet the physical needs of others. They are called the **Corporal Works of Mercy**. The **Spiritual Works of Mercy** name what you can do for others to care for the needs of their heart, mind, and soul. See page 317 in the Our Catholic Tradition section of your book for the full list of Works of Mercy.

Catholic Faith Words

Corporal Works of Mercy actions that show care for the physical needs of others

Spiritual Works of Mercy actions that address the needs of the heart, mind, and soul

Connect Your Faith

Recognize Works of Mercy Draw lines to match the Work of Mercy with an action. Then circle the actions that you have done.

Corporal: Clothe the naked.

Corporal: Shelter the homeless.

Spiritual: Forgive all injuries.

Corporal: Feed the hungry.

Spiritual: Comfort the sorrowful.

Corporal: Visit the sick.

Spiritual: Pray for the living and the dead.

Volunteer to help serve a meal at a shelter.

Attend a funeral.

Donate clothes to those in need.

Listen to a friend who's really sad.

Visit a homebound relative.

Donate money to a homeless shelter.

Accept an apology when someone says they're sorry.

Our Catholic Life

How can you help people as Jesus did?

People all over the world are in need. Some of them are in your parish or neighborhood. If you pay attention, you may find that you know people who need your loving help.

When you think of people in need, do you imagine people who are homeless, hungry, and sick? The Corporal Works of Mercy teach us that there are many kinds of need. It is not always easy to see what those needs are. Here are some people you might see who need your help.

 Write how you could help each of these people in need.

Many Ways to Help

Clothe the naked	A child on the basketball court loses his sweatshirt. _____ _____
Shelter the homeless	A neighbor child forgets her house key. _____ _____
Feed the hungry	A classmate drops his lunch tray. _____
Give drink to the thirsty	A teammate does not have a water bottle. _____
Visit the imprisoned	A neighbor has no way to get to the grocery store. _____
Visit the sick	Your cousin has a broken leg. _____
Bury the dead	The mother of one of your classmates dies. _____

People of Faith

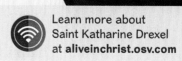

Saint Katharine Drexel, 1858–1955

Saint Katharine Drexel came from a wealthy family, but she devoted her money and her life to those who were poor. She did missionary work among African Americans and Native Americans. She insisted that all people be treated fairly, no matter what their race. She founded the Sisters of the Blessed Sacrament and also established schools on Native American reservations and the first and only Catholic university for African Americans. She believed it was her life's work to live out the Corporal Works of Mercy.

Discuss: What Works of Mercy have you done?

Learn more about
Saint Katharine Drexel
at **aliveinchrist.osv.com**

Live Your Faith

Write or draw one way in which you will try to show your love for God and others on each day next week.

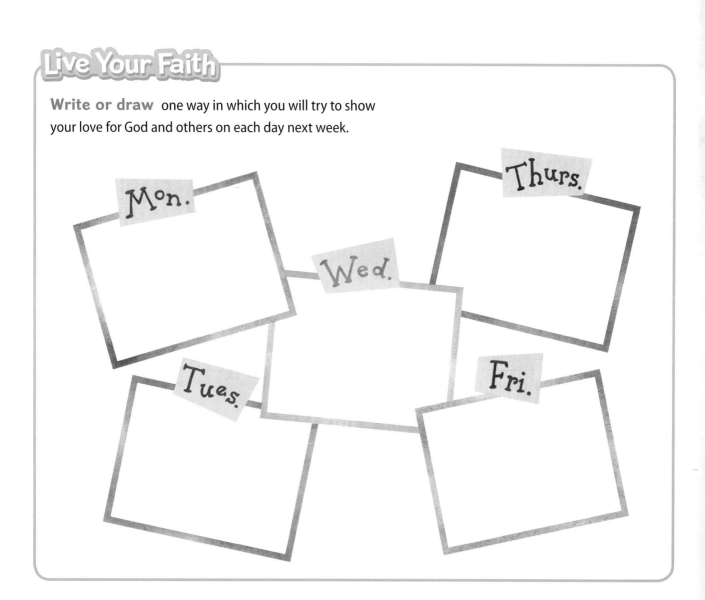

Mon.

Tues.

Wed.

Thurs.

Fri.

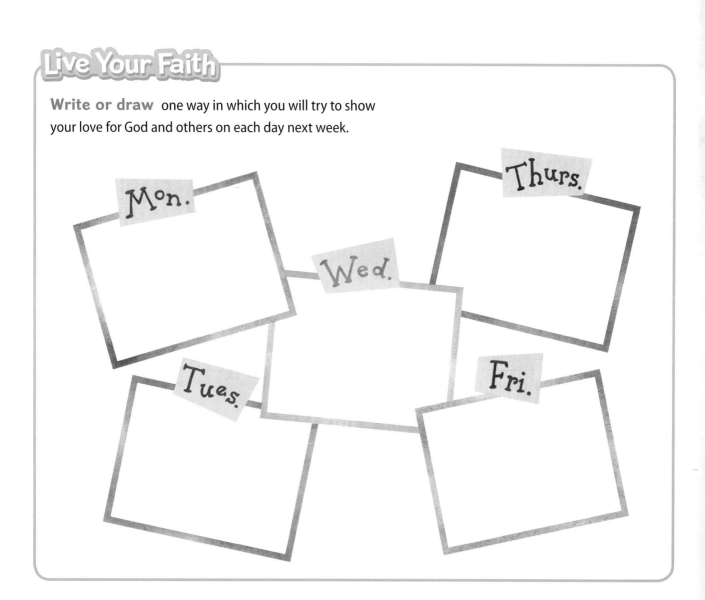

Let Us Pray

Celebration of the Word

Gather and begin with the Sign of the Cross.

Leader: God of Mercy, we gather to remind ourselves of your love and mercy.

Reader 1: A reading from the First Letter to the Corinthians.

Read 1 Corinthians 13:2–7.

The word of the Lord.

All: Thanks be to God.

Reader 2: Lord, give us the gift of patience.

All: We want to live in your love.

Reader 3: Lord, give us the gift of kindness.

All: We want to live in your love.

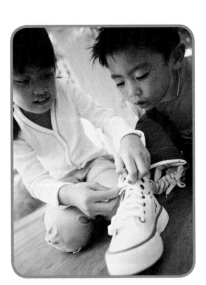

Reader 4: Lord, help us think of others.

All: We want to live in your love.

Leader: Let us pray.

Bow your heads as the leader prays.

All: Amen.

 Sing "Whatsoever You Do"

Whatsoever you do to the least of my people, that you do unto me.

FAMILY+FAITH
LIVING AND LEARNING TOGETHER

© Our Sunday Visitor

YOUR CHILD LEARNED >>>

This chapter helps students deepen their understanding of the Theological Virtues and how these virtues help us live the Great Commandment and practice Works of Mercy.

Scripture

Read **Ephesians 5:1–5** to find out what those who say they love God must have.

Catholics Believe

- The Great Commandment is to love God with all your heart, strength, and mind and to love your neighbor as yourself.
- The Theological Virtues of faith, hope, and charity help us to love God and grow closer to him.

To learn more, go to the *Catechism of the Catholic Church #2055, 2083, 2196* at **usccb.org**.

People of Faith

This week, your child learned about Saint Katharine Drexel, who dedicated her life and her fortune to educating African Americans and Native Americans.

CHILDREN AT THIS AGE >>>

How They Understand the Great Commandment The continued concrete thinking of fourth-graders means that they will probably continue to see love for God and for neighbor as a series of outward actions. This is not far from the truth, for it is certainly the things that we do that tell whether we really have love for God and neighbor. Children your child's age are growing in their ability to see relationships between these larger Commandments and smaller choices in everyday life. They can better determine whether or not an individual action is loving toward God or toward their neighbor. This new ability will help them to begin to make decisions in new situations.

CONSIDER THIS >>>

How does your relationship with God affect how you love others?

The more aware we are of God's love for us, the more that love moves through us. As Catholics, we know that "Scripturally and theologically, the Christian moral life begins with a loving relationship with God, a covenant love made possible by the sacrifice of Christ. The Commandments and other moral rules are given to us as ways of protecting the values that foster love of God and others. They provide us with ways to express love, sometimes by forbidding whatever contradicts love" (*USCCA, p. 318*).

LET'S TALK >>>

- Ask your child to name some of the Works of Mercy.
- Talk about a time of need when someone helped you by performing one of the Works of Mercy.

LET'S PRAY >>>

 Saint Katharine, pray for us that we may follow the way of Jesus. Help us live out the Corporal Works of Mercy in our daily lives. Amen.

For a multimedia glossary of Catholic Faith Words, Sunday readings, seasonal and Saint resources, and chapter activities go to **aliveinchrist.osv.com**.

Chapter 8 Review

A **Work with Words** Use all of the words in the Word Bank to write five of the Corporal Works of Mercy. Use the lines below.

1. _____

2. _____

3. _____

4. _____

5. _____

© Our Sunday Visitor

B **Check Understanding** Circle True if a statement is true, and circle False if a statement is false. Correct any false statements.

6. The Spiritual Works of Mercy show care for the physical needs of others.

   True   **False**

   _____

7. Only adults have the ability to care for and help others.

   True   **False**

   _____

8. Hope makes it possible for us to believe in God and all he has revealed.

   True   **False**

   _____

9. The Great Commandment can be restated in this way: "First love God, and then love others as you love yourself."

   True   **False**

   _____

10. The virtue of charity directs us to love God above all things.

    True   **False**

    _____

Go to **aliveinchrist.osv.com** for an interactive review.

Honoring God

 Let Us Pray

Leader: All glory, praise, and honor to you, great God of grace.

"I will proclaim your name to all I know;
   in the assembly I will praise you:
You who fear the LORD, give praise!
   All descendants of Jacob, give honor."
Based on Psalm 22:23–24a

All: We honor and respect you, Lord, and give to you first place in our lives. Amen.

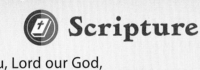 Scripture

"Worthy are you, Lord our God,
   to receive glory and honor and power, for you created all things;
   because of your will they came to be
      and were created.

Blessing and glory, wisdom and thanksgiving,
   honor, power, and might
   be to our God forever and ever. Amen."
Revelation 4:11; 7:12

? What Do You Wonder?

- What can help you honor and worship God?

- Does putting God first mean your family and friends aren't important?

Putting God First

What does it mean to praise and honor God?

God created each person to be unique, but also alike in a most important way. He created everyone in his own image. Once, the Hebrew people forgot to show God the honor and respect due to the giver of such a gift.

📖 Scripture

The Golden Calf

Moses was with God on Mount Sinai for forty days and nights. When the people learned of Moses' delay, they gathered around Aaron and said, "Come, make us a god who will be our leader; as for the man Moses who brought us out of the land of Egypt, we do not know what has happened to him." Aaron collected and melted all their gold, forming it into a golden calf. Then Aaron built an altar before the calf and declared a feast. The people brought sacrifices and worshipped the calf.

God then told Moses to return to the people and tell them how angry he was. Moses returned to the camp and destroyed the calf, turning it to powder. **Based on Exodus 32:1–20**

→ **Why did it not show respect to God to worship the golden calf?**

Astrology contradicts the honor we owe God.

The First Commandment

The sin of worshipping the golden calf occurred while Moses was receiving the stone tablets of the Ten Commandments from God. The First Commandment says, "I am the Lord your God. You shall not have strange gods before me."

The First Commandment requires you to honor and worship only God. **Worship** is the adoration and praise that is due to God. You worship God when you celebrate Mass, when you pray, and when you live a life that puts God first. Worshipping an object or a person instead of God, as the people worshipped the golden calf, is called **idolatry**.

When you worship God, you show your belief in him as the source of creation and salvation. You show that you, and all creatures, rely on him for life. You show your trust and hope in him. This is why fortune-telling or thinking that we can control nature and know the things that God knows are against the First Commandment.

➤ **What are some things that people sometimes place ahead of God?**

Catholic Faith Words

worship to adore and praise God, especially in the liturgy and in prayer

idolatry the sin of worshipping an object or a person instead of God. It is letting anything or anyone become more important than God.

Share Your Faith

Reflect Think about the ways you worship God. Write a sentence that explains why God is deserving of praise.

_____

_____

Share Share your responses with a partner.

Respecting God

What do the Second and Third Commandments tell you to do?

The Second Commandment is connected to the First Commandment: "You shall not take the name of the Lord in vain." God's name is sacred, or holy, because God is sacred. When God called Moses to be the leader of his People, God revealed his name to Moses. God shared his name with his People because he loved and trusted them. In return, God's People are to bless and praise God's holy name.

This Commandment calls you to always use the name of God with reverence and respect. Respecting God's name is a sign of the respect God deserves. It is a sin against God's name to curse or to use God's name to swear to a lie. To seriously dishonor the name of God, Jesus Christ, Mary, or the Saints in words or actions is called **blasphemy**.

You probably use God's name most often in prayer. Calling on God's name strengthens you to live as a child of God and a follower of Christ. The Second Commandment also reminds us that God calls each person by name. A name is a sign of a person's human dignity. You are to use the names of others with respect.

Catholic Faith Words

blasphemy the sin of showing disrespect for the name of God, Jesus Christ, Mary, or the Saints in words or action

Resurrection the event of Jesus being raised from Death to new life by God the Father through the power of the Holy Spirit

Fill in the missing letters in the words below.

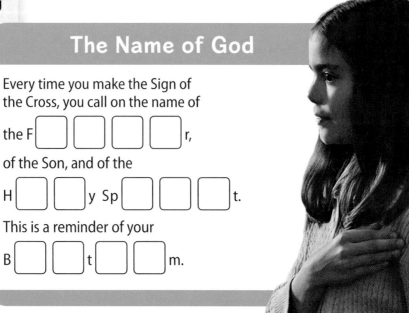

The Name of God

Every time you make the Sign of the Cross, you call on the name of

the F ▢ ▢ ▢ ▢ r,

of the Son, and of the

H ▢ ▢ y Sp ▢ ▢ ▢ t.

This is a reminder of your

B ▢ ▢ t ▢ ▢ m.

© Our Sunday Visitor

Keeping the Lord's Day

Following the First, Second, and Third Commandments helps you love God and grow closer to him. The Third Commandment teaches you to honor God by celebrating Sunday, the greatest and most special day of the week for Christians. The Third Commandment is this: Remember to keep holy the Lord's Day.

Sunday is the first day of the week. Jesus rose to new life on the first day of the week. This is why Sunday is known as the Lord's Day. Gathering on Sunday for the Eucharist has been the center of the Church's life since the time of the Apostles. This is because Sunday is the day of the Lord's **Resurrection**.

The Lord's Day

Participate in the Sunday celebration of the Eucharist. This is the most important way to observe the Third Commandment.

Rest and enjoy time with your family. Share a meal, read the Bible together, or visit a relative you do not often see.

Take part in parish activities, visit a retirement center, visit people in the community who are sick, or perform a work of service as a family.

Respect the rights of others to rest and observe Sunday.

Connect Your Faith

Sunday Suggestions Circle the actions you could take to remember the Lord's Day.

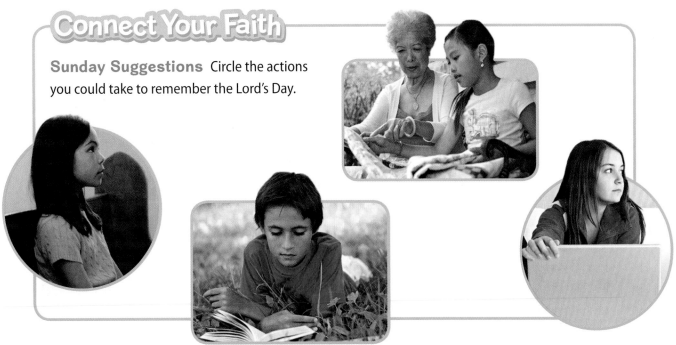

Our Catholic Life

Why are the First, Second, and Third Commandments important?

The first three Commandments are about how you act toward, think about, and worship God. They give you a guide for how you can praise God and show him respect.

Unscramble the letters in the boldfaced words to find some ways to show your respect for God.

Commandments of Respect

God has given you many blessings. In return, he asks that you follow the first three Commandments in worship of him.

Attend Mass Participate in Mass every Sunday or Saturday evening.

Say grace Give thanks to God and ask for his **lbisgssen** before you eat.

_____

Remember the meaning of religious holidays During the holidays, stop and think about why you are celebrating.

Love others Show kindness and love to people around you. They are made in God's **emgia**.

_____

Say a prayer of thanks Thank God for the many blessings in your life.

Do not curse Pay attention to what you are **ysinga**.

_____

People of Faith

Saint Mary Ann of Quito, 1618–1645

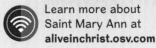

Saint Mary Ann of Quito was born in Quito, a city in Ecuador, South America. She was from a noble family. At an early age, she promised to live a holy life in poverty. She spent much time in prayer and doing penance. At first her name was Mariana de Paredes. Because she wanted to be sure she always showed her respect for the Name of Jesus, she added his name to hers. When earthquakes and disease came to her city, she prayed. The city was saved. She is considered a national hero of Ecuador.

Discuss: How do you show respect for the name of God?

Learn more about
Saint Mary Ann at
aliveinchrist.osv.com

Live Your Faith

Describe how the student in the picture is following one of the Commandments.

Illustrate one way you could love God by following one the first three Commandments.

❤ **Let Us Pray**

Prayer of Praise

Gather and begin with the Sign of the Cross.

Leader: Respond to each name of God by praying:
We praise your name, O God.

Reader: God, our Father,

All: We praise your name, O God.

Reader: All merciful and gracious God,

All: We praise your name, O God.

Reader: God, our Creator,

All: We praise your name, O God.

Reader: Compassionate God,

All: We praise your name, O God.

Reader: God, source of all life,

All: We praise your name, O God.

Leader: Let us pray.

Bow your heads as the leader prays.

All: Amen.

 Sing "Holy God, We Praise Thy Name"

© Our Sunday Visitor

YOUR CHILD LEARNED >>>

This chapter explains how the First, Second, and Third Commandments help us keep God first in our lives and teach us to worship God and honor his name.

Scripture

Read **Revelation 4:11; 7:12** to find out why and how to honor God.

Catholics Believe

- The first three Commandments teach you to honor God above all else, respect his name, and worship him on Sunday.
- These Commandments tell you to believe in, trust, and love God.

To learn more, go to the *Catechism of the Catholic Church #2063–2065* at **usccb.org**.

People of Faith

This week, your child learned about Saint Mary Ann of Quito, one of the national heroes of Ecuador.

CHILDREN AT THIS AGE >>>

How They Understand Honoring God It can be a challenge for many fourth-graders to honor God above everything. Children this age are practical and concrete, so they are usually very focused on material things. Understanding that they should seek God more than they want the newest video game system or other high-tech device can pose a conflict for them. They need to know that if they ask him, God will help them form the desires of their heart so that they are in line with his will.

CONSIDER THIS >>>

What would your calendar indicate are the top priorities in your family's life?

Most of our calendars are filled with work, children's activities, and chores to keep the household running. Yet, the Commandments call us to prioritize with God in mind. As Catholics, we understand that "the first three Commandments treat our relationship to God. . . . The First Commandment calls us to have faith in the true God, to hope in him, and to love him fully with mind, heart, and will. . . . The First Commandment fosters the virtue of religion that moves us to adore God alone because he alone is holy and worthy of our praise" (*USCCA, p. 341*).

LET'S TALK >>>

- Ask your child to tell you one way we honor God in our lives.
- Talk about how your family keeps the Lord's Day.

LET'S PRAY >>>

 Dear God, may we always respect and honor your name and never use it as a swear word. Amen.

 For a multimedia glossary of Catholic Faith Words, Sunday readings, seasonal and Saint resources, and chapter activities go to **aliveinchrist.osv.com**.

Chapter 9 Review

A **Work with Words** Fill in the circle next to the word that best completes each statement.

1. Calling on God's name in _____ helps you live as a child of God and follower of Christ.
   ○ anger
   ○ prayer
   ○ an oath

2. _____ the name of God, Jesus Christ, Mary, or the Saints in words or actions is called blasphemy.
   ○ Dishonoring
   ○ Explaining
   ○ Honoring

3. When you adore and praise God, _____ in the liturgy and in prayer, you are worshipping him.
   ○ except
   ○ only
   ○ especially

4. Fortune-telling is against the _____ Commandment.
   ○ First
   ○ Second
   ○ Third

5. When you worship God, you show your _____ in him as the source of creation and salvation.
   ○ disbelief
   ○ belief
   ○ indifference

B **Check Understanding** Respond briefly to the following questions.

6. Who or what should you worship?
   _____

7. What did God create in his own image?
   _____

8. How can you show respect for God's name?
   _____

9. Who is called to worship at Sunday Mass?
   _____

10. What do the first three Commandments tell you to do?
    _____
    _____
    _____

© Our Sunday Visitor

 Go to **aliveinchrist.osv.com** for an interactive review.

A **Work with Words** Match each description in Column 1 with the correct term in Column 2.

Column 1

1. Loving your neighbor as yourself

2. The meaning of "beatitude"

3. The sin of showing disrespect for the name of God, Jesus Christ, Mary, or the Saints in words or actions

4. Sunday, which is the day Jesus rose to new life

5. Loving God with all your heart

6. Actions that show care for the physical needs of others

7. These tell the way to live in God's Kingdom now and always

8. To adore and praise God, especially in the liturgy and in prayer

9. The virtue of love

10. The sin of worshipping an object or a person instead of God

Column 2

Beatitudes

charity

second part of the Great Commandment

worship

blessing

Corporal Works of Mercy

idolatry

Lord's Day

first part of the Great Commandment

blasphemy

B Check Understanding Complete each sentence with the correct word.

11. _____ received the Ten Commandments from God on Mount Sinai.

12. The _____ Commandment says, "I am the Lord your God. You shall not have strange gods before me."

13. The _____ Commandment says, "You shall not take the name of the Lord in vain."

14. The _____ Commandment says, "Remember to keep holy the Lord's Day."

15. The rich young man in the Scripture story could not think of selling his things and giving the _____ to the poor.

Make Connections Write a response to each question or statement.

16. Write about one of the Theological Virtues.

_____

_____

_____

_____

17. Write about someone who lives out the Theological Virtue you described.

_____

_____

_____

_____

18. Explain what the first three Commandments teach about respect.

_____

_____

_____

_____

_____

19. Explain what the Great Commandment has in common with the Corporal Works of Mercy.

_____

_____

_____

_____

_____

20. What do respect and honor mean to you?

_____

_____

_____

_____

_____

The Church

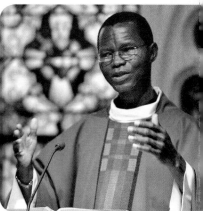

Our Catholic Tradition

- Every person has a vocation to love and honor God, share in his happiness, and become more like Christ as we serve others and work for his Kingdom. (CCC, 1877)

- Mary and the Saints are models and teachers of holiness for all of us. (CCC, 828)

- Jesus gave Church leaders the authority to explain Sacred Scripture and Sacred Tradition to the faithful. The Holy Spirit directs Church leaders in teaching and guiding the faithful. (CCC, 95, 100)

How does your vocation help you to become a Saint?

Called to Serve

 Let Us Pray

Leader: God of love, we gladly honor and obey you.

"Praise, you servants of the LORD,
   praise the name of the LORD." **Psalm 113:1**

All: In our Baptism, we are called to holiness. You call us by name to know you and serve your people. Open our hearts that we may hear your call. Amen.

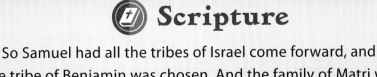 **Scripture**

So Samuel had all the tribes of Israel come forward, and the tribe of Benjamin was chosen. And the family of Matri was chosen. Finally, Saul, son of Kish, was chosen. But they could not find him. Samuel asked, "Has he come here?" The Lord answered, "He is hiding among the baggage." **Based on 1 Samuel 10:20–22**

? What Do You Wonder?

- How does God call people today?
- What will help you respond to God's call?

God's Call

What does it mean to have a vocation?

Everyone has a **vocation**. A vocation is God's plan for our lives: the purpose for which he made us. Sometimes God calls a person to a special role. When Jesus was ready to begin his work, he gathered some friends to help him.

✝ Scripture

The Call of the First Disciples

One day, Jesus was walking by the Sea of Galilee. He saw two brothers, Peter and Andrew. Andrew cast a net into the sea. The brothers were fishermen.

Jesus said to them, "Come follow me. I will make you fishers of men." At once, they left their nets and followed Jesus.

Jesus continued walking. He came upon two more brothers, James and John. They were in a boat with their father, fixing their nets. Jesus called them. Immediately they left their nets and their father and followed Jesus.

Based on Matthew 4:18–22

Vocation and God's Kingdom

Not everyone hears God's call as clearly as the first disciples did. Sometimes it takes many years of praying and listening to know your vocation.

All vocations can make the **Kingdom of God** more visible. God's Reign is the world of love, peace, and justice that God intends. Jesus announced the Kingdom and revealed it in his life and ministry. But God's Kingdom will not be here fully until the end of time when Christ returns in glory. Until then, we are called to help God increase his rule in our lives and in the world.

➜ **What signs can you see of God's Kingdom?**

Ways to Respond to God's Call

The Catholic Church recognizes four ways in which people respond to God's call to serve: through the priesthood, consecrated religious life, committed single life, or the married life. Consecrated religious life is a state of life in which a person usually makes **vows**, or promises, that help them to grow in holiness. Baptism sets us all on the journey of holiness. Priests and married couples take vows as well.

Catholic Faith Words

vocation God's plan for our lives; the purpose for which he made us

Kingdom of God God's rule of peace, justice, and love that exists in Heaven, but has not yet come in its fullness on Earth

vows solemn promises that are made to or before God

Priesthood

Consecrated religious life

Committed single life

Married life

Share Your Faith

Reflect Think about two people you know who serve God.

Share Tell a partner how these people are an example of service for you.

Serving the Church

How can we use our gifts to serve?

The Church recognizes that some people may be called to serve God by remaining single. The dedicated single life is also a vocation. Both single and married people are part of the **laity**. All who are baptized are invited to serve the universal Church and the parish community. Here are some ways we do this.

Catholic Faith Words

laity all of the baptized people in the Church who share in God's mission but are not priests or consecrated sisters or brothers; sometimes called lay people

Circle the roles that interest you or that you have questions about.

Many Gifts

The **pastor** and **pastoral associate** lead and serve the parish community.

The **permanent deacon** is ordained to assist the pastor—especially at Eucharist, marriages, and funerals—and to perform works of charity.

An **extraordinary minister of Holy Communion** not only helps distribute Holy Communion at Mass, but also takes Holy Communion to those who are sick or housebound.

The **lector** proclaims the Word of God at the Liturgy of the Word.

Altar servers assist the priest at Mass by carrying the Roman Missal, the sacred vessels, and the cross.

Musicians practice and lead the assembly in sung prayer.

Catechists teach Scripture and the Catholic faith to members of the parish.

Venerable Anne de Guigné

Venerable Anne de Guigné's beloved "Papa" died when she was four years old. She decided to become as good and as kind as she could. As she grew older, one of her teachers noticed how happy Anne was. The teacher asked Anne for the secret to happiness in life. Anne replied, "Jesus loves me very much, and I love him very much." Anne knew Jesus' love because she had a special gift for prayer. She received her First Holy Communion when she was six. From then on, she offered up her prayers for all those who did not know and love Jesus.

Using Your Gifts

You can already use your gifts from God to make a difference. Discerning your vocation means learning, through prayer, about what God wants you to do. You don't have to do something big and public to make the world a better place. Like Venerable Anne, you can do it quietly and privately.

Connect Your Faith

Sharing Your Gifts What gift do you have to share? Below the cityscape, write how you can help others by using one of God's gifts.

_____

_____

_____

Our Catholic Life

What does your Baptism call you to do?

Like the disciples and Venerable Anne de Guigné, you too have a calling. Your call, like that of all Catholics, came to you at your Baptism.

You probably do not remember your Baptism. You might have heard stories about how you cried or smiled. You know the names of your godparents. Now that you are older, you have learned more about the importance of the Sacrament of Baptism.

Through Baptism, you share in Jesus' ministry as priest, prophet, and king. Here are some ways to live your baptismal commitment.

 Add some other ways to these and fill in your name on the last line.

Live Your Call

As Priest

- Learn about God's plan for all creation.
- Pray with and for others.
- _____

As Prophet

- Learn what the Church teaches about morals and justice.
- Help other people make good choices.
- _____

As King

- Take responsibility for your actions and choices.
- Follow Jesus' example by serving and forgiving others, especially those who are most in need of justice, mercy, and loving care.
- _____

_____, may you live as priest, prophet, and king.

People of Faith

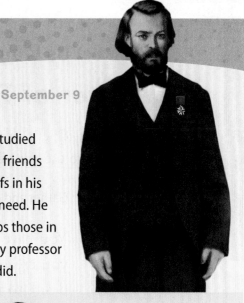

Blessed Frédéric Ozanam, 1813 – 1853

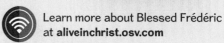
September 9

Blessed Frédéric Ozanam was born in Milan, Italy. For a time, he studied law. When he lived in Paris, he discovered a love for literature. His friends challenged him to find a way to live out his strong Christian beliefs in his everyday life. Frédéric realized that he had a call to help those in need. He helped found the Society of Saint Vincent de Paul, which still helps those in need, especially those who are poor. Frédéric was also a university professor and wrote many books. He tried to live out his vocation in all he did.

Discuss: How do you live your call to holiness?

Learn more about Blessed Frédéric at **aliveinchrist.osv.com**

Live Your Faith

Write On each finger of the hand, write one way you can use your talents in your parish. In the center of the hand, write one way that you can use one of your talents to bring more peace and justice into the world this week. Discuss your idea with a partner and talk next week about how you accomplished your goal.

Let Us Pray

Prayer of Petition for Vocations

This prayer of petition for vocations is a chance to reflect on how God calls each of us to use our gifts, as Jesus did, to build the Kingdom of God.

Gather and begin with the Sign of the Cross.

Leader: You have called each of us, Loving God, to be all that you created us to be. Send your Spirit to give us the desire to use our gifts to make your world a better place.

God's Call—My Vocation
Litany

All: _____, God calls you.

Leader: God, we give you thanks for the gift of our Baptism. In Baptism, you called us to participate in Jesus' ministry as priest, prophet, and king. Give us the courage, through the power of your Spirit, to be faithful to your call.

All: Amen.

▶ Sing "Gifts"
We thank you, God,
for giving talents to us.
Now we use those gifts
to serve others and you.
Singing and teaching,
helping each other.
Caring for needs
of our sisters and brothers.
We thank you, God,
as we give our talents back to you!
© 2010, Chet A. Chambers. Our Sunday Visitor, Inc.

FAMILY+FAITH
LIVING AND LEARNING TOGETHER

YOUR CHILD LEARNED >>>

This chapter explains vocation as God's plan for our lives and the purpose for which he made us; answering God's call and following his plan for us helps us grow in holiness.

Scripture

 Read **1 Samuel 10:20–22** to find out how one person responded to God's call.

Catholics Believe

• God calls every person to a vocation.

• Through your vocation, you can help God increase his Reign.

To learn more, go to the *Catechism of the Catholic Church #941, 2046* at **usccb.org**.

People of Faith

This week, your child learned about Blessed Frédéric Ozanam, who was a cofounder of the Society of Saint Vincent de Paul. Blessed Frédéric is an example for us of someone who answered and lived God's call for his life.

CHILDREN AT THIS AGE >>>

How They Understand Their Call from God As fourth-graders hear that God has a plan for their lives, they are capable of realizing that this plan is different from the one he has for anyone else. They have the free will to choose to follow—or not to follow—God's plan. With help and support from adults like you, your child can begin to better identify the talents and interests that can point to God's plan and also to see the opportunities to further explore God's path for his or her future.

CONSIDER THIS >>>

Do you think of your marriage as part of God's plan for you to grow in holiness?

God invites us to grow in holiness through our vocations. The vocation of marriage helps us become one with God by loving our spouse. As Catholics, we know that "God created man and woman out of love and commanded them to imitate his love in their relations with each other. . . . [Both] are equal in human dignity, and in marriage both are united in an unbreakable bond" (*USCCA, p. 279*).

LET'S TALK >>>

• Ask your child to explain vocation.

• Affirm your child's gifts and talents, naming some ways he or she could use them to bring happiness to others and serve God.

LET'S PRAY >>>

 God, help us answer your call as Blessed Frédéric did, so that we may do your will for our lives. Amen.

 For a multimedia glossary of Catholic Faith Words, Sunday readings, seasonal and Saint resources, and chapter activities go to **aliveinchrist.osv.com**.

Chapter 10 Review

A **Work with Words** Complete the following paragraph.

1–5. Jesus announced that God's _____ was at, hand. By this he meant that God's Reign of _____, _____, and _____ had begun with him, but was still to come in its fullness. All of us are _____ by God to cooperate with him in bringing his Kingdom to fullness.

B **Check Understanding** Fill in the circle next to the answer that best completes each statement.

6. The purpose for which God made us is known as a _____.
   ○ vocation
   ○ vacation
   ○ Commandment

7. _____ people who are baptized can serve a parish.
   ○ Some
   ○ All
   ○ No

8. _____ lead the people in prayer when they celebrate Mass.
   ○ Deacons
   ○ Parishioners
   ○ Priests

9. Deacons do all of the following EXCEPT _____.
   ○ assist at the Sacraments
   ○ perform works of charity
   ○ lead a diocese

10. Both single and married people are part of the _____.
    ○ ordained
    ○ laity
    ○ consecrated

© Our Sunday Visitor

Go to **aliveinchrist.osv.com** for an interactive review.

Models of Virtue

 Let Us Pray

Leader: We know your name, O Lord. It is *Holy, Holy, Holy.*

"I, the LORD, am your God. You shall make and keep yourselves holy, because I am holy."
Leviticus 11:44

All: We are your namesakes, O Lord. Help us live up to our name. Amen.

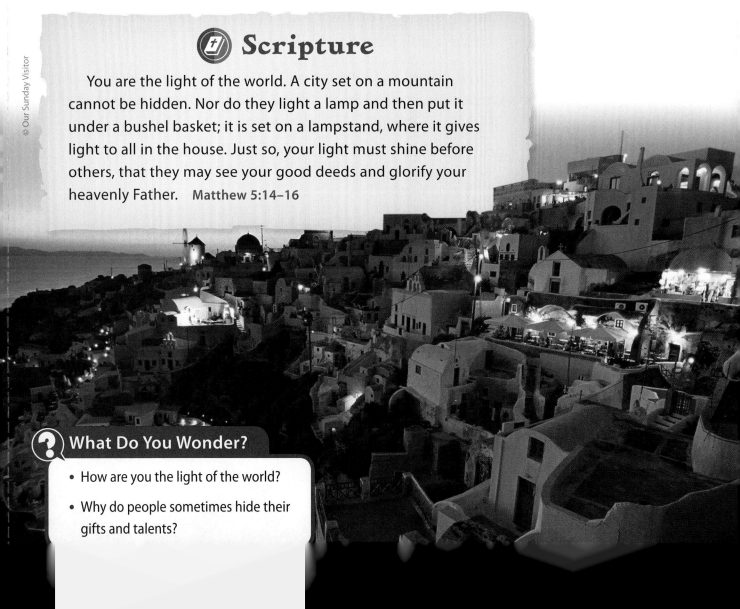

Scripture

You are the light of the world. A city set on a mountain cannot be hidden. Nor do they light a lamp and then put it under a bushel basket; it is set on a lampstand, where it gives light to all in the house. Just so, your light must shine before others, that they may see your good deeds and glorify your heavenly Father. **Matthew 5:14–16**

What Do You Wonder?

- How are you the light of the world?
- Why do people sometimes hide their gifts and talents?

© Our Sunday Visitor

Holy Ones of God

Who models faith for us?

The Church honors certain people whose lives showed others how to do God's will. These models of faith and virtue lived holy lives. To be holy is to be unique and pure, set apart for God and his purposes. These people helped God bring his Reign into the world more fully. Through the process of **canonization**, the Church names each of these people a **Saint**. The second step in the process of canonization is **beatification**. Here is the story of one Saint.

Saint Catherine of Siena

Catherine wanted to serve God through quiet prayer. But Catherine's world was full of problems. God called her to make a difference.

Catherine lived long ago in Siena, Italy. She was very wise and used words well. Although unusual for a woman of her time, Catherine made public speeches and taught priests. She also cared for the sick and those in prison.

© Our Sunday Visitor

Catholic Faith Words

canonization a declaration by the Pope naming a person a Saint. Canonized Saints have special feast days or memorials in the Church's calendar.

Saint a person whom the Church declares has led a holy life and is enjoying eternal life with God in Heaven

beatification the second step in the process of becoming a Saint, in which a venerable person is recognized by the Church as having brought about a miracle through his or her prayers of intercession

Catherine spoke out against injustice. She helped leaders in the Church make peace with one another. For a time, she lived in Rome and served as an adviser to the Pope. Christians learn from Catherine that every member of the Church can make a difference.

Catherine's students called her "Mother" and "Teacher." She has been named a Doctor of the Church, which is an honor that means she is one of the great teachers in our Church. Even though she had no formal education, her writings and teachings have been very influential in the Church.

Catherine of Siena is also a canonized Saint of the Catholic Church. This means that the Church has officially declared that she led a holy life and is enjoying eternal life with God in Heaven.

S. Caterina da Siena

POSTE ITALIANE L.30

➤ **What are some reasons people admire Catherine?**

Share Your Faith

Reflect Name two reasons Saint Catherine is a model of faith for you.

_____

_____

Share Discuss your reasons with a group.

Model of Holiness

How is Mary a model of holiness?

There are many Saints, but **Mary** is the perfect model of holiness. God chose Mary to be the mother of Jesus. After Mary said "yes" to being the Mother of God's Son, she visited her cousin Elizabeth. Here is how Mary described her joy at the great blessing God had given her.

Scripture

The Canticle of Mary

"My soul proclaims the greatness of the Lord;
    my spirit rejoices in God my savior.
For he has looked upon his handmaid's lowliness;
    behold, from now on will all ages call me blessed.
The Mighty One has done great things for me,
    and holy is his name.
                His mercy is from age to age
                to those who fear him."

Luke 1:46–50

Your Will Be Done

God created Mary full of grace. He preserved her from sin from the very first moment of her conception. The Catholic Church calls this gift from God Mary's **Immaculate Conception**.

The word *immaculate* means spotless and clean—without sin. The word *conception* means the very moment when a person's life begins. The Church celebrates the Immaculate Conception of Mary on December 8.

Part of holiness is being able to accept and do the things that God asks. Mary accepted God's will throughout her life. Mary cared for and protected Jesus when he was a child. She stood by him all through his life. She was strong enough to be with him when he was crucified.

After Jesus ascended into Heaven, Mary remained on Earth with Jesus' followers. She was there at Pentecost when the Holy Spirit came. Mary is called the Mother of the Church because she holds her Son's followers close to her heart. She remains an example of love and faith for all.

Catholic Faith Words

Immaculate Conception the truth that God kept Mary free from sin from the first moment of her life

patron Saint a Saint who has a particular connection to a cause, place, type of work, or person. For example, if a person or city shares the name of a Saint, that Saint is a patron.

Circle the ways in which Mary is the perfect model of holiness.

A Guide for You

When you were baptized, you may have received the name of one of the Saints. This person is your **patron Saint**—your model of faith who prays for you from Heaven. You walk in the footsteps of your Saint and continue his or her good works in the way you live.

Connect Your Faith

Model of Holiness With a partner, discuss three qualities of Saints that you want to model.

ST. MARTIN DE PORRES

Our Catholic Life

How can you follow the example of the Saints?

The Church honors Saints from around the world. They have lived holy lives, and many of them have done brave things to spread God's Word. You may think that you cannot be like them until you are older, but all of the Saints were your age once. Some Saints acted heroically at a young age.

You can do things now. To spread God's loving message to others, you must first allow God's love to grow within you. To do so, keep in mind the following steps.

In the boxes, write a D for things you are doing, a G for things you are growing in, and a Q for things you have questions about.

Following the Saints

☐ **Keep Your Eyes on Jesus**
Read in the Bible about Jesus' life. When you face a problem, ask yourself how Jesus would act in that situation. Make Jesus number one in your choices and thoughts.

☐ **Read About the Lives of the Saints**
Think about how these holy men and women chose to love God above everything else. Try to follow their examples of holiness.

☐ **Make Good Decisions**
Follow the Ten Commandments, Jesus' Great Commandment, and the Beatitudes. Avoid sin whenever temptation appears.

People of Faith

April 16

Saint Bernadette, 1844–1879

Saint Bernadette Soubirous came from a very poor French family. She helped her family by herding sheep. One day, she saw a vision of a beautiful young woman. Over the next five months, she saw the woman seventeen more times. The woman led her to a spring of healing water. When Bernadette asked her who she was, the lady said she was "The Immaculate Conception." People then knew that Bernadette was seeing Mary, the Mother of Jesus. Today, people still go to the spring at Lourdes and pray for healing.

Discuss: What do you know about the Immaculate Conception?

 Learn more about Saint Bernadette at **aliveinchrist.osv.com**

Live Your Faith

Name one way you can show how you are growing in holiness.

_____

Create two snapshots of yourself that show ways in which you are still growing.

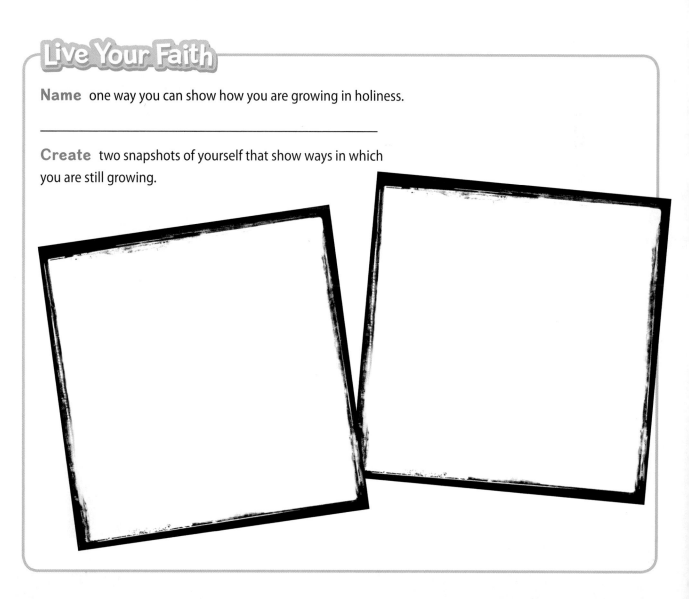

Let Us Pray

Litany of the Saints

A litany is a prayer with one line that is meant to be repeated over and over again so that those praying are caught up in the prayer itself.

Gather and begin with the Sign of the Cross.

Leader: Respond with *Pray for us* after each Saint's name.

Reader 1: Holy Mary, Mother of God

All: Pray for us.

Reader 2: Saint Michael,
Saint John the Baptist,
Saint Joseph,
Saints Peter and Paul,
Saint Mary Magdalene,
Saint Stephen,
Saint Agnes,
Saint Gregory,
Saint Francis,
Saint Dominic,
Saint Catherine,
Saint Teresa,
Saints Perpetua and Felicity,
Saint Martin,

Leader: Let us pray.

Bow your heads as the leader prays.

All: Amen.

▶ Sing "Immaculate Mary"

FAMILY+FAITH
LIVING AND LEARNING TOGETHER

YOUR CHILD LEARNED >>>

This chapter teaches that Saints are people whom the Church declares have lived holy lives and are now with God in Heaven.

Scripture

 Read **Matthew 5:14–16** to find out how living a life of holiness can light the way for others.

Catholics Believe

- The Church's holiness shines in the Saints. All who live their love of God are Saints.

- Mary is the perfect model of holiness, and she is called the Mother of the Church.

To learn more, go to the *Catechism of the Catholic Church #828–829, 963, 967–970* at **usccb.org**.

People of Faith

This week, your child learned about Saint Bernadette of Lourdes, to whom the Virgin Mary appeared.

CHILDREN AT THIS AGE >>>

How They Understand the Saints Your child is probably very interested in stories about the Saints. It is especially intriguing for children this age to hear about Saints who were young or who acted heroically in challenging circumstances. Your child can also understand that the Saints were not perfect, but they allowed God to use them and to form them into what he called them to be.

CONSIDER THIS >>>

Who in your life is open to God's will like Mary?

Saints are ordinary people who live extraordinarily faith-filled lives. Mary's willingness to obey God makes her the perfect model. As Catholics, we know that Mary "occupies a place in the Church which is the highest after Christ and yet very close to us" (*Lumen Gentium*, 54). When God calls Mary to be the Mother of his Son, she consents with deep faith and trust. She is the first and greatest of the disciples (*Based on USCCA p. 143*).

LET'S TALK >>>

- Ask your child to explain why Mary is the perfect model of holiness.

- Share a story about a Saint who means a lot to you or talk about ways your family can honor the Saints.

LET'S PRAY >>>

 Immaculate Mary, keep us safe under your protection. Amen.

 For a multimedia glossary of Catholic Faith Words, Sunday readings, seasonal and Saint resources, and chapter activities go to **aliveinchrist.osv.com**.

Chapter 11 Review

A **Work with Words** Complete each sentence with the correct word from the Word Bank.

Word Bank

Beatification

holy

Mother

preserved

wisdom

1. Catherine of Siena was named a Doctor of the Church because of her _____ .

2. Immaculate Conception is the teaching that recognizes that God _____ Mary from sin from the first moment of her life.

3. _____ is the second step in the process of a person being canonized a Saint.

4. Mary felt great joy at being chosen by God to be the _____ of his Son.

5. A Saint is recognized by the Church for living a _____ life and is in Heaven with God.

B **Check Understanding** Respond briefly to the following questions.

6. What does it mean to be a canonized Saint of the Catholic Church?

_____

_____

7. What makes Mary the perfect model of holiness?

_____

_____

8. What did Catherine of Siena speak out against?

_____

9. What is a patron Saint?

_____

10. What can you learn from reading about the lives of Saints?

_____

Go to **aliveinchrist.osv.com** for an interactive review.

The Church Teaches

 Let Us Pray

Leader: Jesus, Teacher and Lord, send us good teachers and leaders to guide us to you.

"Teach me to do your will,
for you are my God.
May your kind spirit guide me." **Psalm 143:10**

All: Help us to follow our leaders, Lord, so that we, too, might show others the way to you.

Scripture

[Jesus] gave some as apostles, others as prophets, others as evangelists, others as pastors and teachers, to equip the holy ones for the work of ministry, for building up the body of Christ, until we all attain to the unity of faith and knowledge of the Son of God. **Ephesians 4:11–13**

? What Do You Wonder?

- Who are the Church leaders and teachers you know or know about?
- Who guides you in your faith?

Jesus Chooses a Leader

Whom did Jesus choose as the leader of the Apostles?

We have many teachers who help us learn important lessons. Our parents are our first teachers, and the Church is our most important teacher. The Church's authority, or power to teach, was given by Jesus and is guided by the Holy Spirit. Here is a Gospel passage about the beginnings of the Church's authority to teach.

Scripture

You Are the Messiah!

Now Jesus and his disciples set out for the villages of Caesarea Philippi. Along the way he asked his disciples, "Who do people say that I am?" They said in reply, "John the Baptist, others Elijah, still others one of the prophets." And he asked them, "But who do you say that I am?" Peter said to him in reply, "You are the Messiah." Then [Jesus] warned them not to tell anyone about him.   Mark 8:27–30

Peter believed in Jesus and said so. Jesus gave Peter and the other Apostles a share in the authority he had from his Father. Then Jesus sent them out to preach, teach, forgive, and heal in his name.

➜ If Jesus asked you the same question he asked Peter, what would you say?

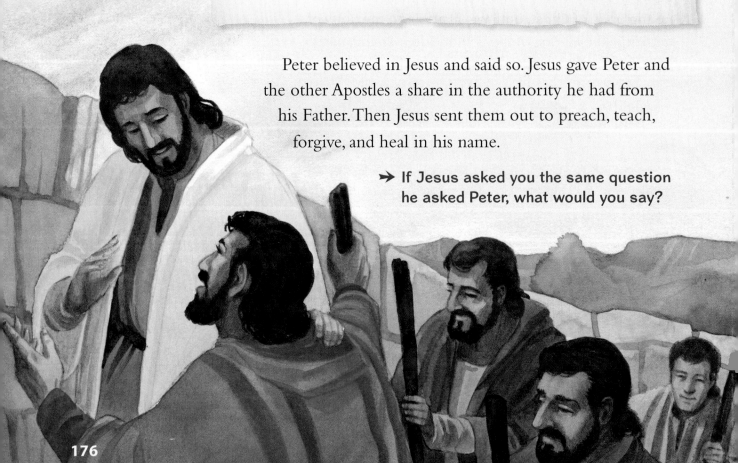

Peter and Jesus

Peter made some mistakes along the way. Much later, at the time of Jesus' crucifixion, Peter and the other disciples were very much afraid. In fact, the night before Jesus died, Peter denied three times that he had ever known Jesus. Afterward, he was ashamed of himself and cried bitterly.

But Jesus never lost faith in Peter. After Jesus' Death and Resurrection, Jesus was talking to Peter and the other disciples on the shore of a lake. Jesus asked three times whether Peter loved him. Of course, Peter said that he did. Jesus said to him, "Feed my lambs. Feed my sheep." (See John 21:15–17.)

In spite of Peter's earlier denials, Jesus made Peter the chief shepherd of all his flock. When he became the leader, Peter made good decisions for the members of the Church.

➡ **Why do you think Jesus asked Peter the same question three times?**

1. **Underline what Peter did the night before Jesus' death.**

2. **Circle what the risen Jesus asked Peter.**

Share Your Faith

Reflect Think of some times when you have been forgiven for mistakes you have made.

Share Write a short prayer of thanks for someone who has forgiven you.

The Church and You

What is your role as a member of the Church?

© Our Sunday Visitor

After Jesus ascended into Heaven, Peter and the Apostles were afraid. Then at Pentecost, the Holy Spirit came and gave them courage to preach the Good News.

The Apostles, with Peter as their head, were the first leaders of the Church. Jesus founded the Church on the Apostles. He gave them the authority to teach and lead his followers. Today, the chief teachers in the Church are the Pope and the bishops, the successors of the Apostles. Their teaching office is called the **Magisterium**. They have the teaching authority to interpret the Word of God found in Sacred Scripture and Sacred Tradition. This is called magisterial authority, and goes back to the authority Christ first gave to the Apostles. The Holy Spirit works through the Church's teachers to keep the whole Church faithful to the teachings of Jesus.

The Church's mission to share the true message of Jesus is not left to the Pope and bishops alone. All members of the Body of Christ have a duty to learn Jesus' message as the Church interprets it and to share it with others. As you do this, you will grow in your love of God and neighbor.

➜ **Who has taught you about the teachings of the Church?**

Catholic Faith Words

Magisterium the teaching office of the Church, which is all of the bishops in union with the Pope

Precepts of the Church some of the minimum requirements given by Church leaders for deepening your relationship with God and the Church

Archbishop Timothy Cardinal Dolan listens to children singing at Mount Carmel—Holy Rosary School in East Harlem, New York.

Rules for Living

Some of the responsibilities of members of the Catholic Church are summed up in the **Precepts of the Church**. The Church's leaders developed these rules and requirements to show you the minimum you should do to live morally and faithfully. As a Catholic, you have a duty to live according to the teachings and Precepts of the Church.

Precepts of the Church

1. Take part in the Mass on Sundays and holy days. Keep these days holy and avoid unnecessary work.

2. Celebrate the Sacrament of Reconciliation at least once a year if you have committed a serious sin.

3. Receive Holy Communion at least once a year during Easter time.

4. Observe days of fasting and abstinence.

5. Give your time, gifts, and money to support the Church.

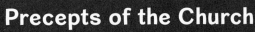

Connect Your Faith

Word Search

Find at least six words in this word search that relate to the teaching authority of the Church.

Use two of these words in a sentence about your role in the Church.

F	A	I	T	H	O	P	E	A	P
B	P	R	E	C	E	P	T	S	E
H	O	L	Y	S	P	I	R	I	T
A	P	O	S	T	L	E	S	C	E
D	E	B	I	S	H	O	P	S	R

Our Catholic Life

How can you help support the Church?

When each person gives time, gifts, or money, the Church can provide for the needs of her members and can grow in helping meet the needs of others as well.

Ways to Support Your Parish

Giving your time could include participating in any activity in which you volunteer your efforts to help with a parish event. You could help decorate the church for a special liturgy, or donate time to the nursery during Sunday Mass.

Write one way you can give your time to the Church.

_____

Sharing your gifts or talents with the Church community is also important. You could use your computer skills to get others involved, or sing in the children's choir or greet people before Sunday Mass.

Write one way you can share your talents with the Church.

_____

Offering some of your money supports the work of the parish, such as ministering to those who are in need. Money is needed to purchase food and other supplies for shelters. It is also needed to run the parish. For example, the parish has to pay for electricity.

Even if your allowance is small, you should give what you can to your parish.

Write one way you can give of your treasure to support the Church's work.

_____

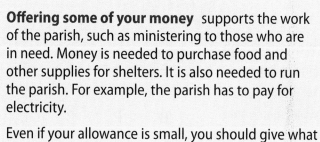

People of Faith

Saint Mary Magdalen Postel, 1756–1846

July 16

Saint Mary Magdalen Postel was educated in a Benedictine convent. At eighteen she opened a school for girls in France. It was just before the French Revolution. During the revolution, her school was closed. At that time, Mary Magdalen helped protect fugitive priests. She knew the importance of teaching people about the faith. She wanted everyone to know what the Church teaches. So after the revolution ended, she continued to work in the field of religious education.

Discuss: How does your parish help you to grow in faith?

 Learn more about Saint Mary Magdalen Postel at **aliveinchrist.osv.com**

Live Your Faith

Think What chances do you have to use your time, talent, or money to help the Church?

Write or draw one thing you will do next week to share these things with the Church.

Let Us Pray

Prayer of Intercession

In an intercession, we ask God to act in some way in the lives of others. This prayer follows the order of the Prayer of the Faithful, which we pray at Mass.

Gather and begin with the Sign of the Cross.

Leader: We gather, knowing that God hears us when we pray.

Reader 1: For our Church, that the Holy Spirit will continue to guide her as she teaches the truth revealed by Jesus, let us pray to the Lord.

All: Lord, hear our prayer.

Reader 2: For those in need, that they will experience our care as we live the Beatitudes, let us pray to the Lord.

All: Lord, hear our prayer.

Reader 3: For each person in our community, that the Great Commandment guides us, let us pray to the Lord.

All: Lord, hear our prayer.

Leader: For what else shall we pray?

Name specific prayers.

All: Amen.

 Sing "The Church"

FAMILY+FAITH
LIVING AND LEARNING TOGETHER

© Our Sunday Visitor

YOUR CHILD LEARNED >>>

This chapter explains the role of Peter and the Apostles continued by the Magisterium and how it interprets Jesus' message through the direction of the Holy Spirit, and describes the Precepts of the Church.

Scripture

Read **Ephesians 4:11–13** to learn about the the diversity of gifts used to build up the Church.

Catholics Believe

- Jesus gave the leaders of the Church the authority to interpret Scripture and Tradition for the faithful.
- The Holy Spirit directs the Church in teaching and guiding the People of God.

To learn more, go to the *Catechism of the Catholic Church #85–87* at **usccb.org**.

People of Faith

This week, your child learned about Saint Mary Magdalen Postel, who is known for her dedication to religious education.

CHILDREN AT THIS AGE >>>

How They Understand Church Teaching For most fourth-graders, the experience of the teaching Church is limited to their own parish or school; for example, the things they learn in faith formation and hear in the Mass. However, your child is likely growing in his or her ability to perceive the larger worldwide Church and to understand the role of the bishops and Pope. Your child's respect for these leaders will be influenced by the respect shown by adults around them.

CONSIDER THIS >>>

Do you recall when you first realized that you didn't have all the answers?

As we grow wiser, we realize we are limited in our understanding. The Church, guided by the Holy Spirit, brings us the fullness of truth. As Catholics, we know the "entire community of Christians received the Apostles' proclamation of the Gospel, and so the church in her entirety is called 'apostolic.' Under the guidance of the Holy Spirit, the church as a whole remains and will always remain faithful to the teaching of the Apostles" (*USCCA, p. 132*).

LET'S TALK >>>

- Ask your child to explain some ways the Church teaches us.
- Share a story about someone who helped you understand a Church teaching.

LET'S PRAY >>>

 Saint Mary Magdalen, pray for us that we may open our hearts and minds to learn more as we grow in faith and in our love for God. Amen.

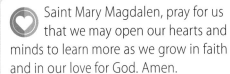 For a multimedia glossary of Catholic Faith Words, Sunday readings, seasonal and Saint resources, and chapter activities go to **aliveinchrist.osv.com**.

Chapter 12 Review

A **Work with Words** Complete each sentence with the correct word or words from the Word Bank.

1. Minimum requirements given by the Church to help you grow closer to God and the Church are called _____ of the Church.

2. Jesus gave the Church the _____ to teach and lead the Body of Christ.

3. You have the duty to _____ the rules and laws of the Church.

4. The _____ is the teaching office of the Church, all the bishops in union with the Pope.

5. The _____ guides the Church and the Magisterium.

B **Check Understanding** Circle True if a statement is true, and circle False if a statement is false. Correct any false statements.

6. Only wealthy people can help support the Church. **(True / False)**

   _____

7. On Christmas, the Holy Spirit came and gave the disciples courage to go out and preach the Good News. **(True / False)**

   _____

8. The Pope and bishops are the chief teachers in the Church. **(True / False)**

   _____

9. When John became the leader of the Church, he made good decisions for the members. **(True / False)**

   _____

10. Jesus sent the Apostles out to preach, teach, forgive, and heal in his name. **(True / False)**

   _____

Go to **aliveinchrist.osv.com** for an interactive review.

Unit Review

A **Work with Words** Solve the puzzle with terms from the Word Bank.

Down

1. _____ is God's plan for our lives. The purpose for which he made us.

2. God's _____ is here now, but has not yet come in its fullness.

3. Observing days of fasting and abstinence is a _____ of the Church.

4. The teaching office of the Church

6. The Immaculate _____ is the teaching that Mary was preserved from sin from the first moment of her life.

7. A person whom the Church declares has led a holy life and is enjoying life with God in Heaven

10. All the baptized who are not priests or religious brothers or sisters

Across

5. An _____ server assists the priest at Mass.

8. The process by which the Church officially declares someone a Saint

9. A Saint who has a particular connection to a cause, place, type of work, or person.

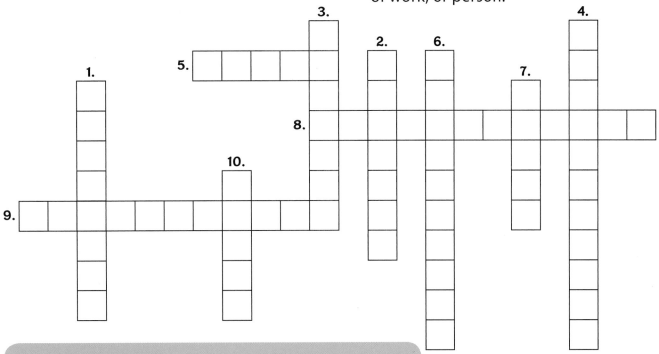

Word Bank

vocation	canonization	Kingdom	altar
Conception	Saint	patron Saint	laity
Magisterium	Precept		

B Check Understanding Complete each sentence with the correct word from the Word Bank.

11. In the story of Catherine of Siena, you learned that Catherine answered God's

    _____ .

12. A declaration by the Pope that names a person a Saint is called

    _____ .

13. Mary is the perfect model of

    _____ .

14. All _____ of the Church have a duty to learn Jesus' message and share it with others.

15. The _____ is the teaching office of the Church, which is all of the bishops in union with the Pope.

Word Bank

holiness

Magisterium

call

members

canonization

C Make Connections Write a response to each question or statement.

16. Through Baptism, you share in Jesus' role as priest, prophet, and king. Think about the accounts of Jesus in the Bible. Describe one account that shows Jesus acting as a priest, a prophet, or a king.

    _____

    _____

    _____

    _____

    _____

17. Name two ways in which you can grow in holiness today.

_____

_____

_____

_____

18. Explain how supporting the Church by offering your time, gifts, and money strengthens the Church community.

_____

_____

_____

_____

19. Why is Mary so important to our Catholic faith?

_____

_____

_____

_____

20. Explain the Church's role as a teacher.

_____

_____

_____

_____

Morality

© Our Sunday Visitor

Our Catholic Tradition

- The virtues help us do what is good, follow God's Commandments, and give the best of ourselves. (CCC, 1803)

- God created humans to live in strong, loving families and communities. These communities are called to respect life and live in the truth. (CCC, 2207)

- All human life is sacred. (CCC, 2319)

- We learn ways of loving our neighbor and respecting others by practicing the Fourth through Tenth Commandments. (CCC, 2196)

Why is it important for families to respect the dignity of each person in their family and in the world?

Family Love

 Let Us Pray

Leader: Loving Father, thank you for our parents and families who love us and teach us.

"Hear, my son, your father's instruction, and reject not your mother's teaching."

Proverbs 1:8

All: Loving God, help us grow with respect and blossom with love. Amen.

© Our Sunday Visitor

 Scripture

Children, obey your parents in everything, for this is pleasing to the Lord. Fathers, support your children, so they may not be discouraged. **Based on Colossians 3:20–21**

? What Do You Wonder?

- What are ways family members help one another?

- Why is obeying your parents important to God?

Honor and Respect

What does the Fourth Commandment require?

It would be hard to imagine our lives without our families. The love of our parents, grandparents, aunts, and uncles helps us to feel cared for and valued. God created humans to live in families. God wants families to be strong, to protect one another, and to live in peace and love.

The Fourth, Sixth, and Ninth Commandments provide basic laws about family love and respect. The Fourth Commandment is this: Honor your father and mother. Jesus is the perfect example for living out this Commandment.

Ⓣ Scripture

The Boy Jesus and His Family

When Jesus was twelve, he went to Jerusalem with his family to celebrate Passover. As Mary and Joseph were returning home, they realized that Jesus was not with them. They finally found him talking with the teachers in the Temple. Mary told Jesus how worried they had been, and Jesus returned to Nazareth with his parents.

Jesus was obedient as he grew in wisdom and age. His actions were pleasing to God and to all who knew him.

Based on Luke 2:41–52

➡ **How did Jesus live out the Fourth Commandment?**

Living the Fourth Commandment

The Fourth Commandment teaches you to honor your parents and guardians. You honor them when you

- listen to and obey them in all that is good.

- show gratitude for all that they do for you.

- respect and care for them as they grow older.

- respect people in authority.

Parents and guardians are to provide for your needs, serve as good role models, love you, and share their faith with you. This sharing makes the family a domestic Church, where we first learn about loving others and following Christ. Parents and guardians also encourage you to grow in faith by sharing their own faith and teaching the **Cardinal Virtues**, good habits that help us live as children of God. They help you make good choices and figure out your vocation.

Catholic Faith Words

Cardinal Virtues the four principal moral virtues—prudence, temperance, justice, and fortitude—that help us live as children of God and from which the other moral virtues flow. We strengthen these good habits through God's grace and our own efforts.

Share Your Faith

Reflect Draw something your family enjoys doing together.

Share Talk with a partner about how this activity keeps your family strong and close.

© Our Sunday Visitor

Faithful Love

What do the Commandments teach about love?

The Sixth Commandment is: You shall not commit adultery. The Ninth Commandment is: You shall not covet your neighbor's wife. These Commandments are about the faithful love and commitment between husband and wife.

When a man and woman marry, they make solemn promises to or before God, called vows. They promise to love and honor each other always and to welcome the gift of children.

Part of being faithful is respecting your vows and those of other married couples. Married couples should not act in ways that would weaken their marriage. Adultery means being unfaithful to these vows. The grace of the Sacrament of Matrimony strengthens the couple to be faithful and true.

➼ **Why is the Sacrament of Matrimony important?**

Virtues and You

The Sixth and Ninth Commandments apply to everyone. You can live out these Commandments by keeping promises to family, friends, and God.

Catholic Faith Words

temperance the Cardinal Virtue that helps us use moderation, be disciplined, and have self-control

fortitude the Cardinal Virtue that helps you show courage, have strength to get through difficult times, and not give up on doing good

modesty a moral virtue and one of the Fruits of the Holy Spirit that helps us dress, talk, and move in appropriate ways

chastity a moral virtue and one of the Fruits of the Holy Spirit that helps us to act and think in ways that are appropriate and pure

The four Cardinal Virtues—prudence, **temperance**, justice, and **fortitude**—help us to act wisely, use self-control, give others their due, stand strong, and be disciplined in our thoughts and actions.

Temperance helps us to practice **modesty** and **chastity**. You can dress, talk, and move in ways that honor your own dignity and that of others. You can respect that the differences between males and females are gifts from God.

God's Love Strengthens

Sometimes it is hard for families to live as God intends. Arguments, hurts, and disappointments can keep families from being signs of God's love. Parents and children sometimes hurt one another. Some families are hurt through separation, divorce, or even death.

But God continues to love all families and to help them grow stronger. Every time families are signs of love, they reflect the love that exists within the Holy Trinity.

1. Underline how the Cardinal Virtues help us.

2. Circle ways you practice modesty and chastity.

Connect Your Faith

Crossword Fill in the crossword using the clues.

Across

3. helps us to act and think in ways that are pure

5. helps us use moderation and self-control

Down

1. helps us dress, talk, and move appropriately

2. Cardinal _____ help you live as children of God

4. showing courage and strength

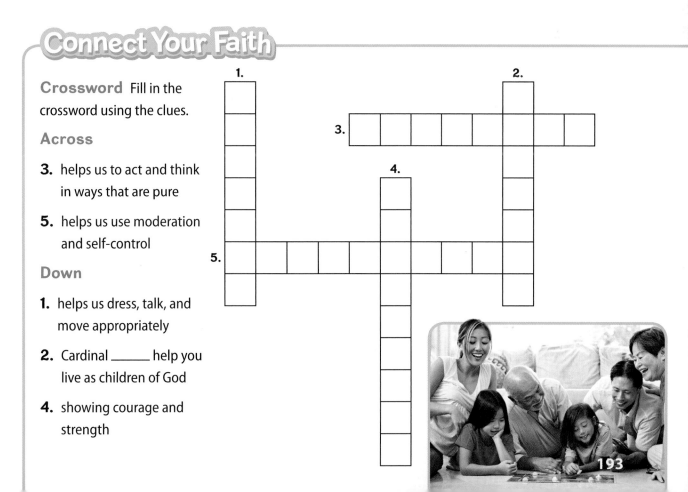

193

Our Catholic Life

How can you follow God's Commandments in your family life?

God asks you to show his love to your family at all times. This is not always easy, but keeping the Fourth, Sixth, and Ninth Commandments will help you.

1. Draw a star next to the hearts that show ways you keep the Commandments now.

2. Discuss how following the Ten Commandments makes family life better.

Remember that being part of a family means forgiving one another as God forgives us when we sin.

Keep the promises you make to your family, friends, and God. Do what you have said you will do.

Practice modesty by dressing decently and by avoiding television programs, movies, books, and music that show disrespect for God's gift of sexuality.

Don't be jealous of other family members. Include others in your friendships.

Share your possessions, your time, and your gifts with family members.

Respect, honor, and obey your parents and other family members. Listen to them, and pay attention to their needs.

© Our Sunday Visitor

People of Faith

July 12

Blessed Louis Martin, 1823–1894
Blessed Marie-Azélie Martin, 1831–1877

God loves all families and wants them to be happy. Blessed Louis Martin and Marie-Azélie Martin fell in love and got married. Louis was a jeweler and watchmaker. Marie-Azélie made a special kind of lace. They promised to live as holy a life as possible and teach their children about Jesus. The Martins did many things with their family, like take walks and tell stories. All of their five daughters became nuns. One, Thérèse de Lisieux, became a Saint.

Discuss: What does your family like to do together?

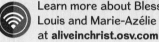 Learn more about Blessed Louis and Marie-Azélie at **aliveinchrist.osv.com**

Live Your Faith

Build with Solid Blocks The family is the building block of the Christian community and of society. In the blocks, write four qualities of good friendships and family love. Tell how your family shows one of these qualities to others.

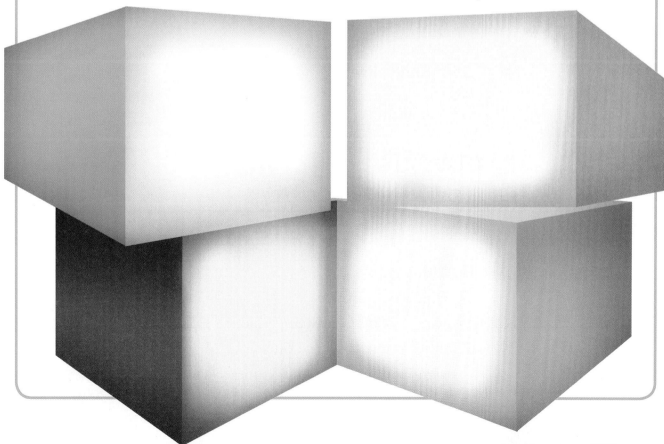

Let Us Pray

Prayer of Petition

A prayer of petition is a prayer in which we ask God for something for another person or for the community.

Gather and begin with the Sign of the Cross.

Leader: God, from you every family learns to love. We ask you to strengthen our families.

All: Hear us, O Lord.

Reader 1: May our parents and those who care for us be blessed in their commitment to love us and each other.

All: Hear us, O Lord.

Reader 2: May we and all children find support and security in their families.

All: Hear us, O Lord.

Reader 3: May all families discover your gift of faithful love.

All: Hear us, O Lord.

Leader: Let us pray.

Bow your heads as the leader prays.

All: Amen.

Sing: "Right and Just"
It is right—the proper thing to do.
It is just—giving God what's due.
When we come to praise our God,
It is right and just.

FAMILY+FAITH
LIVING AND LEARNING TOGETHER

YOUR CHILD LEARNED >>>

This chapter examines the importance of the Sacrament of Matrimony, the role of family in God's plan, and how the Cardinal Virtues help us to act appropriately and be disciplined.

Scripture

 Read **Colossians 3:20** to find out what God's Word says about our parents.

Catholics Believe

- God created humans to live in strong, loving families.
- The Fourth, Sixth, and Ninth Commandments provide basic laws of family love and respect.

To learn more, go to the *Catechism of the Catholic Church #2197–2200, 2204–2206, 2380–2381, 2521–2524* at **usccb.org**.

People of Faith

This week, your child learned about Blessed Louis Martin and Marie-Azélie Martin, the parents of Saint Thérèse of Lisieux.

CHILDREN AT THIS AGE >>>

How They Understand Family Love Fourth-graders usually have a very strong love for their parents. If they live with both parents, they can often pick up on the quality of their mom and dad's relationship with one another. One area in which they often struggle is in their relationship with siblings. Developmental differences, as well as limited space and attention, can cause rivalries between brothers and sisters.

When children understand that the family is like a school where we learn to love each other, they can rise to meet these challenges with God's help.

CONSIDER THIS >>>

How has your understanding of what it means to honor your parents changed?

As our parents age, we have an opportunity to show what they taught us about love. As Catholics, we know that "while adult children may sometimes experience a strain between raising their own children and caring for their parents, they must do what they can to help their parents. . . . While it is right for society to help care for the elderly, the family remains the rightful source of support" (*USCCA, pp. 377–378*).

LET'S TALK >>>

- Ask your child to name one thing about the Fourth, Sixth, or Ninth Commandments.
- Talk about ways your family honors one another.

LET'S PRAY >>>

 Dear God, please help our family to be happy together, to love each other, and to pray for each other. Amen.

 For a multimedia glossary of Catholic Faith Words, Sunday readings, seasonal and Saint resources, and chapter activities go to **aliveinchrist.osv.com**.

Chapter 13 Review

A **Work with Words** Complete each sentence with the correct word from the Word Bank.

1–5. God made humans to live as _____ who love and respect one another. By following the _____ Commandment, children _____ and obey their parents and guardians. The _____ and Ninth Commandments are about being _____ in marriage, keeping promises, and acting appropriately.

Word Bank
. . . .

faithful

Fourth

families

Sixth

honor

B **Check Understanding** Write a definition for each of the following terms.

6. Obey:

_____

_____

7. Vows:

_____

_____

8. Modesty:

_____

_____

9. Adultery:

_____

_____

10. Faithful:

_____

_____

Go to **aliveinchrist.osv.com** for an interactive review.

Respect Life

 Let Us Pray

Leader: God, we thank you for the precious gift of life.

"For with you is the fountain of life,
and in your light we see light." **Psalm 36:10**

All: Brighten our lives with a great love of life and the
courage to cherish and protect it. Amen.

Scripture

"You have heard that it was said to your ancestors, 'You shall
not kill; and whoever kills will have to answer for his actions.'
But I say to you, whoever is angry with his brother will have to
answer for his actions, and whoever says anything mean will
have to answer for his words." **Based on Matthew 5:21–22**

? What Do You Wonder?

• If someone makes you mad, what
should you do?

• Is it okay to be mean to someone
who was mean to you first?

All Human Life is Sacred

How do you respect life?

Catholic
Faith Words

sacred worthy of reverence and devotion

Sometimes we are unsure of people who look or talk differently than we do. And we may not know how to treat people who have illnesses or disabilities. But all people everywhere deserve respect. Here's the story of a woman who could not walk, but her life is an example for all of us.

Blessed Margaret of Castello

Blessed Margaret of Castello could not see or walk. She had a big lump on her back and twisted arms and legs. Her parents were ashamed of her, so they shut her up in a room and left her all alone. Finally, some kind women took Margaret in with them. She lived the rest of her life helping people who were sick and dying. After she died, another girl who could not walk came to her funeral and was miraculously cured! Even though Blessed Margaret had many things wrong with her, she knew that every life is important and that we all can do something to help others.

Highlight how Blessed Margaret showed respect for others.

Choose Life

All human life is **sacred**, worthy of reverence and devotion, and all actions that respect and protect life uphold the Fifth Commandment. At the end of his life, Moses told the people to remember that God's law was life for them.

Scripture

The Choice

I call heaven and earth today to witness against you: I have set before you life and death, the blessing and the curse. Choose life, then, that you and your descendants may live, by loving the LORD, your God, obeying his voice, and holding fast to him. For that will mean life for you . . . **Deuteronomy 30:19–20**

God's laws show the path to life and happiness. The Fifth Commandment reminds us of the fundamental respect for life that is owed to every person. Every person is made in God's image and likeness, therefore every human life is sacred from the moment of conception until the time of death.

Share Your Faith

Reflect Think about what the Fifth Commandment tells you. Unscramble the words below to fill in the sentence about what everyone deserves.

tcpesre	feil	dreasc

Every human _____

is _____ , and deserves

_____ .

Share Then, talk with a partner about how you can follow the Fifth Commandment.

Protect and Respect

How do you keep the Fifth Commandment?

All human life is sacred, including the life of the unborn and the elderly. The life of an unborn child is fragile, and it is deserving of the greatest respect and care. The intentional ending of the life of an unborn child is a grave sin.

The taking of one's own life is suicide. It is contrary to God's gift of life and love. However, one's responsibility may be lessened by certain factors. **Murder**, the intentional killing of an innocent person, is seriously sinful. To kill in self-defense, however, is justified, if it is the only way to protect one's own life.

The Catholic Church teaches that the death penalty, or capital punishment, is almost always wrong. Alternatives, such as life in prison without parole, are preferred.

Respect for the Body

The Church teaches that your body and soul are united. You are a temple in which God's Spirit dwells. The Fifth Commandment teaches you to respect your body and those of others. Eating healthy foods and exercising are important to protect your life and health. At your age, using alcohol is an offense against the Fifth Commandment. The use of tobacco and illegal drugs is harmful to the body. Tempting or encouraging others to disrespect the gift of life is wrong, too.

© Our Sunday Visitor

Catholic Faith Words

murder the deliberate killing of another person when the killing is not in self-defense

Avoid Anger

Jesus said that anger can be sinful if it is not controlled. Anger can harden into hatred and lead to revenge, or getting back at someone, or to violence.

It can be difficult to show love and respect for those who bully or treat you unfairly. Jesus calls you to love in this way.

 Scripture

Love of Enemies

"You have heard that it was said, 'You shall love your neighbor and hate your enemy.' But I say to you, love your enemies, and pray for those who persecute you, that you may be children of your heavenly Father, for he makes his sun rise on the bad and the good, and causes rain to fall on the just and the unjust." **Matthew 5:43–45**

➡ **What did Jesus mean when he said that God makes his sun rise on the bad and the good?**

Connect Your Faith

Choose Life Fill in the missing letters in these examples of life-giving actions.

Protect unborn c ☐ ☐ ☐ d ☐ ☐ n.

Set a ☐ ☐ ☐ ☐ example for others.

Forgive your e ☐ e ☐ ies.

Think of one life-giving action that you will practice today.

Our Catholic Life

How can you act in the spirit of the Fifth Commandment?

The Fifth Commandment may seem easy to follow. But as you have read, there is more to this Commandment than not killing. The Fifth Commandment also asks that you take care of and respect yourself and others.

1. Match the examples with the correct sentence ending.

2. Draw a star next to something you've done this week to follow the Fifth Commandment.

Ways to Respect Life

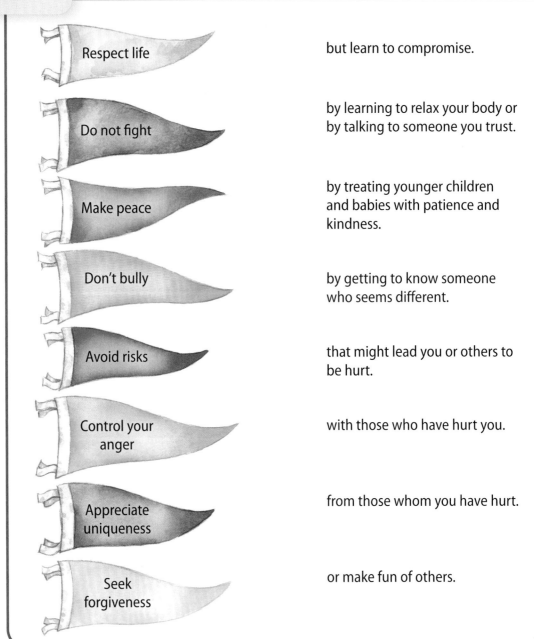

Respect life — but learn to compromise.

Do not fight — by learning to relax your body or by talking to someone you trust.

Make peace — by treating younger children and babies with patience and kindness.

Don't bully — by getting to know someone who seems different.

Avoid risks — that might lead you or others to be hurt.

Control your anger — with those who have hurt you.

Appreciate uniqueness — from those whom you have hurt.

Seek forgiveness — or make fun of others.

People of Faith

April 28

Saint Gianna Molla, 1922–1962

Saint Gianna Molla was a doctor who lived in Italy. She took care of babies and children and had four children of her own. Saint Gianna knew that the way to be happy is to give to others, especially your family. When she was pregnant with her last baby, she had a very dangerous operation. She knew that she might die if she had the surgery, but because she was generous with everything she had, she wanted to make sure she gave her baby the gift of life. She did die after the baby was born, but she was happy her baby lived.

Discuss: Whom do you know who chose life and lived the Fifth Commandment?

Learn more about Saint Gianna at **aliveinchrist.osv.com**

Live Your Faith

Write a note to someone you have treated unfairly. In your note, explain one thing you will or would do differently because of what you've learned this week.

Let Us Pray

Celebration of the Word

Gather and begin with the Sign of the Cross.

Reader 1:   A reading from the First Letter of Peter.

Read 1 Peter 3:9–12.

The word of the Lord.

All: Thanks be to God.

Reader 2:   When we are given the choice to walk away or to stay and fight,

All: Help us choose your way, O Lord.

Reader 3:   When we are given the chance to help people with illnesses or disabilities or an elderly person,

All: Help us choose your way, O Lord.

Leader: Let us pray.

Bow your heads as the leader prays.

All: Amen.

 Sing "Christ, Our Light"

Christ, our Light, you taught us to love.
Christ, our Light, you're always with us.
Together we learn, together we grow,
together we walk in your way.

© 2002, John Burland. All rights reserved.

FAMILY+FAITH
LIVING AND LEARNING TOGETHER

YOUR CHILD LEARNED >>>

This chapter is about respecting and protecting human life at all stages because life is a gift from God.

Scripture

 Read **Matthew 5:21–22** to find out what Jesus teaches us about respecting one another.

Catholics Believe

- All human life is sacred because it comes from God.
- The Fifth Commandment forbids anything that takes a human life.

To learn more, go to the *Catechism of the Catholic Church #2258, 2268–2269* at **usccb.org**.

People of Faith

This week, your child learned about Saint Gianna Molla, who was willing to sacrifice her life for that of her unborn daughter.

CHILDREN AT THIS AGE >>>

How They Understand Respect for Life Respect for human life is foundational to Catholic teaching. Much discussion on this principle, both within the Church and in the public square, focuses on issues such as abortion and the death penalty. Fourth-graders might not yet be ready to confront these issues head on, due to their graphic nature, but respect for human life is also a broader principle that has implications in the everyday lives of children this age. Is there a child who is teased because he or she looks different? Are there times when children feel tempted to hit someone else out of anger? These questions are also relevant to respect for life.

CONSIDER THIS >>>

How does your family acknowledge and celebrate that each person's life is a gift from God?

Family life is the perfect setting to celebrate each person's uniqueness. It is in the heart of family that we experience and appreciate that God creates each of us with imagination and love. As Catholics, we know that "God's creative action is present to every human life and is thus the source of its sacred value…. The Fifth Commandment calls us to foster the physical, spiritual, emotional, and social well-being of self and others" (*USCCA*, *p. 389*).

LET'S TALK >>>

- Ask your child to talk about how anger, teasing, and bullying relate to the Fifth Commandment.
- With your child, name ways we show respect for others and protect others and ourselves, including our bodies.

LET'S PRAY >>>

 Saint Gianna Molla, pray for us that we may be faithful to God's love and always choose the path of life and hope. Amen.

For a multimedia glossary of Catholic Faith Words, Sunday readings, seasonal and Saint resources, and chapter activities go to **aliveinchrist.osv.com**.

Chapter 14 Review

A Work with Words **Complete the following statements.**

1. The Fifth Commandment says this: _____

_____.

2. Every human life is a gift from _____

_____.

3. One serious sin against the Fifth Commandment is _____

_____.

4. All human life is _____

_____.

5. Hatred can lead to _____

_____.

B Check Understanding **Complete each sentence with the correct word from the Word Bank.**

6. One way to live the Fifth Commandment is to make

_____ .

7. Jesus said to love everyone, even your

_____ .

8. Tempting or encouraging others to disrespect the gift

of life is _____ .

9. Jesus explained that uncontrolled _____

is against the Fifth Commandment.

10. Actions that _____ and protect life

uphold the Fifth Commandment.

Word Bank
• • • • • • • • • • •
peace

anger

wrong

enemies

respect

© Our Sunday Visitor

Go to **aliveinchrist.osv.com**
for an interactive review.

Live in the Truth

Let Us Pray

Leader: Your words, O Lord, are precious and true.

"Teach me, LORD, your way
that I may walk in your truth." **Psalm 86:11**

All: May our words echo yours, O Lord, so that your
truth may be told. Amen.

Scripture

"You have heard that it was said to those who came before
you, 'Do not tell lies to each other, but make good to the Lord all
that you promise.' Let your 'Yes' mean 'Yes,' and your 'No' mean
'No.'" **Based on Matthew 5:33, 37**

? What Do You Wonder?

- Is it okay not to tell the truth so you
  don't hurt someone's feelings?
- Is lying really all that bad?

Witness to the Truth

How do people show that they value truth?

Saint Thomas More, an important official in England in the sixteenth century, was imprisoned for refusing to tell a lie.

Saint Thomas More

Saint Thomas had an important decision to make. In a letter to his daughter, he discussed his dilemma.

My dearest Meg,

Your father greets you with all his affection but not much hope. The dilemma I face will not soon go away.

I have been imprisoned now for some months. All I have to do to be set free is to take the Oath of Supremacy. But how can I? If I take the oath, I will be saying that Henry VIII is the supreme head of the Catholic Church in England. You know that my Catholic faith is strong, and I believe that the Pope is the true head of the Catholic Church.

King Henry is angry. He is afraid that if I go against him, other people will follow my example. I am being forced to make a choice: be honest and be killed, or tell a lie and live.

Pray for me.

Your loving father,
Thomas More

➡ What important decision did Saint Thomas More have to make?

➡ What would you do if you were in Thomas' position?

Speak and Act the Truth

Saint Thomas More chose to remain true to his beliefs and speak the truth. As a result, the king had him killed, but the Catholic Church named him a Saint. Many Saints have suffered torture and death for the sake of their faith. A person who stays faithful to Christ and suffers and dies rather than denying the truth is called a **martyr**. Martyrs live the truth by backing up their words with actions.

Catholic **Faith Words**

martyr a person who gives up his or her life to witness to the truth of Christ and the faith. The word *martyr* means "witness."

You will probably not be called on to be a martyr. But every follower of Jesus is called to live in the truth. By your actions, you show your faithfulness to Jesus and the truth of his message.

Jean Donovan was an American missionary martyr. She was killed with three other women in 1980, while working as part of a Diocesan Mission Project in El Salvador.

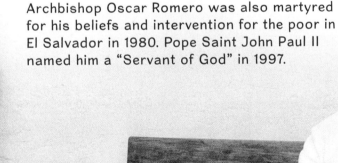

Archbishop Oscar Romero was also martyred for his beliefs and intervention for the poor in El Salvador in 1980. Pope Saint John Paul II named him a "Servant of God" in 1997.

Share Your Faith

Reflect Think about why it is always best to tell the truth.

Share With a partner, create a Top Three list of reasons for telling the truth.

The Eighth Commandment

What does the Eighth Commandment call you to do?

God is the source of all truth. His Word and his law call people to live in the truth. The Eighth Commandment says this: You shall not bear false witness against your neighbor.

The Eighth Commandment forbids lying, or purposely not telling the truth. Lying can take many forms. If a person lies in court when under oath, he or she commits perjury, or false witness. Gossip is talking about another person behind his or her back. Gossip may or may not be a lie, but all gossip can harm the good reputation of another person.

All lies are unjust and unloving. All require **reparation**, or repair. Reparation may be as simple as an apology, or it may take more work, such as trying to help a person get back the reputation you have hurt.

➔ **Why is reparation important?**

Catholic Faith Words

reparation an action taken to repair the damage done from sin

prudence the Cardinal Virtue that helps us be practical and make correct decisions on what is right and good, with the help of the Holy Spirit and a well-formed conscience

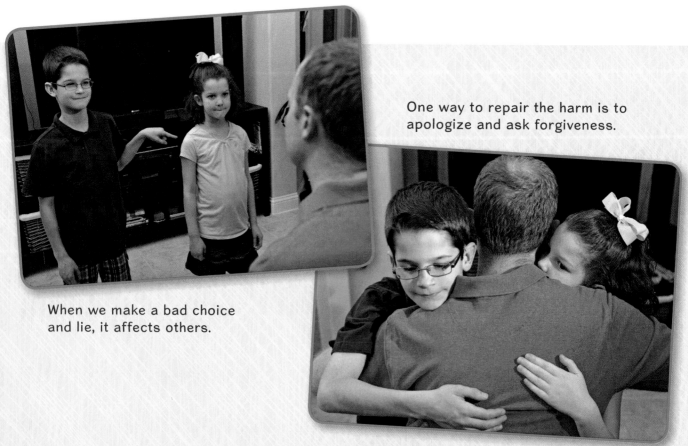

When we make a bad choice and lie, it affects others.

One way to repair the harm is to apologize and ask forgiveness.

© Our Sunday Visitor

Jesus Is the Truth

Living in the spirit of the Eighth Commandment is more than not lying. You must choose to act with **prudence** and make correct decisions on what is right and good. When you are truthful, you are living as a follower of Jesus, who always told the truth.

Scripture

The Truth Will Set You Free

[Jesus said] "If you remain in my word, you will truly be my disciples, and you will know the truth, and the truth will set you free. . . . I am the way and the truth and the life. No one comes to the Father except through me." John 8:31–32, 14:6

People trusted what Jesus did and said. When you are truthful, people trust you. When you promise to tell the truth, you have a special duty. Let your "yes" mean "yes" and your "no" mean "no." Telling the truth will set you free to follow Jesus and to live in love.

Connect Your Faith

Live the Truth Read the following list, and mark an X if a statement talks about living in truth and an O if it does not. For each statement marked with an O, tell one way the person could make up for his or her wrong choice.

_____ Juanita heard an unkind story about a classmate. She did not repeat it.

_____ Scott bragged falsely about how good he was at sports.

_____ Samantha told her parents that she was going to the library, but instead she went to the park.

_____ Matt discovered that his friend had shoplifted, but he did not gossip about it.

Our Catholic Life

How can you live in the spirit of the Eighth Commandment?

Sometimes being honest can be difficult. It is never easy to admit to having done something wrong when you know that you may be punished. But being honest with others and yourself is what God asks of you in the Eighth Commandment.

Imagine what your life would be like if no one trusted you. No friend would tell you a secret. No one would believe anything that you said.

Sounds lonely, doesn't it? Besides, dishonesty is against God's law, and it can lead to hurting others. God's grace and practicing virtues can help us choose honesty.

Use words from the first column to fill in the sentences in the second column.

Choosing Truth

actions respect rumors prejudiced gossip truth	• Use words that show _____ for other people.
	• Do not _____ or tell lies about someone else.
	• Make sure that your _____ reflect your true self. Don't exaggerate, brag, or act better than others.
	• Tell the _____, especially when you have promised to do so.
	• Do not spread _____ about others.
	• Avoid being _____ against those who are different.

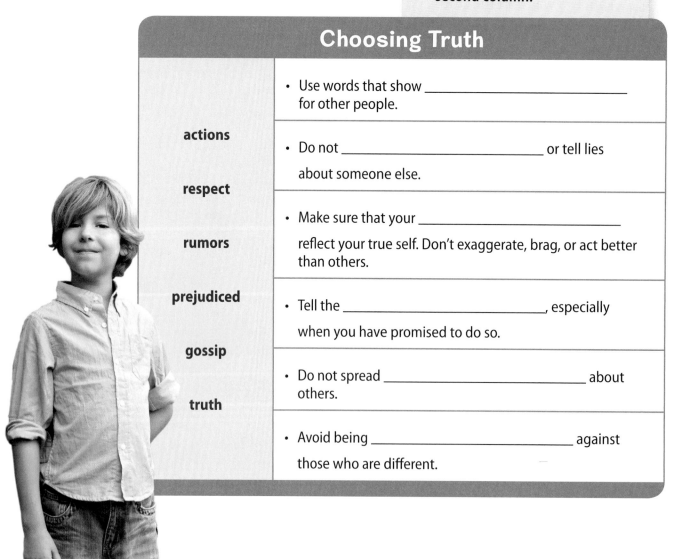

People of Faith

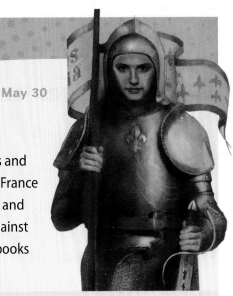

Saint Joan of Arc, 1412–1431

May 30

It isn't always easy to tell the truth. Saint Joan of Arc became a martyr because she told the truth. Joan was a teenager when she had visions and heard voices. They told her to lead an army to fight for truth and save France from invaders. She bravely told the truth about her visions and voices and saved France in many battles. However, Joan was accused of being against the Church and of being a witch. She was burned at the stake. Many books and movies have been written about her.

Discuss: Talk about a time when you told the truth even though it was difficult.

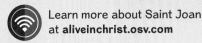

Learn more about Saint Joan at **aliveinchrist.osv.com**

Live Your Faith

Design a poster that explains the importance of telling the truth. Include a slogan to make your message clear, and explain your poster to your family and friends. You may also want to write your slogan on a piece of paper to keep with you in your pocket as a reminder.

Let Us Pray

Prayer to the Holy Spirit

Gather and begin with the Sign of the Cross.

Leader: Whenever we are afraid to tell the truth,

All: Spirit of Truth, guide us!

Leader: Whenever we are tempted to gossip,

All: Spirit of Truth, guide us!

Leader: Whenever we are faced with choices about telling the truth,

All: Spirit of Truth, guide us!

Leader: Whenever we falsely judge another,

All: Spirit of Truth, guide us!

Leader: God of all truth, whenever we face choices about telling the truth, guide us to your light. Give us strength to make good choices. We ask this in Jesus' name.

All: Amen.

 Sing "Spirit, Come Down"
Spirit, Spirit, Spirit,
come down from Heaven.
Spirit, Spirit,
and seal us with your love.
© 2001, Janet Vogt and Mark Friedman.
Published by OCP. All rights reserved.

YOUR CHILD LEARNED >>>

This chapter explains the Eighth Commandment and explores Jesus' call to live in the truth and repair the damage done from sin.

Scripture

Read **Matthew 5:33, 37** to find out about the relationship between grace and truth.

Catholics Believe

- Because God is truth, his people are called to live in the truth.
- The Eighth Commandment forbids lying.

To learn more, go to the *Catechism of the Catholic Church #1741, 2465–2470* at **usccb.org**.

People of Faith

This week, your child learned about Saint Joan of Arc. As a result of her visions, she saved France in many battles. She is the patron of women in the military.

CHILDREN AT THIS AGE >>>

How They Understand Telling the Truth Your child is probably a concrete thinker who understands cause and effect. Unlike preschoolers, children this age know that the truth doesn't change just because we want it to. They also know that adults don't know everything, and that sometimes we can be fooled. It's important for children to see the connection between truth, trust, and relationship. We cannot really be close to people if we tell them lies, no matter how small the lies, because relationship implies trust.

CONSIDER THIS >>>

How important is truth in your relationships?

Most of us expect honesty in our relationships even if we do not always welcome it. Truth is central to our relationship with God. As Catholics, we know that "God is the source of truth. Jesus not only taught the truth; he also said, 'I am the truth' (cf. John 14:6). The Hebrew word for truth, *emeth*, refers to truth in words and truthfulness in deeds. Jesus both personalized truth and spoke nothing but the truth" (*USCCA, p. 431*).

LET'S TALK >>>

- Ask your child to explain the Eighth Commandment.
- Share a time when you had to decide to lie or tell the truth, or when someone else lied to you. How did it feel? What did you do?

LET'S PRAY >>>

 Saint Joan of Arc, pray for us that we may be strong in our faith and always have the courage to speak and live the truth. Amen.

 For a multimedia glossary of Catholic Faith Words, Sunday readings, seasonal and Saint resources, and chapter activities go to **aliveinchrist.osv.com**.

Chapter 15 Review

A **Work with Words** Fill in the circle next to the answer that best completes each statement.

1. A _____ is someone who gives up his or her life to witness to the truth of Christ and the faith.
   - ○ priest
   - ○ deacon
   - ○ martyr

2. _____ are sins against the Eighth Commandment.
   - ○ Lying and gossip
   - ○ Stealing and lying
   - ○ Gossip and murder

3. _____ is the action taken to repair the damage done by sin.
   - ○ Perjury
   - ○ Sin
   - ○ Reparation

4. The Eighth Commandment is "You shall not _____."
   - ○ kill
   - ○ bear false witness against your neighbor
   - ○ keep holy the Lord's Day

5. _____ are called to live in the truth.
   - ○ Only martyrs
   - ○ Only priests and deacons
   - ○ All of us

B **Check Understanding** Complete each sentence with the correct word from the Word Bank.

> ### Word Bank
> martyr   truth
> prudence   gossip
> lying

6. Jesus calls you to live in the
   _____.

7. Thomas More was a
   _____ and
   a Saint.

8. _____ is
   purposely not telling the truth.

9. _____ is
   talking about another person
   behind his or her back.

10. _____ is
    being practical and making
    correct decisions with the
    help of the Holy Spirit and
    a well-formed conscience.

Go to **aliveinchrist.osv.com** for an interactive review.

A **Work with Words** Use the clues to solve the puzzle.

Across

1. This Commandment says: You shall not kill.

3. The deliberate killing of another person

5. This Commandment says: You shall not bear false witness against your neighbor.

6. To do things or act in certain ways that are requested by those in authority

8. The virtue that helps people dress, talk, and move in appropriate ways

9. Action taken to repair the damage done from sin

Down

2. The virtue that helps us be practical and make correct decisions

4. This Commandment specifically addresses sons and daughters.

7. Continuing the cycle of anger and hatred

8. Someone who gives up his or her life to witness to the truth of Christ and the faith

10. Solemn promises that are made to or before God

B **Check Understanding** Fill in the circle next to the best answer.

11. Jesus said, "I am the way and the _____ and the life."

○ light

○ truth

○ leader

12. Saint Thomas More was killed for refusing to say that the king of England was the head of the Catholic Church. More believed that the _____ was the true head of the Church.

○ Pope

○ bishop

○ queen

13. God's plan for humans includes living _____ families.

○ without

○ with

○ around

14. All actions that respect and protect life obey the _____ Commandment.

○ Ninth

○ Sixth

○ Fifth

15. When you are _____, you are living as a follower of Jesus.

○ sinful

○ truthful

○ greedy

C **Make Connections** Write a brief response to each question or statement.

16. List two ways that school helps you respect and take care of your body.

   _____

   _____

   _____

17. List two ways that you respect and take care of your body at home.

   _____

   _____

   _____

18. Why will breaking the Eighth Commandment eventually leave you feeling lonely?

   _____

   _____

   _____

19. Explain what you have learned about family.

   _____

   _____

   _____

   _____

20. What have you learned about being a faithful follower of Christ?

   _____

   _____

   _____

Sacraments

Our Catholic Tradition

- The Paschal Mystery is celebrated in the seasons of the liturgical year and through the Sacraments. (CCC, 1171)

- Christ instituted the Seven Sacraments as effective signs of God's life and love that give us grace. (CCC, 1131)

- The Eucharist is the heart of the Church's life. (CCC, 1407)

- The Sacraments of Healing are about conversion, forgiveness, and healing. (CCC, 1421)

How does Jesus' saving work continue through the Seven Sacraments and the celebration of the liturgical year?

The Liturgical Year

 **Let Us Pray**

Leader: Loving Lord, we praise you and give you thanks no matter the time, no matter the season.

"I will bless the LORD at all times; his praise shall be always in my mouth." **Psalm 34:2**

All: Loving Lord, we praise you and give you thanks no matter the time, no matter the season.

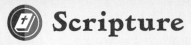 **Scripture**

My deliverance and honor are with God,
my strong rock;
my refuge is with God.
Trust God at all times, my people!
Pour out your hearts to God our refuge!
Psalm 62:8–9

? What Do You Wonder?

- Why does the Church tell the story of Jesus' life over and over again?

- Is Jesus really with you in each moment of your day?

A Time for Everything

What is the Paschal Mystery?

All living things follow a pattern. They come to life, they grow and develop, and finally they die. This pattern is called a life cycle. Every year, as the seasons change, you see changes in the world around you. God tells us about the importance of seasons and cycles in one of the Wisdom Books in the Bible.

Scripture

The Right Time

There is an appointed time for everything,
and a time for every affair under the heavens.
    A time to give birth, and a time to die;
a time to plant, and a time to uproot the plant . . .
    A time to weep, and a time to laugh;
a time to mourn, and a time to dance . . .
    A time to seek, and a time to lose;
a time to keep, and a time to cast away . . .
    A time to love, and a time to hate;
a time of war, and a time of peace.   Ecclesiastes 3:1–8

➤ **What message was God giving us in this poem?**

The Paschal Mystery

Jesus experienced the natural cycle of life, but his cycle did not end with his Death on the Cross. God the Father raised Jesus from the dead and to new life. Then Jesus ascended to join his Father in Heaven. The suffering, Death, Resurrection, and **Ascension** of Jesus are called the **Paschal Mystery**. This mystery reveals that Jesus saved all humans from the power of sin and everlasting death.

The Church celebrates this mystery in every Sacrament and especially at every Eucharist. Every Sunday we gather with the parish community to celebrate the new life that Jesus' Resurrection gives us.

The Liturgical Year

From week to week at Mass, you may notice different readings, hymns, and colors. These mark the seasons of the Church's year, called the **liturgical year**. The liturgical year begins on the first Sunday of Advent, usually around December 1, and ends with the feast of Christ the King.

© Our Sunday Visitor

Catholic Faith Words

Ascension when the Risen Jesus was taken up to Heaven to be with God the Father forever

Paschal Mystery the mystery of Jesus' suffering, Death, Resurrection, and Ascension

liturgical year the feasts and seasons of the Church calendar that celebrate the Paschal Mystery of Christ

Share Your Faith

Reflect Think about what you did last week. In the boxes, sketch one of the symbols for the "times" of your life. If Monday was a happy time, draw a smiling face to show that you were happy. Use different symbols to represent your "times."

Share With a partner, share some of the best and worst times you had last week.

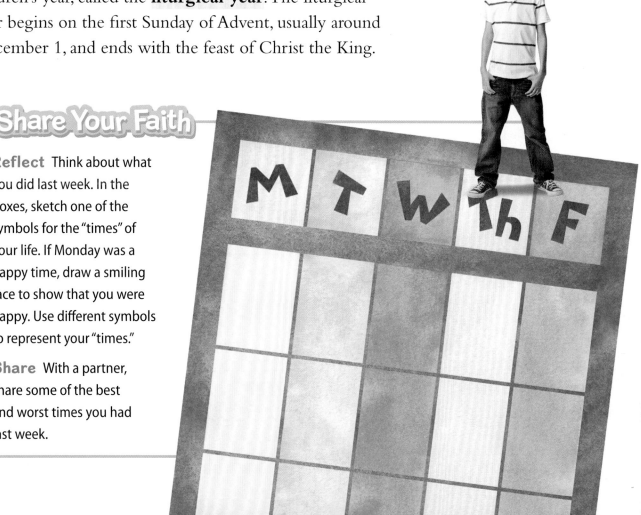

The Church's Seasons

What are the seasons of the liturgical year?

Just as the seasons of the year mark the cycles of life and death in nature, the seasons of the liturgical year mark and celebrate the events of the Paschal Mystery.

➜ **What is your favorite liturgical season? Why?**

Advent

Advent is the beginning of the Church year. The four weeks before Christmas are a time of preparation for the coming of Jesus. The Church asks the Holy Spirit to help people welcome Jesus into their hearts every day. The seasonal color is violet, a sign of waiting.

Christmas

The Christmas season lasts from Christmas Eve through the Sunday after Epiphany, which is twelve days after Christmas. It is a time to be joyful and to thank God the Father for sending his Son to become one of us. White and gold colors are reminders to celebrate the gift of Jesus.

Lent

Lent lasts for forty days. It begins on Ash Wednesday and ends on Holy Thursday. Lent is a time to prepare for Easter by following Jesus more closely. The seasonal color of violet is used as a sign of penance.

Connect Your Faith

Remember His Love On the chart of seasons on these pages, design symbols or write phrases to illustrate the saving actions of Jesus that each season celebrates.

Easter

The Easter Season continues for fifty days until Pentecost. It is a time to remember your Baptism and to give thanks for the Resurrection of Jesus that saved all people from the power of sin and everlasting death. White or gold colors are used during this season as a sign of great joy.

Ordinary Time

Ordinary Time is a season in two parts. The first is between the Christmas season and the First Sunday of Lent. The second is between the Easter season and Advent. Ordinary Time is the time to remember the works of Jesus and listen to his teachings. The color green is used during this season as a sign of hope and growth.

Triduum

The Easter Season is preceded by a three-day celebration of the Paschal Mystery called the Triduum. It starts with the celebration of the Lord's Supper on Holy Thursday and ends with evening prayer on Easter Sunday.

Our Catholic Life

How do you celebrate the seasons of the Church year?

The seasons in nature affect the way you think and act. For example, you would not try to go ice fishing in the middle of summer. The Church also wants you to think and act according to her seasons.

Each season of the Church year gives you a different way to look at Jesus and the people and the world around you. Here are some ways to pray and live according to the seasons.

 In each of the boxes, write one other way you can celebrate that Church season.

Celebrating the Seasons

Christmas	Celebrate Jesus' birth by looking for the love of Jesus in everyone you meet.
Ordinary Time	Learn more about Jesus by reading the Bible. Imitate his love for those who are poor, suffering, or sick.
Advent	Prepare for Jesus' coming into your heart by practicing patience.
Lent	Pray, fast, and focus your attention upon acts of penance. These actions will prepare you to celebrate Easter.
Easter	Celebrate the wonderful news that you have been saved. Share your experiences of how God has worked in your life.

People of Faith

Saint Juan Diego, 1474–1548

December 9

The Church and the year both have seasons. Sometimes God makes special things happen out of season to show his love. Saint Juan Diego lived in Mexico. One December day, while walking to church, he met a woman who said she was the Mother of God and her Son was Jesus, the Savior. She said her title was Our Lady of Guadalupe. When Juan asked for a sign to be sure, roses bloomed even though it was cold and wintery. Juan brought the roses to his bishop, who had a shrine built at the site where Juan had seen Mary.

Discuss: When has God shown you a sign of love?

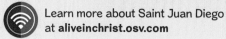
Learn more about Saint Juan Diego at **aliveinchrist.osv.com**

Live Your Faith

Recall the liturgical season the Church is currently celebrating.
Name and draw one thing you can do to celebrate this season now.

Let Us Pray

Prayer of Praise

Gather and begin with the Sign of the Cross.

Leader: God, our good Father, you sent Jesus, your Son, to rescue us from the power of sin and everlasting death.

All: We proclaim your Death, O Lord.

Leader: Jesus, you came into this world of darkness as the light. Your words of love touched those who were sick and weak. You forgave sinners and freed them from shame.

All: Jesus lives with us.

Leader: Jesus, you died on the Cross, a sacrifice of love to set us free from our sins.

All: Jesus died for us.

Leader: Jesus, you were raised from the dead and ascended into Heaven. You sent the Holy Spirit to be with us always. We hope to share eternal life with you.

All: We wait in joyful hope!

Leader: Let us pray.

Bow your heads as the leader prays.

All: Amen.

 Sing "We Proclaim Your Death, O Lord"

YOUR CHILD LEARNED >>>

This chapter explains that the Paschal Mystery is the mystery of Christ's suffering, Death, Resurrection, and Ascension, and that the feasts and seasons of the liturgical year celebrate the Paschal Mystery of Christ.

Scripture

 Read **Psalm 62:8–9** to find out about the importance of giving thanks to God.

Catholics Believe

- The liturgical year celebrates the Paschal Mystery.
- The seasons of the liturgical year include Advent, Christmas, Lent, Triduum, Easter, and Ordinary Time.

To learn more, go to the *Catechism of the Catholic Church #1067–1068, 1168–1171* at **usccb.org**.

People of Faith

This week, your child learned about Saint Juan Diego. Our Lady of Guadalupe appeared to him as he walked to church one morning.

CHILDREN AT THIS AGE >>>

How They Understand the Church Year Your child has a better "internal calendar" than he or she did as a preschooler. Children this age can calculate how long it will be until Christmas or Easter, for example. As they learn about the Church year, their ability to understand time can help them feel involved in the celebrations and seasons of the Church calendar. This is especially true when they have an opportunity to mark time in the home with a sacred space that reflects the current season (for example, cloths of green, purple, red, or white and icons that fit the season).

CONSIDER THIS >>>

When have you longed for a flower to remain in bloom or for a child to not grow up too quickly?

All living things follow a cycle. They come to life, grow and develop, and finally die. The rhythm of the liturgical seasons of the Church flow through our lives just as the cycle of life. As Catholics, we know that "in the Liturgical Year, the Church celebrates the whole mystery of Christ from the Incarnation until the day of Pentecost and the expectation of Christ's second coming. The summit of the Liturgical Year is the Easter Triduum—from the evening of Holy Thursday to the evening of Easter Sunday" (*USCCA, p. 173*).

LET'S TALK >>>

- Ask your child to tell you about the liturgical year.
- Share memories of the ways your family has celebrated different Church holidays.

LET'S PRAY >>>

 O God, help us grow closer to you by our worship at the Eucharist, our learning of our Catholic faith, and our devotion to prayer. Amen.

 For a multimedia glossary of Catholic Faith Words, Sunday readings, seasonal and Saint resources, and chapter activities go to **aliveinchrist.osv.com**.

Chapter 16 Review

A **Work with Words** **Match each description in Column 1 with the correct term in Column 2.**

Column 1

1. a time of penance
2. celebrates the birth of Jesus
3. focuses on the Resurrection of Jesus
4. prepares for the coming of Jesus
5. focuses on Jesus' work and teachings

Column 2

Advent

Christmas

Ordinary Time

Lent

Easter

B **Check Understanding** **Complete each statement with the correct term from the Word Bank.**

> **Word Bank**
> •
> liturgical   Paschal   Thursday
> works   Triduum

6. The _____ Mystery is the mystery of Jesus' suffering, Death, Resurrection, and Ascension.

7. The _____ year is the cycle of feasts and seasons that celebrate the Paschal Mystery of Christ.

8. _____ is a celebration of the Passion, Death, and Resurrection of Christ.

9. In the Church year, the Triduum begins on Holy _____ evening and concludes on Easter Sunday night.

10. Ordinary Time is the time to remember the _____ of Jesus and listen to his teachings.

Go to **aliveinchrist.osv.com** for an interactive review.

The Seven Sacraments

 Let Us Pray

Leader: With joy and gladness, Lord, we celebrate the signs of your great love.

"Shout joyfully to the LORD, all you lands;
    serve the LORD with gladness;
    come before him with joyful song." **Psalm 100:1–2**

All: With wonderful signs of your love, you bless us, Lord. No wonder we shout, "Praise and thanks!" Amen.

 Scripture

Blessed be the God and Father of our Lord Jesus Christ, who has blessed us in Christ with every spiritual blessing in the heavens. . . . In him we have redemption . . . the forgiveness of transgressions, in accord with the riches of his grace that he lavished upon us. **Ephesians 1:3, 7–8**

? What Do You Wonder?

- How do you continue to receive spiritual blessings?

- When do you celebrate Jesus' life and love?

Present Through Time

What is a Sacrament?

Catholic Faith Words

Incarnation the mystery that the Son of God became man in order to save all people

Seven Sacraments effective signs of God's life, instituted by Christ and given to the Church. In the celebration of each Sacrament, there are visible signs and Divine actions that give grace and allow us to share in God's work.

Your life is filled with many signs. However, some signs have a deeper meaning, like a trophy that you worked hard to win or an American flag. Christians received the most precious sign of all in the **Incarnation**, when the Son of God became man. God the Father sent his Son, Jesus, as a sign of his love for all people. He pointed the way to God for all who followed him.

Jesus welcomed people like Peter and Zacchaeus, and they changed their lives for him. Jesus showed people God the Father's forgiveness. He healed some and called others to serve. Through Jesus' words and actions, many people experienced God's saving love. Because he is both Divine and human, Jesus made God and his love present.

"No one comes to the Father except through me," Jesus said to his Apostles at the Last Supper. "If you know me, then you will also know my Father. From now on you do know him and have seen him" (**John 14:6–7**).

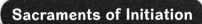

Sacraments of Initiation

Baptism
Forgiveness of sin and new life in Christ

Confirmation
Being sealed and strengthened in the Holy Spirit

Eucharist
Unity and salvation in Christ through the Body and Blood of Christ

Visible Signs and Divine Actions

It was only after Jesus' Resurrection that his Apostles began to understand that Jesus was really God! Jesus had promised his followers that he would always be with them and that they would continue his saving work. A very important way that Jesus does this is through the **Seven Sacraments**. The Sacraments are effective signs of God's life, instituted by Christ and given to the Church. They are actions of the Holy Spirit at work in Christ's Body, the Church. Jesus is present in each of the Sacraments.

In each of the Sacraments, there are visible signs and Divine actions that give grace and allow us to share in God's work. Each one celebrates a way that Jesus' saving work continues in the world.

Underline what Jesus promised the disciples and one way he fulfills this promise today.

Share Your Faith

Reflect Choose a Sacrament you have received.

Share Explain to a partner how Jesus was with you in that Sacrament.

Sacraments at the Service of Communion

Matrimony
Marriage covenant as a sign of Christ's covenant with his Church

Holy Orders
Ministry to Christ's Body, the Church

Sacraments of Healing

Penance and Reconciliation
Conversion and forgiveness through Christ

Anointing of the Sick
Spiritual and physical healing in Christ

The Last Supper, by Remigio Cantagallina

The Eucharist

What is the heart of our Catholic life?

Jesus often ate meals with his friends. On the night before he died, Jesus shared a Passover meal with his Apostles.

Scripture

The Last Supper

Then [Jesus] took a cup, gave thanks, and said, "Take this and share it among yourselves; for I tell you [that] from this time on I shall not drink of the fruit of the vine until the kingdom of God comes." Then he took the bread, said the blessing, broke it, and gave it to them, saying, "This is my body, which will be given for you; do this in memory of me." And likewise the cup after they had eaten, saying, "This cup is the new covenant in my blood, which will be shed for you." **Luke 22:17–20**

After Jesus was raised to new life and returned to the Father, his followers gathered weekly for the "breaking of the bread." They knew, as Catholics do today, that Jesus was present when they blessed and broke bread together as Jesus commanded. This celebration is called the **Eucharist**, the Sacrament in which Jesus gives himself and the bread and wine become his Body and Blood.

Act of Thanksgiving

In the Eucharist, we remember, give thanks for, and share in the life, Death, and Resurrection of Jesus. The word *Eucharist* means "thanksgiving." At the beginning of Mass, you ask God's mercy because of your sins. Your venial sins can be forgiven by your participation in the Eucharist. You listen to the Word of God. You thank God the Father for the great gift of his Son. When you receive Jesus in Holy Communion, you are united with the other members of the Body of Christ.

When Jesus told the Apostles to "do this in memory of me," he did not mean only that they should break bread together. He meant that they should live their lives as he did. Living the Eucharist means loving, welcoming, and forgiving others. You live the Eucharist when you share with those who do not have what you do.

➜ **When did you first receive Jesus in Holy Communion? Tell what you remember about the day.**

Activity

The Sacraments Use some of these terms in a paragraph about the Sacraments.

_____

_____

_____

_____

_____

_____

_____

Word List
• • • • • • • • • •
Eucharist
God's Word
Holy Communion
Divine action
Body of Christ

Catholic
Faith Words

Eucharist the Sacrament in which Jesus gives himself and the bread and wine become his Body and Blood

Our Catholic Life

How can you participate actively in Mass?

Do you go to Mass or do you participate in Mass? Do you know the difference? If you arrive at church on Sunday, slink into the pew, and daydream for the next hour, you are only going to Mass.

Mass is an excellent time for you to take an active role in your relationship with God. It is your chance to join with the rest of your parish in lifting your voices and souls in praise of God.

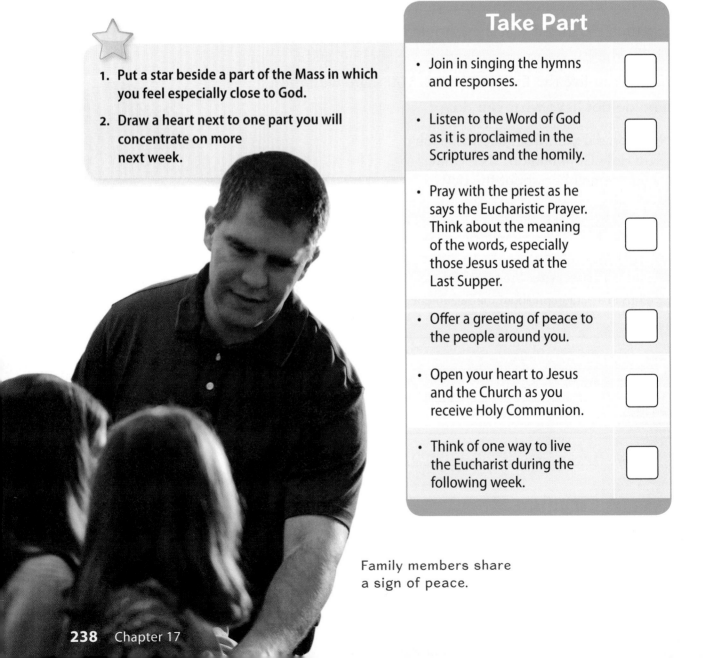

1. Put a star beside a part of the Mass in which you feel especially close to God.

2. Draw a heart next to one part you will concentrate on more next week.

Take Part

- Join in singing the hymns and responses.
- Listen to the Word of God as it is proclaimed in the Scriptures and the homily.
- Pray with the priest as he says the Eucharistic Prayer. Think about the meaning of the words, especially those Jesus used at the Last Supper.
- Offer a greeting of peace to the people around you.
- Open your heart to Jesus and the Church as you receive Holy Communion.
- Think of one way to live the Eucharist during the following week.

Family members share a sign of peace.

People of Faith

Saint Margaret Mary Alacoque, 1647–1690

October 16

Saint Margaret Mary Alacoque was born into a peasant family in France. From the time she was little, she had a special love for Jesus in the Eucharist. When she grew up, she joined a convent. While she was praying, she had several visions in which Jesus told her about his loving heart. He told her that he will give love and mercy to everyone who asks. Saint Margaret Mary taught people about the Devotion to the Sacred Heart of Jesus. It includes going to Mass and receiving the Eucharist on the first Friday of each month.

Discuss: How do you show your devotion to the Eucharist?

 Learn more about Saint Margaret Mary at **aliveinchrist.osv.com**

Live Your Faith

Make a Eucharist Poster Create a poster for your parish hall or church entrance for people to see as they come to Mass. On your poster, draw some ways people can live the Eucharist.

Let Us Pray

Prayer of Petition

This is a traditional prayer by Saint Francis de Sales. It asks God to help us prepare to receive him each time we celebrate the Eucharist.

All: Divine Savior,
we come to Your sacred table
to nourish ourselves,
not with bread but with Yourself,
true Bread of eternal life.
Help us daily to make a good and perfect meal
of this Divine food.
Let us be continually refreshed
by the perfume of Your kindness and goodness.
May the Holy Spirit fill us with his love.
Meanwhile, let us prepare a place
for this holy food by emptying our hearts.
Amen.

 Sing "We Come to the Table"
We come to the table of the Lord,
as one body formed in your love.
© 2005, John Burland. All rights reserved.

YOUR CHILD LEARNED >>>

This chapter explains that in the celebration of each Sacrament, there are visible signs and Divine actions that give grace and allow us to share in God's work.

Scripture

 Read **Ephesians 1:3, 7–8** to find a blessing for God for all the blessings the early Christians received.

Catholics Believe

- The Seven Sacraments are effective signs, instituted by Christ, that give grace and continue his saving work in the world.

- The Sacrament of the Eucharist is at the heart of Christian life.

To learn more, go to the *Catechism of the Catholic Church #1210, 1407* at **usccb.org**.

People of Faith

This week, your child learned about Saint Margaret Mary Alacoque, the promoter of the Devotion to the Sacred Heart of Jesus.

CHILDREN AT THIS AGE >>>

How They Understand the Sacraments Fourth-graders, while still bound to their five senses, are better able than younger children to see the connections between rituals and their meanings. This can help them gain a deeper appreciation of the Seven Sacraments as they know that what they are seeing and hearing in sacramental celebrations is a sign of, and participation in, something invisible as well.

CONSIDER THIS >>>

Who do you know who understands the Eucharist as a sacred gift and not an obligation?

Perhaps we might see it the same way if we became more aware that Jesus' gift of his life is given again for us each time we receive the Eucharist. We need to open our hearts to receive the gift we long for: the gift of knowing we are loved that perfectly, that completely. As Catholics, "we need to remember that the Eucharist is the summit and source of our Christian life. Why? Because in the Eucharist is found the entire treasure of the Church— Jesus Christ" (*USCCA, p.228*).

LET'S TALK >>>

- Ask your child to name the Seven Sacraments.

- Talk about the different Sacraments family members have celebrated.

LET'S PRAY >>>

 Saint Margaret Mary Alacoque, pray for us that we may learn to love Jesus in the Eucharist as much as you did. Amen.

 For a multimedia glossary of Catholic Faith Words, Sunday readings, seasonal and Saint resources, and chapter activities go to **aliveinchrist.osv.com**.

Chapter 17 Review

A **Work with Words** Fill in the circle next to the answer that best completes each statement.

1. There are _____ Sacraments.
   ○ seven
   ○ eight
   ○ nine

2. _____ is present in all of the Sacraments.
   ○ Water
   ○ Jesus
   ○ The Bible

3. The early Christians _____ the Eucharist.
   ○ celebrated
   ○ did not celebrate
   ○ invented

4. Eucharist means " _____ ."
   ○ morality
   ○ Heaven
   ○ thanksgiving

5. When you _____ , you continue Jesus' work in the world.
   ○ go to religion class
   ○ sing hymns
   ○ live the Eucharist

B **Check Understanding** Complete each sentence by circling the correct answer. Then answer the last two questions.

6. After Jesus' Resurrection, the Apostles began to understand that **(he was God/he was gone forever)**.

7. The Sacraments are actions of the **(priest/Holy Spirit)** at work in Christ's Body, the Church.

8. When you receive Jesus in Holy Communion, you **(forgive/are united with)** the other members of the Body of Christ.

9. What are some ways you can live the Eucharist?

   _____

   _____

   _____

10. What are some ways you can participate actively in the Mass?

   _____

   _____

   _____

© Our Sunday Visitor

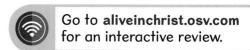
Go to **aliveinchrist.osv.com** for an interactive review.

Healing and Reconciliation

 Let Us Pray

Leader: Merciful God, be always with us as we pray.

"Remember your compassion and your mercy,
O Lord,
for they are ages old." **Psalm 25:6**

All: Jesus, no matter how many times we sin, you call us back to you. Help us to admit our sin and ask for your forgiveness. Amen.

 Scripture

"Blessed is the one whose fault is removed,
whose sin is forgiven.
Blessed is the man to whom the Lord imputes no guilt,
in whose spirit [there] is no deceit.
Because I kept silent, my bones wasted away;
I groaned all day long.
Then I declared my sin to you;
my guilt I did not hide.
I said, 'I confess my transgression to the Lord,'
and you took away the guilt of my sin."
Psalm 32:1–3, 5

? What Do You Wonder?

• Is there a limit to how much God will forgive?

• Why might you feel nervous telling your sins to the priest?

God's Forgiveness

Who is forgiven?

Jesus showed God's forgiveness to others through his words and actions. In this story, Jesus meets a wealthy tax collector who decides to **repent** and become his follower.

Catholic Faith Words

repent to turn our lives away from sin and toward God

Sacrament of Penance and Reconciliation the Sacrament in which God's forgiveness for sin is given through the Church

confession an essential element of the Sacrament of Penance and Reconciliation, when you tell your sins to the priest; another name for the Sacrament

temptation an attraction to sin; wanting to do something we should not or not do something we should

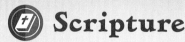 Scripture

The Story of Zacchaeus

One day, Jesus was passing through the town of Jericho. Zacchaeus, a rich tax collector, wanted to see Jesus and learn about him. Zacchaeus was short, so he climbed a tree to see over the crowd.

Jesus noticed Zacchaeus in the tree. He said, "Zacchaeus, come down quickly, for today I must stay at your house." Zacchaeus came down happily.

The crowd complained, saying that Jesus should not stay with Zacchaeus because Zacchaeus was a sinner.

Zacchaeus told Jesus that he would give money to those who were poor. He offered to give anyone he had cheated four times the amount of money that he owed to that person.

"Today salvation has come to this house," said Jesus. "For the Son of Man has come to seek and to save what was lost." **Based on Luke 19:1–10**

➜ **Who has taught you the most about forgiveness? What did the person or persons say or do?**

Conversion

God is always ready and waiting to forgive. He welcomes you back, just as Jesus welcomed Zacchaeus. When you turn away from sin and respond to God's love and forgiveness, you are experiencing conversion. Conversion is about becoming the people God intends us to be.

During his life, Jesus forgave many people in his Father's name. After his Resurrection, Jesus told his disciples that he would send the Holy Spirit, who would give them the power to forgive sins. Today, the Church continues to celebrate God's forgiveness in the **Sacrament of Penance and Reconciliation**. Sometimes this Sacrament is called **confession**, for the element of the Sacrament when we tell our sins to the priest. In this Sacrament, you receive God's forgiveness of sins through the Church. The grace of this Sacrament strengthens you to make peace with those whom you may have hurt. It also strengthens you against the attraction to sin called **temptation**.

Reflect Think of someone who has forgiven you or you have forgiven. Why did you or that person need forgiveness?

Share With a classmate, discuss ways to show you are sorry and make peace with others. Then, tell one way that you can be more forgiving of others.

_____

© Our Sunday Visitor

The Sacraments of Healing

How does the Church celebrate forgiveness and healing?

Celebrating the Sacrament of Penance and Reconciliation is a public sign that you are willing to turn away from sin and toward the love of God and the community.

Begin with an examination of conscience, a prayerful reflection on how you have lived the Ten Commandments, the Beatitudes, and other Church teachings. It helps us know whether what we've done is right or wrong.

When you confess your sins to a priest, you ask for God's forgiveness through the power the Holy Spirit gives to the Church. The priest cannot tell anyone the sins confessed in the Sacrament. This is called the **sacramental seal**, or seal of confession.

Contrition is being sorry for your sins and wanting to live better. God will forgive all sins, even mortal sins, if you are truly sorry and want to change your heart.

God forgives your sins, but the effects of your sins are still in the world. You must do what you can to repair the harm your sin has caused. Part of making up for your sin is to do the prayer, offering, or good work that the priest gives you as a **penance**.

When the priest says the words of **absolution**, he grants you forgiveness of sins in God's name.

Catholic Faith Words

sacramental seal a rule that a priest is not to share anything he hears in confession

penance the prayer, offering, or good work the priest gives you in the Sacrament of Reconciliation

absolution words spoken by the priest during the Sacrament of Penance and Reconciliation to grant forgiveness of sins in God's name

 Underline what God will do for us when we confess our sins and are truly sorry during the Sacrament of Reconciliation.

God's Healing Love

Today, the Church anoints the sick or dying through the **Sacrament of the Anointing of the Sick**. This Sacrament strengthens those who celebrate it and reminds them of God's healing love. God's love and mercy are available to all who turn to him.

In Jesus' time, people thought that sickness was God's punishment for someone's sin. But Jesus taught that this is not the case.

Catholic Faith Words

Sacrament of the Anointing of the Sick the Sacrament that brings Jesus' healing touch to strengthen, comfort, and forgive the sins of those who are seriously ill or close to death

 ## Scripture

The Man Born Blind

One day, Jesus saw a man who had been blind from birth. His disciples asked him, "Why is this man blind? Is it because of his own sin or that of his parents?"

Jesus answered, "Neither he nor his parents sinned; it is so that the works of God might be made more visible through him."

Jesus rubbed clay on the man's eyes and told him to go to a certain place and wash it off. When the man did, he could see!

Many did not believe that Jesus had done this. When the man came back, Jesus asked the man, "Do you believe in the Son of Man? . . . You have seen him and the one speaking with you is he."

The man answered, "I do believe, Lord."   **Based on John 9:1–38**

Connect Your Faith

Think About Healing In the space below, name some things God has provided us for healing. Two examples are provided for you.

doctors, nurses

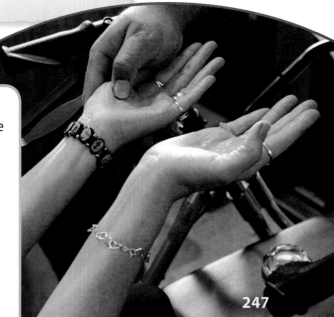

Our Catholic Life

How can you prepare to receive God's forgiveness?

You may feel uncomfortable about telling your sins to a priest. Remember that the priest is not there to scare or punish you. He is acting as a servant of God. He will know your sorrow and grant you God's forgiveness.

Are you wondering how you will know what to say? Here are some suggestions to help you prepare to celebrate the Sacrament of Penance and Reconciliation.

 Match the step with its explanation.

Before You Go

Examine your conscience	Ask for guidance in discovering your weaknesses.
Pray to the Holy Spirit	Pray the Act of Contrition.
Select a Scripture passage	This is a way of healing any hurts or harm you may have caused through your sins.
Make up your mind to do penance	Try to remember as best you can the sins you have committed. Look at the Ten Commandments, the Beatitudes, and the laws of the Church. Ask yourself whether you have followed these laws and guides.
Show your sorrow	Choose one that inspires you to turn away from sin and make a fresh start.
Decide to avoid sin	Resolve that with the help and guidance of the Holy Spirit, you will resist temptation and do better.

People of Faith

Venerable Matt Talbot, 1856–1925

Matt Talbot was born in Dublin, Ireland. Many people in his family drank too much. Matt started drinking when he was young. After years of heavy drinking, he decided to stop. He realized that he had hurt many people and done many bad things. He asked for forgiveness from each person. He also received the Sacrament of Penance and asked God to forgive all his sins. For the rest of his life, he never drank again. He gave away much of his money and prayed for all those that he had hurt.

Discuss: Talk about a time when you hurt someone and had to ask forgiveness.

 Learn more about Venerable Matt at **aliveinchrist.osv.com**

Live Your Faith

Name one friend or family member who needs to hear a message of forgiveness from you. Draft your message in the space below.

_____

_____

_____

_____

_____

_____

_____

_____

_____

_____

_____

Create a card with a handwritten message, and deliver it to that person.

♥ Let Us Pray

Our Lady, Queen of Peace

All: Most holy and immaculate Virgin,
Mother of Jesus and our loving Mother,
being his Mother, you shared in his universal kingship.
The prophets and angels proclaimed him King of peace.
With loving fervor in our hearts we salute and honor
you as Queen of peace.
We pray that your intercession may protect us and all
people from hatred and discord,
and direct our hearts into the ways of peace and justice
which your Son taught and exemplified.
We ask your maternal care for our Holy Father
who works to reconcile the nations in peace.
We seek your guidance for our President and other
leaders as they strive for world peace.
Glorious Queen of peace, grant us peace in
our hearts, harmony in our families, and
concord throughout the world.
Immaculate Mother, as patroness of our
beloved country, watch over us and protect us
with your motherly love.
Amen.

 Sing "Salve Regina (A Litany to Mary)"
Salve, Regína, Mater misericórdiae:
Vita dulcédo et spes nostra, salve.
Hail, Queen of Heaven, our Mother,
kind and merciful:
Pray for your children. Hail, our sweetness
and our hope.

YOUR CHILD LEARNED >>>

This chapter explores reconciliation as it relates to the effect of sin in the world, and explains the necessity of confessing sins to a priest and trusting in Jesus' power to forgive and heal.

Scripture

 Read **Psalm 32:1–3, 5** to find out about the blessing of Reconciliation.

Catholics Believe

- God's forgiveness is offered to all who are truly sorry and seek it.
- The Sacraments of Reconciliation and the Anointing of the Sick celebrate God's healing love.

To learn more, go to the *Catechism of the Catholic Church #1420–1421, 1489–1490* at **usccb.org**.

People of Faith

This week, your child learned about Venerable Matt Talbot, who is known for turning his life around with prayer and self-sacrifice.

CHILDREN AT THIS AGE >>>

How They Understand Healing and Reconciliation For fourth-graders, right and wrong are deeper concepts than they were before. Morality is not just about what other people see us doing. It is also about who we are and what we do when no one seems to be watching. It is important that as children grow in their ability to form their consciences, they have continued opportunity to seek God's forgiveness through the Sacrament of Penance and Reconciliation.

CONSIDER THIS >>>

Have you ever yearned for a relationship to be healed?

We are human, and are not perfect. Our egos or hurt feelings can get in the way of healing a relationship. Yet, God loves perfectly and offers forgiveness to all who have not loved as he asked and therefore hurt ourselves, others, and our relationship with him. As Catholics, we know that "sin should never be understood as a private or personal matter, because it harms our relationship with others and may even break our loving communion with the Church. The Sacrament of Penance repairs this break and has a renewing effect of the vitality of the Church itself" (*USCCA, p. 242*).

LET'S TALK >>>

- Ask your child to name the parts of the Sacrament of Reconciliation (contrition, confession, penance, absolution).
- Discuss how your family shares God's healing love with one another.

LET'S PRAY >>>

 O God, I am heartily sorry for having offended you. Amen.

 For a multimedia glossary of Catholic Faith Words, Sunday readings, seasonal and Saint resources, and chapter activities go to **aliveinchrist.osv.com**.

Chapter 18 Review

 A **Check Understanding** Solve the crossword puzzle.

Down

1. Welcoming someone back after a wrong has been done
2. These separate you from God and others
3. This is done for those who are very sick or dying
4. God's love is available to all who _____ to him.
6. When you tell the priest your sins, you are really _____ to God.

Across

5. The Sacrament that celebrates God's forgiveness of sins is the Sacrament of Penance and _____.
7. Words spoken by the priest to forgive sin in God's name
8. Deciding to turn away from sin and turn back to God
9. The prayer, offering, or good work the priest gives you in the Sacrament of Reconciliation
10. An essential element of Reconciliation when you tell your sins to the priest

 Go to **aliveinchrist.osv.com** for an interactive review.

A Work with Words Complete each sentence with the correct word from the Word Bank.

Word Bank

Triduum

Penance

Eucharist

peace

Anointing

Mystery

Ordinary

forgiveness

Sacraments

liturgical

1. The Sacrament of Penance and Reconciliation strengthens you to make _____ with those whom you may have hurt.

2. Absolution are the words spoken by a priest to grant God's _____ of sins.

3. Jesus' healing touch strengthens and forgives the sins of those who are seriously ill in the Sacrament of the _____ of the Sick.

4. _____ is the Sacrament in which Jesus gives himself and the bread and wine become his Body and Blood.

5. The cycle of the Church's feasts and seasons which celebrate the Paschal Mystery is the _____ year.

6. Through the Paschal _____, Jesus' suffering, Death, Resurrection, and Acension, we are saved from sin and death.

7. _____ is the prayer, offering, or good work the priest gives you to help you make up for the effects of your sins.

8. The _____ are effective signs of God's life, instituted by Christ and given to the Church, to give grace.

9. The _____ celebrates the Passion, Death, and Resurrection of Christ.

10. _____ Time is a season of the Church year.

B **Check Understanding** Fill in the circle next to the answer that best completes the sentence.

11. Early Christians honored Jesus with "the breaking of the bread." Today this is known as _____.

    ○ the breaking at the table

    ○ a feast day

    ○ the Eucharist

12. Jesus showed that the most generous gift is to _____.

    ○ spend all your money on presents

    ○ make your own greeting cards

    ○ give your life for others

13. Two of the Seven Sacraments are _____.

    ○ Contrition and Holy Orders

    ○ Eucharist and Study

    ○ Baptism and Matrimony

14. The seasonal color for Advent and Lent is _____.

    ○ green

    ○ violet

    ○ red

15. The seasonal colors for _____ are white and gold.

    ○ Christmas and Easter

    ○ Ordinary Time and Lent

    ○ Pentecost and Advent

C **Make Connections** **Write responses on the lines below.**

16. Name two different seasons of the Church year, and tell one way you can grow closer to God during each.

_____

_____

_____

_____

17. Why is it important to participate actively in Mass?

_____

_____

_____

18. Name three things you can do to prepare for the Sacrament of Penance and Reconciliation.

_____

_____

_____

19. Why is it important to celebrate the Sacrament of Penance and Reconciliation?

_____

_____

_____

20. How do the Sacraments help you grow in faith?

_____

_____

_____

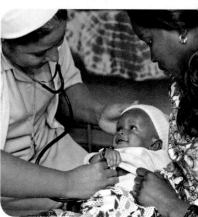

Kingdom of God

Our Catholic Tradition

- All Church members share in her mission to spread Jesus' message of God's love and promote the Kingdom of God. (CCC, 863)

- We do this by proclaiming the Gospel and being a sign of Christ to others. (CCC, 942)

- We are called to be generous stewards of our possessions and to work for the good of all people. (CCC, 2238)

- We live in God's love and do his will so that we can live forever with him in Heaven. (CCC, 1821)

How does living in God's Kingdom on Earth prepare us for God's Kingdom in Heaven?

A Generous Spirit

 Let Us Pray

Leader: Create in us, O God, a generous spirit, a kind and caring heart.

"Happy is the one who is kind to the poor!
Those who are kind to the needy honor [God]."
Based on Proverbs 14:21, 31

All: Create in us, O God, a generous spirit, a kind and caring heart. Amen.

Scripture

"Give and gifts will be given to you; a good measure, packed together, shaken down, and overflowing, will be poured into your lap. For the measure with which you measure will in return be measured out to you." Luke 6:38

? What Do You Wonder?

- How do you share your gifts with others?

- Which of the Ten Commandments helps you grow in generosity?

What Really Matters

What does Jesus want you to know about riches?

The difference between needs and wants is not always clear. Commercials constantly show us things that we don't really need. Sometimes it can feel like we need everything we want to make us happy. Jesus helps us to understand how much is too much through this parable.

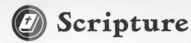

Scripture

The Parable of the Rich Fool

There was a rich man whose land produced a bountiful harvest. He asked himself, "What shall I do? I do not have space to store my harvest." And he said, "This is what I will do. I will tear down my barns and build larger ones. There I will store all my grain and other goods. Afterward, I will say to myself, 'You have so many good things stored up for many years. It is time to rest, eat, drink, and be merry!'"

But God said to him, "You fool. Tonight your life will be taken from you. The things you have stored, to whom will they belong?"

Thus will it be for the one who stores up treasure for himself but is not rich in what matters to God.   **Based on Luke 12:16–21**

→ **How could the Rich Fool have been richer in what matters to God?**

Poor in Spirit

Everything that God made is good. People are good. The things that people create with love and care are good. But Jesus taught that possessions are not the most important things. Do you remember the story found in Matthew 19:16–22 about the rich young man? Jesus loved him and wanted him to be happy.

Sometimes people need to leave behind their material possessions in order to have the time and energy to do good. The Apostles left their homes, families, and jobs in order to follow Jesus and help him spread God's Word.

The first Beatitude says, "Blessed are the poor in spirit, for theirs is the kingdom of heaven" (**Matthew 5:3**). Those who do not become too attached to their possessions are able to work for love and peace in the world and help bring about God's Kingdom.

Share Your Faith

Reflect Describe a right and wrong choice for each of the following situations.

Share In a small group, role-play the right choice in one of these situations.

A video game that you want is on an outdoor table during a sidewalk sale.

Right _____

Wrong _____

Someone else wins an award that you wanted.

Right _____

Wrong _____

Generosity and Humility

What do the Seventh and Tenth Commandments teach you?

Catholic Faith Words

envy the sin of resenting what others have or being sad from wanting for yourself what belongs to others

greed the sin of desiring to gain earthly goods without limits or beyond what you need

humility the moral virtue that helps us to know that God is the source of everything good. Humility helps us to avoid being prideful.

justice giving God what is due him, and giving each person what he or she is due because that person is a child of God

There are two Commandments that teach us about the right attitude to have toward our material possessions. The Seventh Commandment says this: You shall not steal. The Tenth Commandment tells us: You shall not covet your neighbor's goods.

Theft, greed, and envy are all sins against the Seventh and Tenth Commandments. Theft is taking what is not yours. When you have **envy**, you resent or are sad because someone else possesses something that you really want. Envy harms the Body of Christ because it divides God's People rather than bringing everyone together. **Greed** is the desire to gain earthly possessions without concern for what is reasonable or right.

Called to Share

Humility helps us to know that God is the source of everything good. It can help us overcome both envy and greed. Caring too much about material possessions almost always brings unhappiness and disappointment.

Justice is giving God and others what is their due. Because everything comes from God, all people have a right to what they need to live comfortably. As a member of the Body of Christ, you are called to share your possessions with others, especially those who do not have food, shelter, or decent clothing.

→ **In what ways are people your age tempted to be envious or greedy?**

Called to Stewardship

The Seventh and Tenth Commandments require us to be generous with others. Being generous means giving more than is necessary.

God created the world for all creatures and called humans to **stewardship**. This means people are called to use natural resources well and protect the environment for everyone now and in the future; to respect all life as a gift from God; and to share time, money, and talent to help others.

Catholic Faith Words

stewardship the way we appreciate and use God's gifts, including our time, talent, and treasure, and the resources of creation

Scripture

The Poor Widow's Contribution

Jesus watched people put money into the Temple treasury. Many rich people put in large sums of money. A poor widow put in two small coins worth only a few cents. Jesus said to his disciples, "I say to you, this poor widow put in more than all the others. They contributed their extra money, but the widow has given all she had."   **Based on Mark 12:41–44**

> On the coin label, write the name of someone you know who has a generous spirit.

➔ **Why do you think the widow contributed more than the rest?**

Connect Your Faith

Be a Good Steward Match the categories of stewardship on the left to the examples on the right.

Time	•	• Singing in the choir
Talent	•	• Putting money in the collection basket
Treasure	•	• Handing on faith to children as a catechist

Our Catholic Life

How can you learn to have a more generous spirit?

God knew that it would be easier for you to help and care for one another if you did not let possessions get in the way. He gave you the Seventh and Tenth Commandments to encourage good habits and help build a world of peace, love, and justice.

You have the ability to be as generous as God wants you to be. Here are some ideas that can help you be more generous every day.

In the open sections, write ways you can follow some of these suggestions this week.

If you have a book or video game that someone else would enjoy, lend it to that person. Perhaps he or she cannot afford to buy this item.

SHARE

Before you ask for or buy something new, stop and think, "Do I really need that, or do I just want it?"

SEPARATE NEEDS FROM WANTS

Reduce the clutter in your room. Look for things that you no longer use, and give them to the Saint Vincent de Paul society, Goodwill Industries, or another local charity.

LIVE SIMPLY

When you see someone who has something you want, be happy for that person rather than being envious.

DO NOT ENVY OTHERS; BE GLAD FOR WHAT THEY HAVE

© Our Sunday Visitor

People of Faith

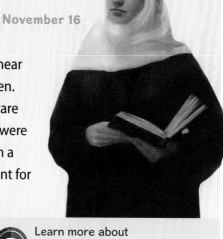

Saint Margaret of Scotland, 1045–1093

November 16

Saint Margaret was a princess who was shipwrecked with her family near Scotland. She married Malcolm, the Scottish king, and became a queen. Margaret was rich, but she used her money to help others. She took care of children who didn't have parents. She helped repair churches that were falling down. She even built a bridge so people didn't have to wade in a river to cross it. Saint Margaret knew that the Earth's goods were meant for the benefit of the whole human family, not just for some people.

Discuss: How does it feel when you give away something you own?

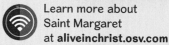

Learn more about Saint Margaret at **aliveinchrist.osv.com**

Live Your Faith

Design and Decorate In the space below, design and decorate an ad that will remind people to be generous with one another.

Let Us Pray

Beatitudes for the Poor in Spirit

This prayer calls us to remember that our relationships are far more important than things. We ask God for the strength to help us to put him and his People first in our lives.

Gather and begin with the Sign of the Cross.

Leader: Jesus calls us to be poor in spirit. We ask you, God, for the grace to allow us to see the needs of others and a heart that wants to help.

Side 1: Blessed are the poor in spirit,

Side 2: for theirs is the Kingdom of Heaven.

Side 1: Blessed are those who

Side 2: share their possessions.

All: Help us to love and care for others.

Side 2: Blessed are the poor in spirit,

Side 1: for theirs is the Kingdom of Heaven.

Side 2: Blessed are those who

Side 1: find ways to care for those who have little.

All: Help us to love and care for others.

 Sing "God's Greatest Gift"
Love, love, Jesus is love.
God's greatest gift is the gift of love.
All creation sings together,
praising God for love.
© 1995, 1999, Owen Alstott. Published by OCP.
All rights reserved.

FAMILY+FAITH
LIVING AND LEARNING TOGETHER

YOUR CHILD LEARNED >>>

This chapter examines generosity and humility and discusses theft, greed, and envy in relationship to the Seventh and Tenth Commandments, deepening the understanding that the Earth's good are meant for all.

Scripture

 Read **Luke 6:38** to find out about the importance of generosity.

Catholics Believe

- The Commandments call you to be generous and to have the right attitude toward possessions.
- Stewardship is the way we appreciate and use God's gifts, including our time, talent, and treasure, and the resources of creation.

To learn more, go to the *Catechism of the Catholic Church #299, 2402–2405* at **usccb.org**.

People of Faith

This week, your child learned about Saint Margaret of Scotland, who used her wealth to benefit the Scottish people.

CHILDREN AT THIS AGE >>>

How They Understand Being Generous Because they are still concrete thinkers, fourth-graders can be very materialistic. However, they also love opportunities to give to others. Giving them practical ways to be generous helps them feel a sense of purpose and can be an important foundation for pursuing their God-given vocation as they grow.

CONSIDER THIS >>>

Do you think your family has too much stuff?

Most desires such as for food, shelter, and loving relationships are good and natural. But when we focus too much on material things, we can become selfish and even greedy. As Catholics, we know that "the Tenth Commandment calls us to practice poverty of spirit and generosity of heart. These virtues liberate us from being slaves to money and possessions. They enable us to have a preferential love for the poor and to be witnesses of justice and peace in the world" (*USCCA pgs. 449–450*).

LET'S TALK >>>

- Ask your child to explain what envy, being poor in spirit, and humility have to do with the Seventh and Tenth Commandments.
- Talk about ways your family might change its attitude toward possessions and be even more generous with one another.

LET'S PRAY >>>

 Saint Margaret, pray for us that we may always be generous with everything we have. Amen.

 For a multimedia glossary of Catholic Faith Words, Sunday readings, seasonal and Saint resources, and chapter activities go to **aliveinchrist.osv.com**.

Chapter 19 Review

A **Work with Words** Fill in the circle next to the answer that best completes each statement.

1. The _____ Commandment states that you should not steal.
   - ○ Sixth
   - ○ Seventh
   - ○ Eighth

2. The way we appreciate and use God's gifts is called _____ .
   - ○ stewardship
   - ○ conscience
   - ○ generosity

3. The _____ Commandment states that you should not desire what others have.
   - ○ Eighth
   - ○ Ninth
   - ○ Tenth

4. _____ is being sad or resentful when someone else possesses something you want.
   - ○ Stealing
   - ○ Generosity
   - ○ Envy

5. _____ is the unlimited gathering of material possessions.
   - ○ Greed
   - ○ Generosity
   - ○ Stewardship

B **Check Understanding** Below are examples of how you can keep the Seventh and Tenth Commandments. In the space provided, write the number of the Commandment that the example refers to.

6. ☐ Donating your outgrown clothing to charity

7. ☐ Finding a toy in the parking lot of a store, and turning it in to the lost and found

8. ☐ Sharing your possessions with a brother or sister

9. ☐ Not eating food in a grocery store until after you have paid for it

10. ☐ Being thankful for what you have

© Our Sunday Visitor

Go to **aliveinchrist.osv.com** for an interactive review.

The Church in the World

 Let Us Pray

Leader: Lord God, you invite us to take part in the mission of your Son to share the Good News with all the world.

"I heard the voice of the Lord saying, 'Whom shall I send? Who will go for us?' 'Here I am,' I said; 'send me!'" **Isaiah 6:8**

All: Here we are, Lord. Send us to be your witnesses. Amen.

 Scripture

[Jesus said,] "You will receive power when the holy Spirit comes upon you, and you will be my witnesses in Jerusalem, throughout Judea and Samaria, and to the ends of the earth."

Acts of the Apostles 1:8

? What Do You Wonder?

- What is one thing you want to tell someone about Jesus?
- What unifies Catholics around the world?

Make Disciples of All Nations

How does the Church reach out to the world?

At the Last Supper, Jesus told his Apostles that the Holy Spirit would come to strengthen them and guide them when he was gone. After his Resurrection, before he ascended into Heaven, Jesus gave his Apostles the following command.

Scripture

The Commissioning of the Disciples

"All power in heaven and on earth has been given to me. Go, therefore, and make disciples of all nations, baptizing them in the name of the Father, and of the Son, and of the holy Spirit, teaching them to observe all that I have commanded you. And behold, I am with you always, until the end of the age."
Matthew 28:18–20

Jesus wanted his followers to go out to all places and share the **Gospel** message of the Good News of God's Kingdom. Today, no matter where you go in the world, you will find followers of Jesus. Jesus' universal, or worldwide, **mission** on Earth was to share God's love with all people. All Catholics share in the Church's mission to announce this Good News and to share it in words and actions through her work of **evangelization**.

➡ Think about three places you will go this week. How will you live out Jesus' mission in each place?

Jesus' Universal Mission

Jesus reached out to all people, especially people who were poor and those who were left out by others. He healed, forgave, and loved people, especially those who were considered sinners. Jesus treated everyone with dignity and respect. An important part of Jesus' mission was justice, the virtue of giving to God and people what is due to them.

Unity in the Church

There are differences in the ways the people of other countries and cultures practice their faith. Even in your parish you may notice a diversity, or variety, in the ways that people express their faith. These cultural differences strengthen the Church. She is united because of her faithfulness to the common belief handed down from the Apostles through their successors, the bishops. The Church is united in the celebration of the Mass, in the Sacraments, in prayer, and when people in every culture help bring justice to the world. You bring justice to the world by working to give others what is rightfully theirs.

Catholic Faith Words

Gospel a word that means "Good News." The Gospel message is the Good News of God's Kingdom and his saving love.

mission a job or purpose. The Church's mission is to announce the Good News of God's Kingdom.

evangelization sharing the Good News of Jesus through words and actions in a way that invites people to accept the Gospel

Share Your Faith

Reflect Think of all the ways that Jesus taught about and worked for justice. Write a newspaper headline that describes how Jesus brought justice to the world.

_____

_____

Share With a partner, talk about ways that you can bring justice into the world like Jesus did.

ANDES

The Church in Bolivia

How does the Church include different cultures?

Catholic missionaries bring the Catholic faith to people all over the world. They are careful to respect and include the customs of different groups in prayer and worship. Missionaries preach the Gospel of Jesus in word and deed.

In the following story told by a missionary, you will find some ways that the Church in Bolivia is like your parish and some ways that it is different from your parish.

A Floating Church

I work with other missionaries in the jungle region of northeast Bolivia. We travel in our parish boat to visit the people who live far apart along the Beni River. Most of the people work deep in the jungle. Some work with rubber trees, and others harvest Brazilian nuts.

On our way up the river, we tell whoever is home to gather their neighbors together for Mass, Baptisms, and marriages on the day we will return downstream. When we return, the people gather near the river. There we baptize people, celebrate Mass, and perform marriages.

CHILE

© Our Sunday Visitor

The People and the Mission

The people are happy to have us come and celebrate the Sacraments with them. Ninety-five percent of Bolivians are Catholic. Their ancestors converted to Christianity a long time ago. Many of the people we meet along the river still speak their native Indian languages. The people we meet also bring some of their native customs into their religious life.

BOLIVIA

My coworkers and I have learned the languages of the people. We spend time talking and listening to the people. We are able to help them take care of their health in a clinic, and we educate them in a school. We have helped them set up a type of company called a *cooperative*, which is owned by the people who use its services. For example, we helped the farmers set up a cooperative so that they could get fair prices for their rubber and nut crops.

Bolivia has a lot of troubles. Once, there was an uprising in a town, and I was asked to be mayor for four months. Another time, I was arrested with another priest because we had helped the people form a cooperative.

➤ **What about the missionaries' experience in Bolivia is different from the experience in your parish?**

➤ **How does the Church include different cultures?**

PARAGUAY

Connect Your Faith

Support the Missions Research what connections your parish has to mission work. Write a short prayer to support missionaries around the world.

_____

_____

_____

Our Catholic Life

How can you help missionaries spread God's Word?

Jesus told his Apostles to go and spread his message all around the world. Today, missionaries continue this work in all corners of the world.

Missionaries give up lives of comfort to live with and help people in need. The missions provide food, medical care, and education in addition to spreading the Word of God. Many missions have very little money to buy the items needed to care for the people. Below are some ways you can help missionaries in their good work.

Ways to Help

Put a check mark next to one thing you could do this week to help support missions. Underline what you might do in the future.

Collect Medical Supplies
Collect bandages, first aid cream, or used eyeglasses.

Raise Money
Organize projects to raise money to help missionaries purchase supplies.

Send Your Support
Write a letter to a missionary, thanking him or her for doing God's work.

Gather Bibles
Collect Bibles or old hymnbooks to help missions share the Word of the Lord.

Pray for a Missionary
Say a prayer to bless a missionary and the work that he or she is doing.

People of Faith

Blessed Junípero Serra, 1713–1784

July 1

We think missionaries go to faraway places, but two hundred years ago, the United States *was* a faraway place! Blessed Junípero Serra, a Spanish priest, came to America and lived in what is now California. He built many churches and named them after Saints. Many cities still have those names, like San Diego (Saint Diego) and Santa Monica (Saint Monica). Father Serra walked from mission to mission. Once he was bitten by a snake! Although his foot hurt for the rest of his life, he still kept walking to his churches.

Discuss: How have you helped support missions?

 Learn more about Blessed Junípero at **aliveinchrist.osv.com**

Live Your Faith

Make a List Missionaries are often gone from home for a long time. What might they need? Make a list of items you would include in a care package to a missionary.

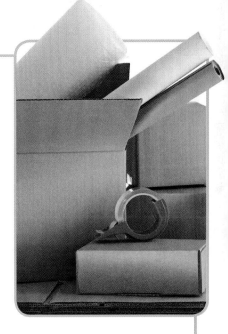

© Our Sunday Visitor

 **Let Us Pray**

Prayer of Praise

This prayer helps us reflect on and appreciate the diversity of God's people, a gift of God to each of us.

Gather and begin with the Sign of the Cross.

Leader: Lord of the Nations, all the people of the world glorify you. We are your one family, all sisters and brothers.

Prayer statements about our sisters and brothers around the world:

- I pray for the people of _____, who _____.
- I give thanks for the people of _____, who _____.
- God created the people of _____, who _____.
- The people of God in _____ praise God by _____.

Leader: Loving God, we marvel at the diversity of the world, all people, all creation, showing your greatness. May each of us always bring your love and your Good News with us wherever we are.

All: Amen.

 Sing "Somos el Cuerpo de Cristo/We Are the Body of Christ"
Somos el cuerpo de Cristo.
We are the body of Christ.
Hemos oído el llamado;
we've answered "Yes" to the call of the Lord.
Somos el cuerpo de Cristo.
We are the body of Christ.
Traemos su santo mensaje.
We come to bring the good news to the world.

FAMILY+FAITH
LIVING AND LEARNING TOGETHER

YOUR CHILD LEARNED >>>

This chapter discusses the mission and unity in diversity of the Catholic Church.

Scripture

Read **Acts of the Apostles 1:8** to find out what Jesus promises to send.

Catholics Believe

- The mission of the People of God is to proclaim the Gospel and to work for the good of all people.
- The Church is made up of people of many cultures, but all are united by their belief in Christ.

To learn more, go to the *Catechism of the Catholic Church #849, 858–859, 1934–1938* at **usccb.org**.

People of Faith

This week, your child learned about Blessed Junípero Serra, the founder of the California mission chain.

CHILDREN AT THIS AGE >>>

How They Understand Mission Your child is probably learning more about the world and its diverse cultures. Children this age often are growing in their ability to understand distances and the different experiences and living conditions of people around the world. For this reason, your child is ready to learn more about the Church's missionary activity and ways in which they can participate, through praying and supporting missionaries and looking for God's call to share the Gospel in everyday life.

CONSIDER THIS >>>

Do you believe unity in diversity is a possibility?

Differences are part of the beauty of creation. Imagine if all the roses in the world were red. The Church is made up of many cultures, but we are all united in our belief in Christ. As Catholics, we know that "the word *catholic* means 'universal.' The Catholic Church has lived and continues to live in a diversity of cultures and languages because she is led by the Spirit of Christ to bring the Gospel to all peoples" (*USCCA, p. 129*).

LET'S TALK >>>

- Ask your child to explain how the Catholic faith is brought to the whole world.
- Talk about how your family participates in Jesus' mission to spread the Good News.

LET'S PRAY >>>

 Dear God, thank you for the missionaries like Blessed Junípero Serra who teach others about God and the saving grace of Jesus. Amen.

 For a multimedia glossary of Catholic Faith Words, Sunday readings, seasonal and Saint resources, and chapter activities go to **aliveinchrist.osv.com**.

Chapter 20 Review

A **Work with Words** Complete each sentence with the correct word from the Word Bank.

Word Bank

justice

world

mission

diversity

respect

1. Jesus' _____ was to share God's love with all people.

2. The Church is one body, made up of a great _____ of members.

3. The mission of every person in the Church is to bring the Good News of Jesus to the _____ .

4. The virtue of _____ challenges followers of Jesus to work to provide for the needs and rights of others.

5. Missionaries must _____ the culture and customs of the local people.

B **Check Understanding** List five things that missionaries do for the people they serve.

6. _____

_____

7. _____

_____

8. _____

_____

9. _____

_____

10. _____

_____

Go to **aliveinchrist.osv.com**
for an interactive review.

Eternal Life with God

 **Let Us Pray**

Leader: God, teach us to live so that some day we might share eternal life with you.

"Turn from evil and do good;
 seek peace and pursue it." **Psalm 34:15**

All: Give us gifts to help us see you, love you, and follow you, Lord, until the day your Kingdom comes in fullness. Amen.

📖 Scripture

Everyone who believes that Jesus is the Christ has been born of God, and everyone who loves the father also loves the child. We know that we love the children of God when we love God and obey his Commandments. For the love of God is this, that we obey his Commandments. And his Commandments are not burdensome. And this is the testimony: God gave us eternal life, and this life is in his Son. Whoever has the Son has life; whoever does not have the Son of God does not have life. **Based on 1 John 5:1–3, 11–12**

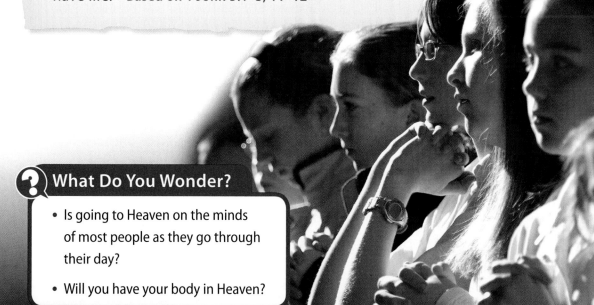

❓ What Do You Wonder?

- Is going to Heaven on the minds of most people as they go through their day?

- Will you have your body in Heaven?

© Our Sunday Visitor

Being with God

How do the Gifts of the Holy Spirit help you live in friendship with God?

Heaven is not a place in the sky among the clouds. **Heaven** is the full joy that all holy people who have lived in God's grace will share with him forever.

To spend eternity with God, you first must grow in friendship with God. Through the Holy Spirit, God helps you grow in friendship with him and with others. You receive the **Gifts of the Holy Spirit** at Baptism, and in Confirmation these gifts are strengthened in you. The seven Gifts of the Holy Spirit are wisdom, understanding, counsel, fortitude, knowledge, piety, and fear of the Lord.

These seven powerful gifts help you show care and respect to God and holy persons and things, and to follow Jesus more closely. They open your heart so that the Holy Spirit can guide you to make good and unselfish choices and live the Christian life. When we allow the Gifts of the Holy Spirit to work in our hearts, the Fruits of the Holy Spirit (see page 306 in the Our Catholic Tradition section of your book) can be seen in us.

The Gifts of the Holy Spirit

The Gift of	Helps You
WISDOM	• see yourself as God sees you and act as God wants you to act • live in the image and likeness of God
Understanding	• get to know God, yourself, and other people better • see why you sometimes make wrong choices • learn to make better choices and forgive more freely
COUNSEL	• give good advice to others • hear the Holy Spirit, who speaks to you through the good advice and good example of others
FORTITUDE	• stand up for what is right even when doing so is difficult • face and overcome your fear, which sometimes leads to making a bad choice or failing to love
Knowledge	• be open to God's loving communication • know God in the way that you come to know someone you love and someone who loves you
Piety	• show faithful love and honor to God • recognize the importance of spending time talking and listening to God in prayer
Fear of the Lord	• know that God is greater and more wonderful than any created thing • remember to be open to the surprising and powerful goodness of God

© Our Sunday Visitor

Share Your Faith

Reflect Think and write about a time when you used one of the Gifts of the Holy Spirit.

_____

_____

Share With a partner, discuss this time in your life.

The Last Judgment

How does a person prepare for the Last Judgment?

The Gifts of the Holy Spirit help you turn away from selfish actions and prepare you to be with God forever. All through your life, you have the choice of accepting or rejecting the grace offered through Jesus. At the time of your death, God will judge how well you have accepted and used his gifts. This is called the **Particular Judgment**.

Jesus asks you to love God above all things and your neighbor as yourself. If you have faith in God and are open to the grace he gives you to live his plan for your life, the everlasting happiness of Heaven will eventually be yours. Sometimes people are in friendship with God but need to be purified to be with him in Heaven. This period of final cleansing is called **Purgatory**. Some people sin greatly and reject God's love. They refuse his grace and forgiveness. These sinners will be separated forever from God because of their own choices. That separation is called **Hell**.

Catholic Faith Words

Particular Judgment the individual judgment by God at the time of a person's death; when God decides, after a person's death, where that person will spend eternity according to his or her faith and works

Purgatory a state of final cleansing after death and before entering Heaven

Hell being separated from God forever because of a choice to turn away from him and not seek forgiveness

Highlight the words *forever* and *everlasting* in the text. Talk about what these words mean to us and in our life with God today.

All Souls Day celebrations remember those who have died and celebrate their lives.

© Our Sunday Visitor

At the end of time, all people who have ever lived will rise again and appear before God for judgment. This **Last Judgment** will not change each person's Particular Judgment. Rather, it will mark the coming of God's Kingdom in its fullness. This is the time when Christ will come again in glory.

© Our Sunday Visitor

Scripture

The Judgment of the Nations

"Then the king will say to those on his right, '. . . Inherit the kingdom prepared for you. . . . For I was hungry and you gave me food, I was thirsty and you gave me drink, a stranger and you welcomed me, naked and you clothed me, ill and you cared for me, in prison and you visited me.' Then the righteous will answer him and say, 'Lord, when did we see you hungry and feed you, or thirsty and give you drink? When did we see you a stranger and welcome you, or naked and clothe you? When did we see you ill or in prison, and visit you?' And the king will say to them in reply, 'Amen, I say to you, whatever you did for one of these least brothers of mine, you did for me.'"

Matthew 25:34–40

➡ **Who is the king in this story? Who are the righteous?**

Connect Your Faith

Express Yourself Design a car magnet with a saying about living according to how you will be judged.

Our Catholic Life

How can you grow in friendship with God?

God our Father, by the Holy Spirit, has given you seven powerful gifts to help you grow in friendship with him. He is always there to help and encourage you as you use these gifts in your life.

Sometimes you might feel lonely or unsure of what you should do. During these times, you can reach out to God and to others. Here are some examples.

In the spaces below, write about a time when you did these things.

Using the Gifts of the Spirit

Look for Guidance
When you are faced with a difficult choice, remember the Gifts of the Holy Spirit. Pray for the Spirit's help.

Reach Out
When you meet a person who is lonely, afraid, or suffering, reach out with words and actions of love.

_____

_____

Stop and Pray
When you are rushed or stressed, stop and pray. Feel God's presence and find comfort.

_____

_____

Notice the Beauty
When you experience sadness, look around at the beauty of God's creation and the blessings you have been given.

_____

_____

Give Thanks
When you feel joy or happiness, thank God, the source of all goodness.

© Our Sunday Visitor

People of Faith

Saint Martin de Porres, 1579–1639

November 3

Saint Martin de Porres was born in Lima, Peru. His father was Spanish, and his mother was a freed black slave. Martin became a Dominican brother. He spent his life doing good works. He went throughout the city, caring for those who were sick and poor. He was a blessing to all he met, even animals. Because he was meek and pure of heart, he saw that the simplest work honored God if it served others. He would ask people for donations to help the poor, as well. Saint Martin lived the Beatitudes and worked for the Kingdom his whole life.

Discuss: How will you prepare for eternal life with God?

Learn more about Saint Martin de Porres at **aliveinchrist.osv.com**

Live Your Faith

Name and Describe Look at the pictures and name the Gift of the Holy Spirit represented in each one. Then, in the space below, describe how you could use these gifts in your everyday life.

_____ helps me _____ at home.

_____ helps me _____ at school.

When I feel _____ , _____ helps

me _____ .

♡ Let Us Pray

Prayer for the Kingdom

Gather and begin with the Sign of the Cross.

Leader: Because you call us, All-Loving God, we want to live each day working for the justice, love, and peace of your Reign.

All: We will be followers of Jesus, praying and living each day: "Your Kingdom come."

Remembering
Our Summer Promise

Leader: Your Kingdom come.

Side 1: May your Kingdom come

Side 2: into our hearts and into our world.

Side 1: Open our hearts

Side 2: to those who are poor, sick, lonely, and suffering.

Side 1: Make us one Body in Christ

Side 2: through the gifts of your Spirit.

All: Help us ready ourselves for the banquet of Heaven. Amen.

 Sing "Holy Spirit"

© Our Sunday Visitor

FAMILY+FAITH
LIVING AND LEARNING TOGETHER

YOUR CHILD LEARNED >>>

This chapter examines the Gifts of the Holy Spirit, defines Heaven as the state of eternal happiness with God, and recognizes that acting as members of God's Kingdom on Earth prepares us for the fullness of God's Kingdom in Heaven.

Scripture

 Read **1 John 5:1–3, 11–12** to find out more about the connection between the Son of God and eternal life.

Catholics Believe

• To spend eternity with God, we first must grow in friendship with him and accept his grace.

• The Last Judgment will mark God's final triumph over evil when Christ returns in glory and judges all the living and the dead.

To learn more, go to the *Catechism of the Catholic Church #681–682* at **usccb.org**.

People of Faith

This week, your child learned about Saint Martin de Porres, who spent his life working for the Kingdom.

CHILDREN AT THIS AGE >>>

How They Understand Death and Resurrection

Your child probably has a clear sense of death as an irreversible state and knows that everyone will eventually die. Fear of their parents' death is one of the most common fears of children this age, though they rarely voice it. Some children have had experience with the deaths of grandparents and great aunts and uncles. It is helpful for them to know that death is not the end, and that by faith we know that we will be reunited with those we love and can look forward to an eternity with God.

CONSIDER THIS >>>

How many times have you thought, "Why isn't someone holding him accountable?"

An important lesson that you will teach your children is the need for consequences. We are accountable for what we choose and the consequences that follow our words and actions. The need for accountability stretches past this lifetime into the next world. God, our perfect parent, will allow us the consequences of a lifetime of choices. As Catholics, we understand that "immediately after death, each person comes before God and is judged individually (the particular judgment) and enters into heaven, Purgatory, or hell" (*USCCA, p. 156*).

LET'S TALK >>>

• Ask your child to tell you about the seven Gifts of the Holy Spirit.

• Share how these gifts help you to follow Jesus.

LET'S PRAY >>>

 Saint Martin, help us do simple things with love, so that we may always be prepared to meet God at the end of time. Amen.

For a multimedia glossary of Catholic Faith Words, Sunday readings, seasonal and Saint resources, and chapter activities go to **aliveinchrist.osv.com**.

Chapter 21 Review

A **Work with Words** Fill in the circle of the choice that best completes each sentence.

1. _____ Judgment is the individual judgment by God at the time of a person's death.
   - ○ **Last**
   - ○ **Particular**
   - ○ **Strong**

2. The _____ Judgment will occur when Jesus returns to judge all who have ever lived.
   - ○ **Last**
   - ○ **Particular**
   - ○ **Lord's**

3. A separation from God forever is called _____ .
   - ○ **sin**
   - ○ **Hell**
   - ○ **Purgatory**

4. The Last Judgment _____ change your Particular Judgment.
   - ○ **will**
   - ○ **will not**
   - ○ **should**

5. Heaven is the _____ of full joy, living eternally in God's presence.
   - ○ **state**
   - ○ **place**
   - ○ **room**

B **Check Understanding** For each statement, write the correct Gift of the Holy Spirit being used.

6. Josh gives his best friend good advice, telling him not to shoplift.

   _____

7. Kim didn't do her homework, but she decides to tell her teacher the truth.

   _____

8. Tasha was ready to steal a DVD. When she remembered what she learned in religion class, she put the DVD back.

   _____

9. Madison is overwhelmed with the beauty of the night sky, and she thinks of God.

   _____

10. Amelia is struggling with a decision. She thinks about what Jesus would do.

   _____

 Go to **aliveinchrist.osv.com** for an interactive review.

A **Work with Words** Complete each sentence with the correct term.

1. To _____ or want for yourself what belongs to others is called envy.

2. Variety, especially among people, is known as _____.

3. The _____ _____ will occur at the end of time, when Christ returns to judge the living and the dead.

4. The virtue of giving to God and people what is due them is called

   _____.

5. _____ is the desire to gain earthly goods without limits or beyond what you need.

6. The _____ _____ _____ are those who do not become too attached to their possessions and are able to help bring about God's reign.

7. The job or purpose of sharing the Good News of Jesus and the Kingdom of God is known as a _____.

8. _____ is the way we appreciate and use God's gifts and the resources of creation.

9. The full joy of living eternally in God's presence is _____.

10. _____ _____ is the individual judgment by God at the time of a person's death.

B **Check Understanding** Fill in the circle next to the answer that best completes each statement.

11. In the Parable of the Rich Fool, Jesus teaches that the rich man is not concerned with _____ .

    ○ **what matters to God**

    ○ **being merry**

    ○ **riches**

12. _____ left their homes, families, and jobs in order to follow Jesus and help him spread God's Word.

    ○ **The Israelites**

    ○ **Adam and Eve**

    ○ **The Apostles**

13. Missionaries follow Jesus' example by reaching out to _____ people, especially those who are sick and those who are poor.

    ○ **most**

    ○ **all**

    ○ **some**

14. Being separated from God forever as a result of a person's choice to sin and reject God's forgiveness is called _____ .

    ○ **Hell**

    ○ **greed**

    ○ **Heaven**

15. You receive the Gifts of the Holy Spirit in Baptism and Confirmation, including _____ .

    ○ **wisdom**

    ○ **piety**

    ○ **both wisdom and piety**

C **Make Connections** Use the five words in the Word Bank to write a brief paragraph that answers the following question: What can you do in your life now to prepare for when you will see God?

16–20. _____

_____

_____

_____

_____

_____

_____

_____

_____

_____

_____

_____

_____

_____

_____

_____

_____

_____

_____

Word Bank

generous

mission

Heaven

judgment

Holy Spirit

Life and Dignity of the Human Person

In Scripture God tells us, "Before I formed you in the womb I knew you" (Jeremiah 1:5). God created each of us. Every person is unique and unrepeatable. God has a special plan for each of our lives. He knows what he made us to be.

Because God made each person, we should treat each person with dignity. Every life is valuable to God. We should take care of the bodies and minds God gave us and use them to do good things. God calls us to be kind toward others and to solve problems peacefully instead of fighting. If we see someone being bullied, teased, or disrespected, we need to speak up and get help from an adult if necessary. We should help protect others because every life is important to God.

NO BULLY ZONE

Life and Dignity

All humans have a special place in God's plan. As followers of Jesus, you have a duty to help one another use God's gifts to live as he has called you to live.

God wants all people to have the food, water, and shelter they need to live happy and healthy lives. He also wants you to treat all people with respect. Part of showing respect for people is asking them what they need and then helping them to help themselves.

≫ **What are some ways you can show respect for human life and dignity?**

© Our Sunday Visitor

Needs Around the World

What types of aid are needed by people who are poor around the world? How would these types of aid improve the people's lives? Discuss these issues with a partner and then answer the following questions.

1. When we help the poor, we also learn valuable lessons. What is something we can learn from helping others?

   _____

   _____

2. How might this lesson help us be better followers of Jesus?

   _____

   _____

Call to Family, Community, and Participation

From the very beginning, God made people to be in relationship with one another. Scripture tells us, "The LORD God said: It is not good for the man to be alone. I will make a helper suited to him" (Genesis 2:18). God gave us communities so that we could take care of one another.

The family is a very special type of community. Our Church teaches that the family is the "school of holiness" and the "domestic Church." These names reflect the Catholic teaching that the family is where we learn who God is and how to live a Christian life. It is the first place where we learn what it means to live in a community. The family is where we learn how to love others.

Call to Community

God made people to live with and for others. Humans belong to one another because God is Father of all, and Jesus is everyone's brother and Savior.

A community is a group of people who share common beliefs and activities. The first community you belong to is your family. You belong to the Church community through Baptism. You also belong to other communities, such as neighborhoods, towns or cities, and the world. Baptized Christians have a responsibility to participate in all of these communities.

An Ideal Community

Use the diagram to design an ideal community. The diagram represents the main street and two cross streets in a neighborhood. Draw housing, schools, parks, stores and services the community might need.

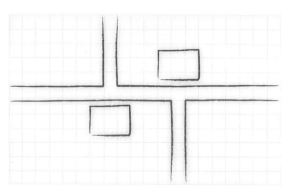

1. How can you and your friends take more responsibility for your community?

   _____

2. What are you willing to do to help others in the neighborhood or world community live better lives?

   _____

Rights and Responsibilities of the Human Person

Because God made every person, everyone has rights and responsibilities. Rights are the freedoms or things every person needs and should have. Responsibilities are our duties, or the things we must do.

Jesus tells us to "love your neighbor as yourself" (Mark 12:31). The *Catechism* teaches that "respect for the human person considers the other 'another self'" (CCC, 1944). We respect the rights that come from people's dignity as human beings. Everyone has a right to food, shelter, clothing, rest, and the right to see a doctor if they need one. We also have a responsibility to treat others well and work together for the good of everyone.

Rights and Responsibilities

God's plan is that every person should be treated with dignity. Every person, everywhere, has a right to life and to the things needed to live, such as food, clothing, shelter, and education.

With human rights come human responsibilities. Part of your mission to follow Jesus is to work for the human rights of all people. It is not fair that some people have things they do not need while others have nothing. All Christians have the responsibility to see that people everywhere are treated fairly and have what they need to live. The Catholic Church calls all of its members to find ways to fight hunger and homelessness. One way to work for human rights is to care for the needs of those who are homeless.

≫ **What human rights and responsibilities can you name?**

Sharing Food

Another way to work for human rights is to gather food for a local food bank. To accomplish this, you will need a plan. Check off each task as you complete it.

1. ☐ Find a food bank nearby and ask what kinds of food are needed.

2. ☐ Decide when and where you will collect the food, and how you will let people know about your food drive.

3. ☐ Get containers for the food, and encourage class members to collect and arrange to have it delivered.

4. ☐ Make cards to thank those who have donated, and think about how to collect food other times during the year.

Do Your Part Ask yourself: Which of the project jobs could I do best? Do I have my own money that I can use to buy food? Can I earn money to buy food for the poor?

Option for the Poor and Vulnerable

In Scripture, Jesus says, "whatever you did for one of these least brothers of mine, you did for me" (Matthew 25:40). Whatever we have done for people who are poor or needy, we have also done for him, and what we have not done for them, we haven't done for Jesus. This means we should treat people in need the same way we would treat Jesus himself. We should give special priority to people who are hungry, thirsty, homeless, or alone.

Saint Rose of Lima said, "When we serve the poor and the sick, we serve Jesus." Our Church teaches that we should have special love and care for those who are poor, and put their needs first. This is called the preferential option for the poor. The *Catechism* teaches that "God blesses those who come to the aid of the poor and rebukes those who turn away from them … It is by what they have done for the poor that Jesus Christ will recognize his chosen ones" (CCC, 2443).

Option for the Poor

The crowds that came to hear Jesus preach included many people who were poor or sick. Jesus wanted his Church to be a Church for the poor. Jesus told people who were poor that they were blessed in God's eyes. God's Kingdom belonged to them.

For Catholics, the needs of those who are poor come first. Every Catholic parish is called to serve people who are poor. This is a job that parishioners must do in order to live their faith.

A family that has plenty of money or belongings has a duty to share its good fortune and help meet the needs of those who have less. Every country has a duty to use its wealth to help its citizens who are poor. Rich countries have a duty to help countries that do not have as much.

>> **What are some ways that families, parishes, and countries could show that they put the needs of the poor first?**

How Can You Help?

Tell about a time when you put the needs of others before your own. What good thing happened because of your action?

_____

_____

Think of ways that you, or a group to which you belong, might help in the following situations:

1. A friend hurt themselves on the way home from school.

2. A woman is poor and has a sick child.

3. A homeless person is outside on a cold night.

4. A shelter is running low on supplies such as blankets and clothes.

Live Your Faith
Catholic Social Teaching

The Dignity of Work and Rights of Workers

All adults have a right and responsibility to work. Work helps people earn money to buy food and other necessities. It also helps to give their lives meaning as they cooperate with God's creation. Everyone should have access to meaningful work, whether that work is within the home or outside the home.

Scripture and Catholic Tradition teach that workers deserve to be treated with justice by their employers: "you shall not exploit a poor and needy hired servant" (Deuteronomy 24:14). Workers have a right to a fair wage for their work (see Leviticus 19:13; Deuteronomy 24:15). When there is a conflict between workers and employers, workers have a right to get together and express their opinions. Workers and their employers should treat one another with respect and solve conflicts peacefully.

© Our Sunday Visitor

The Dignity of Work

Work is more than just a way to make money or complete a task. God calls you to discover your unique gifts and talents and to use them in your work. When you do this, your work becomes part of God's continuing work of creation. Through work, people can see that they have dignity as gifted children of God.

≫ **When have you used your gifts and talents along with those of others?**

One kind of work is no more important than another. Each person's work can help his or her community and the people who live there. How much a job pays is not important. Every worker and every kind of work is important and worthy of respect.

≫ **What kinds of work do you respect most? Why?**

Design an Action Plan

In your group, you may have people with several different gifts and talents, all of which are important and deserve respect. These gifts can be put to good use in a parish ministry or community outreach to help others. Work together to design an action plan that will benefit your community.

Who	What
_____	_____
When	**Where**
_____	_____
Why	
_____	
_____	

Solidarity of the Human Family

Our world includes people of different nations, races, cultures, beliefs, and economic levels. But God created each one of us. We are one. In fact, Scripture tells us that "there is no partiality with God" (Romans 2:11). The differences that we see between others and ourselves are not important to him. God calls everyone to be his children.

Because God created all people, we have an obligation to treat everyone with love, kindness, and justice. In the Beatitudes, Jesus says, "blessed are the peacemakers, for they will be called children of God" (Matthew 5:9). Working for justice between people will help us to live in peace with one another.

Solidarity

When you look at the word solidarity, you can see the word solid. To stand in solidarity with others means to stand strong, or solid, next to them, helping them with their problems and sharing their joys. United, both groups of people become brothers and sisters in the one family of God.

The Call to Unity

Sometimes it may be difficult to see God's plan for solidarity and unity. Countries fight one another in wars. Family members argue. Friends sometimes walk away angry. But Christians are called to look for ways to grow in unity and peace. Bringing people together to solve problems is one way.

> ≫ **How can you help your family live in unity? How can you help the world live in solidarity?**

Building It Up

Building a house is hard work. It takes lots of time, many people, and special tools. Building solidarity can be hard work, too. Many people must work together to build solidarity, and they need to have the right tools. Tell how each of these "tools" could help people build solidarity.

1. teaching and learning

   _____

2. listening and talking

   _____

3. praying

   _____

4. helping

   _____

5. receiving help

   _____

Care for God's Creation

When God created the world—the animals, plants, and all natural things—he looked at what he had made and called it "very good" (Genesis 1:31). God made people the stewards of the "fish of the sea, the birds of the air, and all the living things that crawl on the earth" (Genesis 1:28). That means humans have a responsibility to care for all of God's creation.

Catholic Tradition teaches us that God created the Earth and all living things for the common good—the good of everyone. God asks us to take care of the environment and all living things, so that they can be enjoyed by everyone today and in future generations. The *Catechism* teaches us that we owe animals kindness, because they give glory to God just by being what they were made to be.

Care for Creation

You show that you care for creation by taking care of resources such as land and plants and by using them well. This is a way to thank God for the many gifts he has given you.

Humans are part of creation, too. In fact, humans are a very special part of creation because God created people in his image.

When you take care of other people and treat them with love, you are doing your part in God's plan. Helping other people shows that you recognize his creation of human life as a special and precious gift.

Kinds of Care

In the spaces below, list some things that are necessary for God's creation to grow.

1. What does a plant need to grow healthy and strong?

   _____

2. What does a person need to grow healthy and strong?

   _____

3. What does a pet need to grow healthy and strong?

   _____

Compare the lists. Which items are the same?

_____

Scripture

About the Old Testament

The Pentateuch is the first five books of the Old Testament—Genesis, Exodus, Leviticus, Numbers, and Deuteronomy. The word *pentateuch* means "five containers." In the beginning the Pentateuch was written on leather or papyrus and each book was kept in a separate container. Jewish people call these books the Torah. The books of the Pentateuch tell of the beginning of human relationship with God. They also tell us the story of God's loving actions for humans.

The Wisdom books of the Old Testament provide guidance in human behavior. Wisdom is a spiritual gift that allows a person to know God's purpose and plan. These books remind us that God's wisdom is always greater than human knowledge.

Many prophets were authors of Old Testament books. A prophet is a person sent by God to call people back to their covenant with God.

The New Testament

Stages of Formation

1 The life and teaching of Jesus—Jesus' whole life and teaching proclaimed the Good News. As Catholics, we are called to walk in Christ's footsteps. To follow his example and to become more like him, we need to get to know him— to learn about his life and teachings.

2 The oral tradition—After the Resurrection the Apostles preached the Good News. Then the early Christians passed on what the Apostles had preached. They retold the teachings of Jesus and the story of his life, Death, and Resurrection.

3 The four Gospels and other writings— The stories, teachings, and sayings of Jesus were collected and written down in the four Gospels. The actions and lessons of the early Church were recorded in the Acts of the Apostles and Epistles.

The Covenant

The covenant is the sacred agreement joining God and humans. When God made the covenant with Noah after the flood, he promised never to destroy the Earth again. God renewed the covenant with Abram (Abraham), promising him that his descendants would be "as numerous as the stars in the sky" (Genesis 26:4).

Years later, when the descendants of Abraham were slaves in Egypt, God used Moses to lead his People away in the Exodus, or "the road out." At Mount Sinai the covenant was renewed with Moses. God guided the Israelites to the Promised Land. In return, the Israelites were called to love only God and to follow his Law, the Ten Commandments.

Finally, through the Paschal Mystery—Jesus' life, Death, Resurrection, and Ascension—the covenant was fulfilled and a new covenant was created. The new covenant is open to all who remain faithful to God.

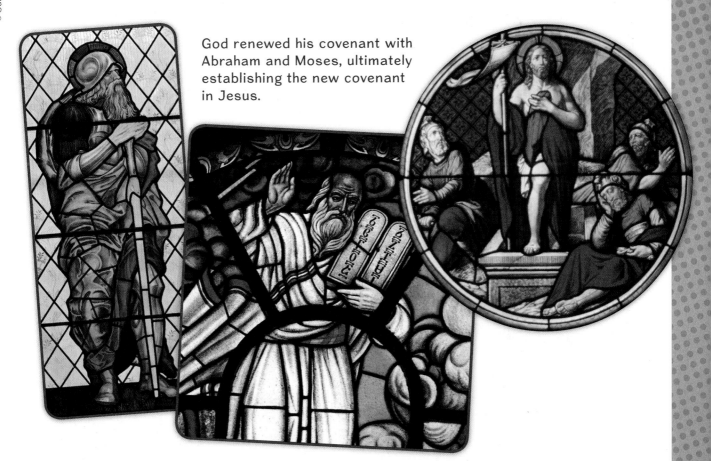

God renewed his covenant with Abraham and Moses, ultimately establishing the new covenant in Jesus.

The Creeds

A creed is a statement of the Church's belief.

Apostles' Creed

This is one of the Church's oldest creeds. It is a summary of Christian beliefs taught since the time of the Apostles. This creed is used in the celebration of Baptism and is often used at Mass during the Season of Easter and in Masses with children. This creed is part of the Rosary.

I believe in God,
the Father almighty,
Creator of heaven and earth,
and in Jesus Christ, his only Son,
    our Lord,

At the words that follow, up to and including the Virgin Mary, all bow.

who was conceived by the Holy Spirit,
born of the Virgin Mary,
suffered under Pontius Pilate,
was crucified, died and was buried;
he descended into hell;
on the third day he rose again from the
    dead;
he ascended into heaven,
and is seated at the right hand
of God the Father almighty;
from there he will come to judge
the living and the dead.
I believe in the Holy Spirit,
the holy catholic Church,
the communion of Saints,
the forgiveness of sins,
the resurrection of the body,
and life everlasting. Amen.

Nicene Creed

This creed, which is prayed at Mass, was written over a thousand years ago by leaders of the Church who met at a city named Nicaea. It is a summary of basic beliefs about God the Father, God the Son, and God the Holy Spirit, the Church, and other teachings of our faith.

I believe in one God,
the Father almighty,
maker of heaven and earth,
of all things visible and invisible.

I believe in one Lord Jesus Christ,
the Only Begotten Son of God,
born of the Father before all ages.
God from God, Light from Light,
true God from true God,
begotten, not made, consubstantial
    with the Father;
through him all things were made.
For us men and for our salvation
he came down from heaven,

At the words that follow up to and including and became man, *all bow.*

and by the Holy Spirit was incarnate
    of the Virgin Mary,
and became man.

For our sake he was crucified under
    Pontius Pilate,
he suffered death and was buried,

and rose again on the third day
in accordance with the Scriptures.
He ascended into heaven
and is seated at the right hand of
    the Father.
He will come again in glory
to judge the living and the dead
and his kingdom will have no end.

I believe in the Holy Spirit, the Lord,
    the giver of life,
who proceeds from the Father and
    the Son,
who with the Father and the Son is
    adored and glorified,
who has spoken through the prophets.

I believe in one, holy, catholic and
    apostolic Church.
I confess one Baptism for the
    forgiveness of sins
and I look forward to the resurrection
    of the dead
and the life of the world to come.
    Amen.

The Holy Trinity

God is revealed in three Divine Persons: God the Father, our Creator and sustainer; God the Son, our Savior; and God the Holy Spirit, our guide. Each of the Persons of the Trinity is separate from the other Persons. However, the Father, Son, and Holy Spirit are one and the same God. The Holy Trinity is the central mystery of the Catholic faith.

The mission of God the Son and God the Holy Spirit is to bring people into the love of the Trinity— the perfect love that exists in the Father, Son, and Holy Spirit.

The Holy Trinity is often represented by an equilateral triangle, three interwoven circles, a circle of three fish, or a shamrock.

God the Father

God created all things. The beauty of creation reflects the beauty of the Creator. He cares for and loves all. In his Divine providence, God guides everything toward himself.

God the Son

Jesus is the Son of God. The Son of God became man in order to save all people from the power of sin and everlasting death. Jesus was truly man and yet was truly God, fully divine while fully human. He became human, being born of the Virgin Mary. Except for sin, Jesus was human in every way.

Through the teachings of Jesus, people come to know about the Kingdom of God and how to live for God's reign. From the Sermon on the Mount and other teachings, people learn to live in love. Jesus taught everyone how to live the Ten Commandments—by loving God and all of his creation.

Jesus' Resurrection showed him as the Messiah, the Savior. By his Death Jesus conquered sin. By rising to new life, Jesus conquered death and so saved all humans from the power of sin and everlasting death.

The Ascension happened forty days after the Resurrection, when Jesus ascended to Heaven to join the glory of God the Father. At the Ascension Jesus commanded the Apostles to continue his mission by teaching and guiding people toward God's Kingdom.

God the Holy Spirit

The Holy Spirit continues to guide people in the Christian life. Through the teachings of Jesus, we learn how to live in love. Through the strength and wisdom of the Holy Spirit, we are able to lead this life of love. The Holy Spirit breathes into the faithful his Gifts.

Gifts of the Holy Spirit	Fruits of the Holy Spirit
You receive the Gifts of the Holy Spirit through the Sacraments of Baptism and Confirmation. These gifts help you grow in relationship with God and others.	The qualities that can be seen in us when we allow the Holy Spirit to work in our hearts.
Wisdom Understanding Right judgment (Counsel) Courage (Fortitude) Knowledge Reverence (Piety) Wonder and awe (Fear of the Lord) 	Charity Joy Peace Kindness Patience Goodness Gentleness Faithfulness Modesty Self-Control Chastity Fortitude 

Church

Church authority is based on the authority Jesus gave to Peter when he gave him the "keys to the kingdom" (**Matthew 16:19**) and the authority Jesus gives his disciples to forgive sins in his name (see John 20:23). Church authority also flows from the command from Jesus to his Apostles to make disciples of people everywhere, teaching them to live as Jesus taught and baptizing them in the name of the Father, Son, and Holy Spirit. (See Matthew 28:18–20). Speaking to his Apostles, Jesus also promised to send the Holy Spirit as the Spirit of Truth that would guide them "into all truth." The official teaching authority of the Church is the Magisterium, which is made up of the Pope and the bishops. The Magisterium teaches with the authority given by Jesus and the guidance of the Holy Spirit.

Mission

The Church has the mission to help bring justice to everyone. The principles of social justice are respect for all persons, equality for all persons, and oneness in the family of God with responsibility for one another. These principles can be accomplished with the fair distribution of goods, fair wages for work, and fair resolution in conflicts.

Pope

The Pope's title of "Servant of the Servants" began with Pope Gregory the Great. The Bible says that "[W]hoever wishes to be first among you will be the slave of all" (**Mark 10:44**). The many titles for the Pope include: Bishop of Rome, Vicar of Christ, Supreme Pontiff of the Universal Church, Patriarch of the West, Primate of Italy, Successor of Saint Peter, Prince of the Apostles, Servant of the Servants of God, and Sovereign of Vatican City.

Saints

Canonization is the process by which the Church recognizes faithful people as Saints. During each of the three stages of becoming a Saint, the faithful person has a different title—first Venerable, then Blessed, and finally Saint.

Mary is the greatest of Saints. We have many teachings about her. The Immaculate Conception means that Mary was preserved from Original Sin from the first moment of conception. The Feast of the Immaculate Conception is December 8. On this date, the Catholics of Paraguay celebrate the feast day of the Virgin of Caacupe. Centuries ago, the Virgin Mary appeared in the Paraguayan countryside. A church was built in the place where she had appeared, and many pilgrims to that church have experienced miracles. Today December 8 is as special a celebration to the Catholics of Paraguay as Christmas is. Many honor Mary every year by making a pilgrimage, or long walk, to the church of the Virgin of Caacupe.

Last Things

Purgatory

At death most people are not ready for Heaven and God's eternal friendship. However, they have not broken their relationship with God. These souls are given time in Purgatory. Purgatory means "purifying." Purgatory helps the soul prepare for life with God. The soul becomes more faithful and loving.

Particular Judgment

When people die, they are judged by how fully they have responded to God's call and the grace he has offered through Jesus. This judgment is called Particular Judgment. Souls will be given reward or punishment at this time.

General Judgment

General Judgment, or the Last Judgment, will occur at the Second Coming of Christ. This judgment represents God's triumph over evil. General Judgment will mark the arrival of God's Kingdom in its fullness. General Judgment will happen to all people, living and dead. However, this judgment will not change the Particular Judgment received by each soul.

The Liturgical Year

Advent

Four Sundays of Advent

Christmas

Christmas Day
Feast of the Holy Family
Feast of Epiphany

Ordinary Time

Sundays between Epiphany and
Ash Wednesday

Before Lent begins, the palms from Palm Sunday from the prior year are collected and burned. The ashes are then used for the Ash Wednesday service.

Please place last year's blessed palms here

Lent

Lent begins on Ash Wednesday, and continues with the Five Sundays of Lent, including Passion or Palm Sunday.

Lent is a time of fasting, prayer, and almsgiving. The forty days of Lent remind Christians of the number of days Jesus spent fasting in the desert. The forty days also represent the number of years the Israelites spent wandering in the desert after the Exodus.

Lent begins with Ash Wednesday, a day of penance. The last Friday in Lent, Good Friday, is also a day of penance. All Catholics from their eighteenth to their fifty-ninth birthdays must fast on days of penance: They eat light meals and have no food between meals. On Ash Wednesday and on all Fridays during Lent, abstinence is required for Catholics fourteen years of age or older. This means that they may not eat meat. Fasting, abstinence, and personal reflection during Lent help prepare Catholics for the celebration of Easter.

Triduum

The Triduum, which means "three days," starts with the celebration of the Lord's Supper on Holy Thursday. Good Friday is observed with a Liturgy of the Word, Veneration of the Cross, and a Communion service. On Holy Saturday evening the Easter Vigil is celebrated. The Triduum ends with evening prayer on Easter Sunday. Because the Triduum celebrates the Paschal Mystery—the life, Death, and Resurrection of Jesus—it is the high point of the entire Church year.

Easter Season

The Easter season begins on Easter Sunday and continues with the Second through Seventh Sundays of Easter, culminating with Pentecost Sunday (fifty days after Easter).

The Paschal Candle is a symbol of Christ and of Easter. This candle is lit from the Easter fire during the Easter Vigil. Throughout the fifty days of the Easter Season, the candle burns during the liturgy. After the Easter Season it is used during Baptisms and funerals as a symbol of the Resurrection.

Ordinary Time

Sundays between Pentecost and the First Sunday of Advent

The Seven Sacraments

The Catholic Church celebrates Seven Sacraments—special signs and celebrations of Jesus' presence. Jesus gave us the Sacraments to allow us to share in God's life and work. There are three groups of Sacraments.

Sacraments

Sacraments of Initiation

These are the three Sacraments that celebrate membership into the Catholic Church.	• Baptism • Confirmation • Eucharist

Sacraments of Healing

In these Sacraments, God's forgiveness and healing are given to those suffering physical and spiritual sickness.	• Penance and Reconciliation • Anointing of the Sick

Sacraments at the Service of Communion

These Sacraments celebrate people's commitment to serve God and the community and help build up the People of God.	• Holy Orders • Matrimony (Marriage)

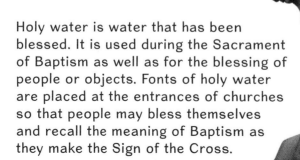

Holy water is water that has been blessed. It is used during the Sacrament of Baptism as well as for the blessing of people or objects. Fonts of holy water are placed at the entrances of churches so that people may bless themselves and recall the meaning of Baptism as they make the Sign of the Cross.

The Sacrament of Penance and Reconciliation

The Sacrament of Reconciliation is also known as the Sacrament of Penance or the Sacrament of Confession. In this Sacrament, sin is forgiven and the one who has sinned is reconciled with God, with himself or herself, and with the Church community. The essential elements for Reconciliation are contrition (sorrow for the sin), confession, absolution by the priest, and satisfaction (attempting to correct or undo the wrong done).

Rite for Reconciliation of Individual Penitents

1. Welcome
2. Reading from Scripture
3. Confession of Sins and Acceptance of a Penance
4. Act of Contrition (See page 324.)
5. Absolution
6. Closing Prayer

Rite for Reconciliation of Several Penitents

1. Greeting
2. Celebration of the Word
3. Homily
4. Examination of Conscience
5. General Confession of Sin/ Litany of Contrition
6. The Lord's Prayer

7. Individual Confession of Sins, Acceptance of a Penance, and Absolution:

Prayer of Absolution

God, the Father of mercies,
through the death and resurrection
    of his Son
has reconciled the world to himself
and sent the Holy Spirit among us
for the forgiveness of sins;
through the ministry of the Church
may God give you pardon and peace,
and I absolve you from your sins
in the name of the Father, and of
    the Son,
and of the Holy Spirit.

8. Closing Prayer

Examination of Conscience

For help with examining your conscience, use the following steps:

1. Pray for the Holy Spirit's help in making a fresh start.
2. Look at your life in the light of the Beatitudes, the Ten Commandments, the Great Commandment, and the Precepts of the Church.
3. Ask yourself these questions: Where have I fallen short of what God wants for me? Whom have I hurt? What have I done that I knew was wrong? What have I not done that I should have done? Have I made the necessary changes in bad habits? What areas am I still having trouble with? Am I sincerely sorry for all my sins?

God's Laws

God gives us laws to help us live by the covenant. These laws guide us in loving God and our neighbor.

Laws are rules that help people live as members of a community and behave in an acceptable manner.

Divine law is the eternal law of God. It includes physical law and moral law. The law of gravity is an example of physical law. A moral law is one that humans understand through reasoning (you may not steal) and through Divine Revelation (keep holy the Lord's Day).

Natural moral law consists of those decisions and duties that all humans accept as right. For example, people everywhere understand that no one may kill another unjustly. Everyone must obey natural moral law.

The Ten Commandments

1. I am the Lord your God: you shall not have strange gods before me.

2. You shall not take the name of the Lord your God in vain.

3. Remember to keep holy the Lord's Day.

4. Honor your father and your mother.

5. You shall not kill.

6. You shall not commit adultery.

7. You shall not steal.

8. You shall not bear false witness against your neighbor.

9. You shall not covet your neighbor's wife.

10. You shall not covet your neighbor's goods.

The Beatitudes

The Beatitudes are sayings of Jesus that show us the way to true happiness in God's Kingdom. The Beatitudes are listed in the Gospel according to Matthew (see Matthew 5:3–10). See also Chapter 7.

The New Commandment

Jesus also gave his followers a New Commandment: "love one another. As I have loved you, so you also should love one another" (John 13:34).

Corporal and Spiritual Works of Mercy

The Corporal Works of Mercy draw Catholics to the care of the physical needs of others. The Spiritual Works of Mercy guide us to care for the spiritual needs of people.

Corporal

- Feed the hungry
- Give drink to the thirsty
- Clothe the naked
- Shelter the homeless
- Visit the sick
- Visit the imprisoned

Spiritual

- Warn the sinner
- Teach the ignorant
- Counsel the doubtful
- Comfort the sorrowful
- Bear wrongs patiently
- Forgive injuries
- Pray for the living and the dead

Precepts of the Church

The following precepts are important duties of all Catholics.

1. Take part in the Mass on Sundays and holy days. Keep these days holy and avoid unnecessary work.

2. Celebrate the Sacrament of Reconciliation at least once a year.

3. Receive Holy Communion at least once a year during the Easter Season.

4. Fast and abstain on days of penance.

5. Give your time, gifts, and money to support the Church.

Free Will and Conscience

God's image is his likeness that is present in you because you are his creation. You are called to respect the dignity of all people because everyone is made in God's image.

- Freedom means you are able to choose and act with few limitations. We are given freedom by God that we may choose to do good things.

- Free will is the gift from God that allows humans to make their own choices. Because you are free to choose between right and wrong, you are responsible for your choices and actions.

- Conscience is a gift from God that helps us judge whether actions are right or wrong. It is important for us to know God's laws so our conscience can help us make good decisions. Conscience helps you choose what is right. It involves free will and reason working together. You must form your conscience properly. If not formed properly, your conscience can lead you to choose what is wrong.

Forming your conscience is a lifelong process. It involves practicing virtues and avoiding sin and people or situations that may lead you to sin. You can turn to good people for advice, to Church teachings for guidance, and to God for help in educating your conscience.

Grace

God gives you two types of grace. Sanctifying grace is the gift of God's life in you. It gives you the desire to live and act within God's plan.

Actual grace is the gift of God's life in you that helps you think or act in a particular situation according to God's plan. Actual grace opens you to understanding and strengthens your will.

Virtue and Sin

Virtues are good qualities or habits of goodness. The word virtue means "strength." Practicing virtue can give you the strength to make loving choices.

Types of Virtues	
Theological Virtues	**Cardinal Virtues**
Faith Hope Charity (Love)	Prudence (careful judgment) Fortitude (courage) Justice (giving people their due) Temperance (moderation, balance)

Sin is a turning away from God and a failure to love. Sin affects both the individual and the community. A person may be sorry for his or her sin, ask forgiveness for it, accept punishment for it, and resolve to do better. In this case, the experience may actually help the person develop as a Christian and avoid sin in the future. However, a person who makes a habit of sin will harm his or her development, set a poor example, and bring sorrow to others. Society suffers when people disobey God's law and the just laws of society. There are many types of sin.

- Original Sin is the human condition of weakness and the tendency toward sin that resulted from the choice of Adam and Eve, our first parents, to disobey God. Baptism restores the relationship of loving grace in which all people were created.

- Actual sin is any thought, word, act, or failure to act that goes against God's law. Sin is always a choice, never a mistake.

- Mortal sin causes a person's relationship with God to be broken.

A mortal sin is a serious act, such as murder. In order for it to be a mortal sin, there must be a deliberate choice to commit the act; it is never an accident.

- Venial sin weakens a person's relationship with God but does not destroy it. Venial sin often comes from bad habits. It can lead to mortal sin.

- Social sin happens when one person's sins affect the larger community. Poverty and racism are examples of social sin.

Basic Prayers

These are essential prayers that every Catholic should know. Latin is the official, universal language of the Church. As members of the Catholic Church, we usually pray in the language that we speak, but we sometimes pray in Latin, the common language of the Church.

Sign of the Cross

In the name of the Father,
and of the Son,
and of the Holy Spirit.
Amen.

Signum Crucis

In nómine Patris
et Fílii
et Spíritus Sancti.
Amen.

The Lord's Prayer

Our Father, who art in heaven,
hallowed be thy name;
thy kingdom come,
thy will be done
on earth as it is in heaven.
Give us this day our daily bread,
and forgive us our trespasses,
as we forgive those who trespass
   against us;
and lead us not into temptation,
but deliver us from evil.
Amen.

Pater Noster

Pater noster qui es in cælis:
santificétur Nomen Tuum;
advéniat Regnum Tuum;
fiat volúntas Tua,
sicut in cælo, et in terra.
Panem nostrum
cotidiánum da nobis hódie;
et dimítte nobis débita nostra,
sicut et nos
dimíttus debitóribus nostris;
et ne nos indúcas in tentatiónem;
sed líbera nos a Malo.

© Our Sunday Visitor

The Hail Mary

Hail, Mary, full of grace,
the Lord is with thee.
Blessed art thou among women
and blessed is the fruit of thy womb,
   Jesus.
Holy Mary, Mother of God,
pray for us sinners,
now and at the hour of our death.
Amen.

Glory Be

Glory be to the Father
and to the Son
and to the Holy Spirit,
as it was in the beginning
is now, and ever shall be
world without end.
Amen.

Angelus

V. The angel spoke God's message to
Mary,
R. and she conceived of the Holy
Spirit.
Hail, Mary . . .
V. "I am the lowly servant of the Lord:
R. let it be done to me according to
your word."
Hail, Mary . . .
V. And the Word became flesh,
R. and lived among us.
Hail, Mary . . .
V. Pray for us, holy Mother of God,

Ave Maria

Ave, María, grátia plena,
Dóminus tecum.
Benedícta tu in muliéribus,
et benedíctus fructus ventris
   tui, Iesus.
Sancta María, Mater Dei,
ora pro nobis peccatóribus,
nunc et in hora mortis nostræ.
   Amen.

Gloria Patri

Gloria Patri
et Filio
et Spíritui Sancto.
Sicut erat in princípio
et nunc et semper
et in sæcula sæculorum.
Amen.

R. that we may become worthy of the
promises of Christ.
Let us pray.

Lord,
fill our hearts with your grace:
once, through the message of an angel
you revealed to us the Incarnation of
your Son;
now, through his suffering and death
lead us to the glory of his resurrection.

We ask this through Christ our Lord.
Amen.

Memorare

Remember, most loving Virgin Mary, never was it heard that anyone who turned to you for help was left unaided. Inspired by this confidence, though burdened by my sins, I run to your protection for you are my mother. Mother of the Word of God, do not despise my words of pleading but be merciful and hear my prayer. Amen.

Hail, Holy Queen

Hail, Holy Queen, Mother of Mercy,
our life, our sweetness and our hope.
To you do we cry,
poor banished children of Eve.
To you do we send up our sighs,
mourning and weeping in this valley of tears.
Turn then, most gracious advocate,
your eyes of mercy toward us,
and after this exile
show unto us the blessed fruit of thy womb, Jesus.
O clement, O loving,
O sweet Virgin Mary.

Prayer to the Holy Spirit

Come, Holy Spirit, fill the hearts of your faithful.
And kindle in them the fire of your love.
Send forth your Spirit and they will be created.
And you will renew the face of the earth.
Let us pray.
Lord, by the light of the Holy Spirit you have taught the hearts of your faithful. In the same Spirit help us to relish what is right and always rejoice in your consolation. We ask this through Christ our Lord. Amen.

Prayers from the Sacraments

I Confess/*Confiteor*

I confess to almighty God
and to you, my brothers and sisters,
that I have greatly sinned,
in my thoughts and in my words,
in what I have done and in what I have
failed to do,

Gently strike your chest with a closed fist.

through my fault, through my fault,
through my most grievous fault;

Continue:

therefore I ask blessed Mary ever-
Virgin,
all the Angels and Saints,
and you, my brothers and sisters,
to pray for me to the Lord our God.

Gloria

Glory to God in the highest,
and on earth peace to people of
    good will.
We praise you, we bless you, we adore
    you, we glorify you, we give you
    thanks for your great glory,
Lord God, heavenly King, O God,
    almighty Father.
Lord Jesus Christ,
Only Begotten Son,
Lord God, Lamb of God,
Son of the Father,

you take away the sins of the world,
    have mercy on us;
you take away the sins of the world,
    receive our prayer;
you are seated at the right hand of
    the Father, have mercy on us.
For you alone are the Holy One,
you alone are the Lord,
you alone are the Most High,
    Jesus Christ, with the Holy Spirit,
in the glory of God the Father.
    Amen.

Holy, Holy, Holy Lord

Holy, Holy, Holy Lord God of hosts.
Heaven and earth are full of your glory.
Hosanna in the highest.
Blessed is he who comes in the name of
    the Lord.
Hosanna in the highest.

Sanctus, Sanctus, Sanctus

Sanctus, Sanctus, Sanctus
Dominus Deus Sabaoth.
Pleni sunt coeli et terra gloria tua.
Hosanna in excelsis.
Benedictus qui venit in nomine
    Domini.
Hosanna in excelsis

Lamb of God

Lamb of God, you take away the
sins of the world,
have mercy on us.
Lamb of God, you take away the
sins of the world,
have mercy on us.
Lamb of God, you take away the
sins of the world,
grant us peace.

Agnus Dei

Agnus Dei, qui tollis peccata mundi:
miserere nobis.
Agnus Dei, qui tollis peccata mundi:
miserere nobis.
Agnus Dei, qui tollis peccata mundi:
dona nobis pacem

Act of Contrition

Contrition is the sorrow that rises up in
the soul, making you repent past sins and
plan not to sin again. To repent is to turn
back from the sin and ask God's mercy.

My God, I am sorry for my sins with all
my heart.
In choosing to do wrong
and failing to do good,
I have sinned against you
whom I should love above all things.
I firmly intend, with your help,
to do penance,
to sin no more,
and to avoid whatever leads me to sin.
Our Savior Jesus Christ
suffered and died for us.
In his name, my God, have mercy.

The Jesus Prayer

Lord Jesus Christ, Son of God,
have mercy upon me, a sinner.

The Apostles' Creed

See page 306 for this prayer.

The Nicene Creed

See page 307 for this prayer.

Personal and Family Prayers

Act of Faith

O God, we firmly believe that you are one God in three Divine Persons, Father, Son, and Holy Spirit; we believe that your Divine Son became man and died for our sins, and that he will come to judge the living and the dead. We believe these and all the truths that the holy Catholic Church teaches because you have revealed them, and you can neither deceive nor be deceived.

Act of Hope

O God, relying on your almighty power and your endless mercy and promises, we hope to gain pardon for our sins, the help of your grace, and life everlasting, through the saving actions of Jesus Christ, our Lord and Redeemer.

Act of Love

O God, we love you above all things, with our whole heart and soul, because you are all good and worthy of all love. We love our neighbor as ourselves for the love of you. We forgive all who have injured us and ask pardon of all whom we have injured.

Grail Prayer

Lord Jesus,
I give you my hands to do your work.
I give you my feet to go your way.
I give you my eyes to see as you do.
I give you my tongue to speak your words.
I give you my mind that you may think in me.

Above all, I give you my heart
that you may love in me your Father
and all mankind.
I give you my whole self that
you may grow in me,
so that it is you, Lord Jesus,
who will live and work and pray in me.
Amen.

Morning Prayer

God be in my head, and in my understanding;
God be in my eyes, and in my looking;
God be in my mouth, and in my speaking;
God be in my heart, and in my thinking;
God be at my end, and at my departing.
Amen.

Evening Prayer

Lord, from the rising of the sun to its setting your name is worthy of all praise. Let our prayer come like incense before you. May the lifting up of our hands be as an evening sacrifice acceptable to you,
Lord our God.
Amen.

Praying with the Saints

When we pray with the Saints, we ask them to pray to God for us and to pray with us. The Saints are with Christ. They speak for us when we need help.

One of the most popular devotions to Mary is the Rosary. It focuses on the twenty mysteries that describe events in the lives of Jesus and Mary.

How to Pray the Rosary

1. Pray the Sign of the Cross and say the Apostles' Creed.
2. Pray the Lord's Prayer.
3. Pray three Hail Marys.
4. Pray the Glory Be to the Father.
5. Say the first mystery; then pray the Lord's Prayer.
6. Pray ten Hail Marys while meditating on the mystery.
7. Pray the Glory Be to the Father.
8. Say the second mystery; then pray the Lord's Prayer.

Repeat 6 and 7 and continue with the third, fourth, and fifth mysteries in the same manner.

9. Pray the Hail, Holy Queen.

© Our Sunday Visitor

The Mysteries of the Rosary

The Joyful Mysteries

The Annunciation

The Visitation

The Nativity

The Presentation in the Temple

The Finding in the Temple

The Sorrowful Mysteries

The Agony in the Garden

The Scourging at the Pillar

The Crowning with Thorns

The Carrying of the Cross

The Crucifixion and Death

The Luminous Mysteries

The Baptism of Jesus

The Wedding at Cana

The Proclamation of the Kingdom

The Transfiguration

The Institution of the Eucharist

The Glorious Mysteries

The Resurrection

The Ascension

The Descent of the Holy Spirit

The Assumption of Mary

The Coronation of Mary in Heaven

Litany of St. Joseph

A litany is a prayer with one line that is meant to be repeated over and over again so that those praying are caught up in the prayer itself. In Litanies of the Saints we call to the Saints to intercede for us.

Lord, have mercy.   Lord, have mercy.
Christ, have mercy.   Christ, have mercy.
Lord, have mercy.   Lord, have mercy.

Good Saint Joseph,   pray for us.
Descendant of the House of David,   pray for us.
Husband of Mary,   pray for us.
Foster father of Jesus,   pray for us.
Guardian of Christ,   pray for us.
Support of the holy family,   pray for us.
Model of workers,   pray for us.
Example to parents,   pray for us.
Comfort of the dying,   pray for us.
Provider of food to the hungry,   pray for us.
Companion of the poor,   pray for us.
Protector of the Church,   pray for us.

Merciful God,
grant that we may learn from Saint Joseph
to care for the members of our families
and share what we have with the poor.
We ask this through Christ our Lord. Amen.

Catholic Faith Words

A

absolution words spoken by the priest during the Sacrament of Penance and Reconciliation to grant forgiveness in God's name **(246)**

ark of the covenant a wooden chest that housed the tablets of the Ten Commandments. The Israelites carried it wherever they went as a reminder that God was with them. **(76)**

Ascension when the Risen Jesus was taken up to Heaven to be with God the Father forever **(225)**

B

beatification the second step in the process of becoming a Saint, in which a Venerable person is recognized by the Church as having brought about a miracle through his or her prayers of intercession **(166)**

Beatitudes teachings of Jesus that show the way to true happiness and tell the way to live in God's Kingdom now and always **(122)**

blasphemy the sin of showing disrespect for the name of God, Jesus Christ, Mary, or the Saints in words or action **(144)**

C

canonization a declaration by the Pope naming a person a Saint. Canonized Saints have special feast days or memorials in the Church's calendar. **(166)**

Cardinal Virtues the four principal moral virtues —prudence, temperance, justice, and fortitude—that help us live as children of God and from which the other moral virtues flow. We strengthen these good habits through God's grace and our own efforts. **(191)**

charity the Theological Virtue of love. It directs us to love God above all things and our neighbor as ourselves, for the love of God **(134)**

chastity a moral virtue and one of the Fruits of the Holy Spirit that helps us to act and think in ways that are appropriate and pure **(192)**

common good the good of everyone, with particular concern for those who might be most vulnerable to harm **(100)**

confession another name for the Sacrament of Penance and Reconciliation; an essential element of the Sacrament when you tell your sins to the priest **(244)**

conscience the God-given ability that helps us judge whether actions are right or wrong. It is important for us to know God's laws so our conscience can help us make good decisions. **(110)**

Corporal Works of Mercy actions that show care for the physical needs of others **(135)**

covenant a sacred promise or agreement between God and humans **(3, 67)**

D – E

Divine Revelation the way God makes himself, and his plan for humans, known to us **(57)**

envy the sin of resenting what others have or being sad from wanting for yourself what belongs to others **(260)**

eternal life life forever with God for all who die in his friendship **(122)**

Eucharist the Sacrament in which Jesus gives himself and the bread and wine become his Body and Blood **(237)**

evangelization sharing the Good News of Jesus through words and actions in a way that invites people to accept the Gospel (269)

faith the Theological Virtue that makes it possible for us to believe in God and all that he helps us understand about himself. Faith leads you to obey God. (134)

faithful to be constant and loyal in your commitments to God and others, just as he is faithful to you (67)

fortitude the Cardinal Virtue that helps you show courage, have strength to get through difficult times, and not give up on doing good (192)

free will the God-given freedom and ability to make choices. God created us with free will so we can have the freedom to choose good. (109)

Gifts of the Holy Spirit seven powerful Gifts God gives us to follow the guidance of the Holy Spirit and live the Christian life (278)

Gospel a word that means "Good News." The Gospel message is the Good News of God's Kingdom and his saving love. (269)

grace God's free and loving gift to humans of his own life and help (109)

Great Commandment the twofold command to love God above all and your neighbor as yourself. It sums up all God's laws. (132)

greed the sin of desiring to gain earthly goods without limits or beyond what you need (260)

Heaven the joy of living eternally in God's presence (278)

Hell being separated from God forever because of a choice to turn away from him and not seek forgiveness (280)

Holy Trinity the mystery of one God in three Divine Persons: Father, Son, and Holy Spirit (98)

hope the Theological Virtue that helps us trust in the true happiness God wants us to have and in Jesus' promises of eternal life, and to rely on the help of the Holy Spirit (134)

human dignity the worth each person has because he or she is made in the image of God (88)

humility the moral virtue that helps us to know that God is the source of everything good. Humility helps us to avoid being prideful. (260)

idolatry the sin of worshipping an object or a person instead of God. It is letting anything or anyone become more important than God. (143)

Immaculate Conception the truth that God kept Mary free from sin from the first moment of her life (169)

Incarnation the mystery that the Son of God became man in order to save all people (234)

justice giving God what is due him. This virtue also means giving each person what he or she is due because that person is a child of God. (260)

Kingdom of God God's rule of peace, justice, and love that exists in Heaven, but has not yet come in its fullness on Earth (157)

laity all of the baptized people in the Church who share in God's mission but are not priests or consecrated sisters or brothers; sometimes called lay people (158)

Last Judgment God's final triumph over evil that will occur at the end of time, when Christ returns and judges all the living and the dead (281)

liturgical year the feasts and seasons of the Church calendar that celebrate the Paschal Mystery of Christ (225)

Magisterium the teaching office of the Church, which is all of the bishops in union with the Pope (178)

martyr a person who gives up his or her life to witness to the truth of Christ and the faith. The word martyr means "witness." (211)

Mary the Mother of Jesus, the Mother of God. She is also called "Our Lady" because she is our Mother and the Mother of the Church. (168)

mercy kindness and concern for those who are suffering. God has mercy on us even though we are sinners. (122)

mission a job or purpose. The Church's mission is to announce the Good News of God's Kingdom. (269)

modesty a moral virtue and one of the Fruits of the Holy Spirit that helps us dress, talk, and move in appropriate ways (192)

morality living in right relationship with God, yourself, and others. It is putting your beliefs into action. (100)

mortal sin serious sin that causes a person's relationship with God to be broken (91)

murder the deliberate killing of another person when the killing is not in self-defense (202)

Original Sin the sin of our first parents, Adam and Eve, which led to the sinful condition of the human race from its beginning (64)

Particular Judgment the individual judgment by God at the time of a person's death; when God decides, after a person's death, where that person will spend eternity according to his or her faith and works (280)

Paschal Mystery the mystery of Jesus' suffering, Death, Resurrection, and Ascension (225)

patron Saint a Saint who has a particular connection to a cause, place, type of work, or person. For example, if a person or city shares the name of a Saint, that Saint is a patron. (169)

peace a state of calm when things are in their proper order and people settle problems with kindness and justice (125)

penance the prayer, offering, or good work the priest gives you in the Sacrament of Penance (246)

Precepts of the Church some of the minimum requirements given by Church leaders for deepening our relationship with God and the Church (178)

providence God's loving care for all things; God's will and plan for creation (56)

prudence the Cardinal Virtue that helps us be practical and make correct decisions on what is right and good, with the help of the Holy Spirit and a well-formed conscience (212)

Purgatory a state of final cleansing after death and before entering Heaven (280)

reparation an action taken to repair the damage done from sin (212)

repent to turn our lives away from sin and toward God (244)

Resurrection the event of Jesus being raised from Death to new life by God the Father through the power of the Holy Spirit **(144)**

Sacrament of Penance and Reconciliation the Sacrament in which God's forgiveness for sin is given through the Church **(244)**

Sacrament of the Anointing of the Sick the Sacrament that brings Jesus' healing touch to strengthen, comfort, and forgive the sins of those who are seriously ill or close to death **(247)**

sacramental seal a rule that a priest is not to share anything he hears in confession **(246)**

sacred worthy of reverence and devotion **(200)**

Sacred Scripture another name for the Bible; Sacred Scripture is the inspired Word of God written by humans **(4, 57)**

Sacred Tradition God's Word to the Church, safeguarded by the Apostles and their successors, the bishops, and handed down verbally—in her creeds, Sacraments, and other teachings—to future generations **(57)**

Saint a person whom the Church declares has led a holy life and is enjoying eternal life with God in Heaven **(166)**

salvation the loving action of God's forgiveness of sins and the restoration of friendship with him brought by Jesus **(64)**

Seven Sacraments effective signs of God's life, instituted by Christ and given to the Church. In the celebration of each Sacrament, there are visible signs and Divine actions that give grace and allow us to share in God's work. **(234)**

sin a deliberate thought, word, deed, or omission contrary to the law of God. Sins hurt our relationship with God and other people. **(91)**

soul the spiritual part of a human that lives forever **(88)**

Spiritual Works of Mercy actions that address the needs of the heart, mind, and soul **(135)**

stewardship the way we appreciate and use God's gifts, including our time, talent, and treasure, and the resources of creation **(261)**

temperance the Cardinal Virtue that helps us use moderation, be disciplined, and have self-control **(192)**

temptation an attraction to sin; wanting to do something we should not or not do something we should **(244)**

Ten Commandments the summary of laws that God gave Moses on Mount Sinai. They tell what is necessary in order to love God and others. **(76)**

Theological Virtues the virtues of faith, hope, and charity, which are gifts from God that guide our relationship with him **(134)**

venial sin a sin that weakens a person's relationship with God but does not destroy it **(91)**

vocation God's plan for our lives; the purpose for which he made us **(157)**

vows solemn promises that are made to or before God **(157)**

worship to adore and praise God, especially in the liturgy and in prayer **(143)**

Index

Photo Credits

Music selections copyrighted or administered by OCP Publications are used with permission of OCP Publications, 5536 NE Hassalo, Portland, OR 97213. Please refer to songs for specific copyright dates and information.

Music selections copyright John Burland, used with permission, and produced in partnership with Ovation Music Services, P.O. Box 402 Earlwood NSW 2206, Australia. Please refer to songs for specific copyright dates and information.

© Our Sunday Visitor